THE
Practical
Stylist

THE Practical Stylist

Second Canadian Edition

Sheridan Baker
The University of Michigan

Canadian Edition prepared by

KEN LEDBETTER
University of Waterloo

LAWRENCE B. GAMACHE
University of Ottawa

1817

HARPER & ROW, PUBLISHERS, New York
Cambridge, Philadelphia, San Francisco,
London, Mexico City, São Paulo, Singapore, Sydney

Sponsoring Editor: Phillip Leininger
Project Editor: Lucy Zakarian
Text Design: Leon Bolognese
Cover Design:
Text Art: Vantage Art, Inc.
Production: Jeanie Berke
Compositor: ComCom Division of Haddon Craftsmen, Inc.
Printer and Binder: R. R. Donnelley and Sons, Inc.

The Practical Stylist: Second Canadian Edition

Library of Congress Cataloging in Publication Data

Baker, Sheridan Warner, 1918-
  The practical stylist.

  Bibliography: p.
  Includes index.
  1. English language—Rhetoric. 2. English language—
Style. I. Ledbetter, Ken. II. Gamache, Lawrence B.
III. Title.
PE1408.B283 1986b   808'.042   85-14077
ISBN 0-06-040468-X

        88 9 8 7 6 5 4 3

Contents

Preface to the Second Canadian Edition

In preparing this edition of *The Practical Stylist,* we have tried again to keep the needs and interests of Canadian students in mind by using Canadian examples, traditional Canadian spelling based more conservatively on the British model than on standard American spelling, and Canadian research materials. We have not, however, attempted to remove all references to the history and people of the United States. Canada is a part of North America, and we have tried to retain a sense of this fact while giving the text a clearly Canadian orientation—by including, for example, a distinctively Canadian sample research paper and a list of Canadian resource materials, something we hope will be particularly useful to Canadian students.

Lawrence B. Gamache
Ken Ledbetter

Preface

The process makes the product—the essay, the poem, the painting, the home, the achievement awarded, the effort satisfied. Teachers and students in thousands of classrooms, and many others who have faced a blank page and the problems of exposition, have found *The Practical Stylist* useful in achieving the essentials of composition and the graces of good prose. But many faithful adherents have recently asked for more help with the process; hence, this new edition.

I have thoroughly revised and arranged the first three chapters into a smoother and more helpful progress through the process of writing—finding oneself and one's subject, making a thesis, the inner organizer, and managing the outer structure. In easy steps, we begin with the whole essay. Many books on writing begin with small steps then lead the student cautiously up to the ominous essay ahead. But students find early confidence in the opposite approach: "Why yes, even I can do it!" Once they see how easily one turns any familiar subject from ping-pong to nuclear energy into a thesis and then see the simple essentials of structure, they can proceed effectively to the smaller and more powerful elements—to paragraphs to sentences, and to words, where the real dynamite of writing is.

I continue to emphasize argument because argument indeed subsumes all other expository principles and teaches easily the firmest organization of one's ideas. To the chapters on paragraphing, I have added the inductive and deductive structures, and what I call the "hybrid," the more open-ended arrangement of many seasoned essayists, but I also include the classic modes of description, narration, and exposition, with additional explanation of analogy, comparison and contrast, cause and effect, and process. A chapter on common-sense logic leads to the sentence and on to words.

Throughout, I have included exercises in thesis-making, in paragraphing, in writing various kinds of sentences and punctuating them, in using words and spelling them, in handling various figures of speech. I have encouraged the student to play with language, to write unusual and complicated sentences for exercise, to juggle with words, and especially to achieve clarity by learning to recognize and eliminate the various endemic kinds of wordiness, which everywhere befogs modern prose. The chapter on the research paper draws everything together, and includes for the first time the Modern Language Association's newly simplified system of citation, explained in simple steps and illustrated by a paper on Louis Riel.

The book concludes with a handbook of grammar, punctuation, spelling, capitalization, and usage—for supplementary teaching and permanent reference—with further exercises as needed. It also includes a surprise (Chapter 13)—a well-kept secret on how to answer an essay-question, how to improve one's grade on examinations—well worth a preliminary peek before midsemester. Inside the front cover is a "do's" list against which students may check their work; inside the back cover, a set of symbols for marking the "don'ts."

The teacher will find plenty of room here for any convenient approach, and ample opportunity for that almost necessary bonus of academic gratification, disagreeing with the book, out of which much of our best teaching comes. A great deal will certainly be familiar. Nothing here is really new. I am simply describing the natural linguistic facts discovered again and again by the heirs of Aristotle, in which lineage I seem inescapably to belong. For I have found that one practical need in all writing is to mediate gracefully between opposite possibilities—between simplicity and complexity, clarity and shade, economy and plenitude, the particular and the general.

I wish to acknowledge my great and unending debt to the teachers who, from the responses of more than two million students, have given me their encouragement and suggestions. I continue to be no less grateful to the individual students and private citizens who have written me from as far away as Kenya and as near home as Ann Arbor.

Sheridan Baker

1
Overview:
The Point of It All

WRITE FOR YOUR SHARE

Writing is one of the most important things we do. It helps us
catch our ideas, realize our thoughts, and stand out as fluent
persuasive people both on paper and on our feet in front of the
meeting or the boss. Reading and writing have already enlarged
your education and your speech. Even television, in its news and
advertising, and in most of its shows, pours into our thoughts the
words and habits that literacy—and written scripts—has built into
our speech and thinking.

This language we share is Standard English—somewhere
between what is customary in Britain and what is sometimes
called "edited Standard American English" south of our border.
But it is our living language, in speech as well as print. Actually,
even our most local and private dialects partake of its forms and
vocabulary, as do our silent thoughts, however fragmentary, our
"inner speech," as several psychologists and linguists have recently called it.* In fact, we automatically "edit" all our fragmentary thoughts for even our most spontaneous expressions, intui-
tively selecting from our store of possibilities, filling in the
grammar, expanding, rephrasing, just as if we were writing and
rewriting: ". . . er . . . I mean . . . but really. . . ." So writing is
an extension of the way we naturally handle language. Writing
simply straightens out and clarifies our intuitive editing, and in

---

*Lev Vygotsky, *Thought and Language* (Cambridge, Mass.: MIT Press, 1962), with
"Comments" by Jean Piaget; James Moffett, "Writing, Inner Speech, and Medita-
tion," *College English* 44 (1982): 231–246.

turn makes the editing itself more fluent. Writing perfects thought and speech. Indeed, over the millions of years from our first emotive screams and gurgles of pleasure to the bright dawn of literacy, writing—thinking in full dress—seems to be where speech has been going all the time.

Your writing course prepares you for the challenges not only of university but of the business of life ahead, whether in the executive suite or the courtroom, the hospital or the consulate, the legislature or the press room. You must write in almost every course. You must write for admission to postgraduate studies. You must write proposals for grants and programs. You must write to persuade people of your worth—demonstrated in your literacy—and of the worth of your ideas. You must write to develop and advance them—and yourself. You must write for your share of life. Thinking and persuasion are your business, and the business of your course in writing. All communication is largely persuasion. Even your most factual survey as engineer or educator must persuade its audience to approval by its perception and clarity and organization—in short, by its writing.

ATTITUDE

Writing well is a matter of conviction. You learn in school by exercises, of course; and exercises are best when taken as such, as body-builders, flexions, and extensions for the real contests ahead. But when you are convinced that what you write has meaning, that it has meaning for you—and not in a lukewarm, hypothetical way, but truly—then your writing will stretch its wings and have the whole wide world in range. For writing is simply a graceful and articulate extension of the best that is in you. Writing well is not easy. As it extends the natural way we express ourselves, it nevertheless takes unending practice. Each essay is a polished exercise for the next to come, each new trial, as T. S. Eliot says, a new "raid on the inarticulate."

In writing, you clarify your own thoughts, and strengthen your conviction. Indeed, you probably grasp your thoughts for the first time. Writing is a way of thinking. Writing actually creates thought, and generates your ability to think: you discover thoughts you hardly knew you had, and come to know what you know. You learn as you write. In the end, after you have rewritten and rearranged for your best rhetorical effectiveness, your words will carry your readers with you to see as you see, to believe as you believe, to understand your subject as you now understand it.

Don't Take Yourself Too Seriously

Take your subject seriously—if it is a serious subject—but take yourself with a grain of salt. Your attitude is the very center of your prose. If you take yourself too importantly, your tone will go hollow, your sentences will go moldy, your page will go fuzzy with *of*'s and *which*'s and nouns clustered in passive constructions. In your academic career, the worst dangers lie immediately ahead. Freshmen usually learn to write tolerably well, but during the upper years the academic mildew frequently sets in, and by graduate school you can cut it with a cheese knife.

You must constantly guard against acquiring the heavy, sober-sided attitude that makes for wordiness along with obscurity, dullness, and anonymity. Do not lose your personality and your voice in the monotone of official prose. You should work like a scholar and scientist, but you should write like a writer, one who cares about the economy and beauty of language, and has some individual personality. Your attitude, then, should form somewhere between a confidence in your own convictions and a humorous distrust of your own rhetoric, which can so easily carry you away. You should bear yourself as a member of humankind, knowing that we are all sinners, all redundant, and all too fond of big words. Here is an example from—I blush to admit—the pen of a professor:

> The general problem is perhaps correctly stated as inadequacy of nursing personnel to meet demands for nursing care and services. Inadequacy, it should be noted, is both a quantitative and qualitative term and thus it can be assumed that the problem as stated could indicate insufficient numbers of nursing personnel to meet existing demands for their services; deficiencies in the competencies of those who engage in the various fields of nursing; or both.

Too few good nurses, and a badly swollen author—that is the problem. "Nursing personnel" may mean nurses, but it also may mean "the nursing of employees," so that the author seems to say, for a wildly illogical moment, that someone is not properly pampering or suckling people. Notice the misfiring *it* (fourth line), which seems to refer to *term* but actually refers to nothing. And the ponderous jingle of "deficiencies in the competencies" would do for a musical comedy. The author has taken the wrong model, is taking herself too seriously, and taking her readers almost nowhere.

Consider Your Readers

If you are to take your subject with all the seriousness it deserves and yourself with as much skeptical humour as you can bear, how are you to take your readers? Who are they, anyway? Some teachers suggest using your classmates as your audience. This is a good beginning. But the problem remains with all those other classes, with those papers in history or social science, with the reports, the applications for jobs and grants, the letters to the editor. At some point, you must become a writer facing the invisible public.

To some extent, your audiences will vary. You imagine yourself addressing slightly different personalities when you write about snorkeling and when you write about nuclear reactors. Hypothetically, your vocabulary and your tone would vary all the way from Skid Row to Oxford as you turn from social work to Rhodes scholarship; and certainly the difference of audience would reflect itself somewhat in your language. Furthermore, you must indeed sense your audience's capacity, its susceptibilities and prejudices, if you are to win even a hearing. No doubt our language skids a bit when down on the Row, and we certainly speak different tongues with our friends, and with the friends of our parents.

But the notion of adjusting your writing to a whole scale of audiences, though attractive in theory, hardly works out in practice. You are *writing,* and the written word presupposes a literate norm that immediately eliminates all the lower ranges of mere talk. Even when you speak, you do not so lose your identity as to pass for a total illiterate. You stand on your own linguistic feet, in your own linguistic personality, and the only adjustment you should assiduously practice in writing and speaking is the upward one toward verbal adulthood, a slight grammatical tightening and rhetorical heightening to make your thoughts clear, emphatic, and attractive.

Consider your audience a mixed group of intelligent and reasonable adults. You want them to think of you as well informed and well educated. You wish to explain what you know and what you believe. You wish to persuade them pleasantly that what you know is important and what you believe is right. Try to imagine what they might ask you, what they might object to, what they might know already, what they might find interesting. Be simple and clear, amusing and profound, using plenty of illustration to show what you mean. *But do not talk down to them.* That is the great flaw in the slumming theory of communication. Bowing to your readers' supposed level, you insult them by assuming their inferiority. Thinking yourself humble, you are actually haughty. The best solution is simply to assume that your readers are as intelligent as you. Even if they are not, they will be flattered by the assumption. Your written language, in short, will be respectful toward your subject, considerate toward your readers, and somehow amiable toward human failings.

THE WRITTEN VOICE

Make Your Writing Talk

That the silent page should seem to speak with the writer's voice is remarkable. With all gestures gone, no eyes to twinkle, no notation at all for the rise and fall of utterance, and only a handful of punctuation marks, the level line of type can yet convey the writer's voice, the tone of his personality.

To achieve this tone, to find your own voice and style, simply try to write in the language of intelligent conversation, cleared of all the stumbles and weavings of talk. Indeed, our speech, like thought, is amazingly circular. We can hardly think in a straight line if we try. We think by questions and answers, repetitions and

failures; and our speech, full of *you know's* and *I mean's,* follows
the erratic ways of the mind, circling around and around as we
stitch the simplest of logical sequences. Your writing will carry
the stitches, not those editorial loopings and pauses and re-
threadings. It should be literate. It should be broad enough of
vocabulary and rich enough of sentence to show that you have
read a book. It should not be altogether unworthy to place you
in the company of those who have written well in your native
tongue. But it should nevertheless retain the tone of intelligent
and agreeable conversation. It should be alive with a human
personality—yours—which is probably the most persuasive rhetorical force on earth. Good writing should have a voice, and the
voice should be unmistakably your own.

Suppose your spoken voice sounded something like this (I
reconstruct an actual response in one of my classes):

> **Well, I don't know, I like Shakespeare really, I guess—
> I mean, well, like when Lear divides up his kingdom like a
> fairy tale or something, I thought that was kind of silly,
> dividing his kingdom. Anyone could see that was silly if you
> wanted to keep your kingdom, why divide it? But then like,
> something begins to happen, like a real family, I mean.
> Cordelia really gets griped at her older sisters, I mean, like
> all older sisters, if you've ever had any. There's a kind of
> sibling rivalry, you know. Then she's kind of griped at her
> father, who she really loves, but she thinks, I mean, like
> saying it right out spoils it. You can't really speak right out,
> I mean, about love, well, except sometimes, I guess, without
> sounding corny.**

Your written voice might then emerge from this with something of the same tone, but with everything straightened out,
filled in, and polished up:

> **The play begins like a fairy tale. It even seems at first
> a little abstract and silly. A king has three daughters. The
> two elder ones are bad; the youngest is good. The king
> wishes to keep his kingdom in peace, and keep his title as
> king, by dividing his kingdom in a senseless and almost
> empty ceremonial way. But very soon the play seems like
> real life. The family seems real, complete with sibling ri-
> valry. The king, not the play, now seems foolish and senile.
> The older daughters are hypocrites. Cordelia, the youngest,**

is irritated at them, and at her father's foolishness. As a result, she remains silent, not only because she is irritated at the flattering words of her sisters, but also because anything she could say about her real love for her father would now sound false.

You might wish to polish that some more. You might indeed have said it another way, one more truly your own. The point, however, is to write in a tidy, economical way that wipes up the lapses of talk and fills in the gaps of thought, and yet keeps the tone and movement of good conversation, in your own voice.

Establish a Firm Viewpoint

"In my opinion," the beginner will write repeatedly, until he seems to be saying "It is only *my* opinion, after all, so it can't be worth much." He has failed to realize that his whole essay represents his opinion—of what the truth of the matter is. Don't make your essay a personal letter to Diary, or to Mother, or to Teacher, a confidential report of what happened to you last night as you agonized upon a certain question. *"To me,* Irving Layton is a great poet"—this is really writing about yourself. You are only confessing private convictions. To find the public reasons often requires no more than a trick of grammar: a shift from *"To me,* Irving Layton is . . ." to "Irving Layton is . . . ," from *"I thought* the book was good" to "The book is good," from you and your room last night to your subject and what it *is. Generalize* your opinions and emotions. Change "I cried" to "The scene is very moving." The grammatical shift represents a whole change of viewpoint, a shift from self to subject. You become the informed adult, showing the reader around firmly, politely, and persuasively.

Once you have effaced yourself from your assertions, once you have erased *to me* and *in my opinion* and all such signs of amateur terror, you may later let yourself back into the essay for emphasis or graciousness: "Mr. Watson errs, I think, precisely at this point." You can thus ease your most tentative or violent assertions, and show that you are polite and sensible, reasonably sure of your position but aware of the possibility of error. Again: the reasonable adult.

You go easy on the *I,* in short, to keep your reader focused on your subject. But you can use the *I* as much as you like to *illustrate* your point, once established, using a personal experience among several other pieces of evidence, or even all by itself. Of course, your instructors will sometimes ask for a wholly autobiographical essay. Indeed, some courses focus altogether on the *I* of personal experience. And your autobiographical résumés in applying for medical and law school, for grants and jobs, will of course require the *I.* But for the usual essay, I repeat, use the personal anecdote and the *I* to illustrate a point or to interject a tactful remark.

Effacing the *I,* then letting it back in on occasion, fixes your point of view. But what about the other pronouns, *we, you, one? One* objectifies the personal *I,* properly generalizing the private into the public. But it can seem too formal, and get too thick:

> **FAULTY:** *One* **finds** *one*'s **opinion changing as** *one* **grows older.**
> **REVISED: Opinions change with age.**
> **REVISED:** *Our* **opinions change as** *we* **grow older.**

That *we* is sometimes a useful generalizer, a convenient haven between the isolating *I* and the impersonal *one. We* can seem pompous, but not if it honestly handles those experiences we know we share, or can share. Suppose we wrote:

> **As I watched program after program, I got bored and began to wonder what values, if any, they represented.**

We can easily transpose this to:

> **As** *we* **watch program after program,** *we* **are progressively bored, and** *we* **begin to wonder what values, if any, they represent.**

(Notice that shifting to the present tense is also part of the generalizing process.) Thus, *we* can generalize without going all the way to *one,* or to the fully objective:

> **Program after program, TV bores its audiences and leaves its sense of values questionable.**

We also quite naturally refers to earlier parts of your demonstration, through which you have led your reader: *as we have already seen.* But you will have noticed from the preceding examples that *we* tends slightly toward wordiness. Used sparingly, then, *we* can ease your formality and draw your reader in. Overused, it can seem too presumptuous or chummy. Try it out. See how it feels, and use it where it seems comfortable and right.

You raises two different problems. The first is the one we have been discussing: how to generalize that *I* effectively into something else, either *one* or *we* or full objectivity. The indefinite *you*, like the indefinite *they*, is usually too vague, and too adolescent.

FAULTY: **You have your own opinion.**
FAULTY: **They have their own opinion.**
REVISED: **Everyone has his own opinion.**
REVISED: **We all have our own opinions.**

You as direct address to the reader poses a different problem. I have consistently addressed this book to *you*, the reader. But this is a special case, the relationship of tutor to student projected onto the page. None of my essays, I think, contains any *you* at all. Our stance in an essay is a little more formal, a little more public. We are better holding our pronouns to *one* or *we*, an occasional *I*, or none at all, as we find a comfortable stance between our subject and audience, and find our written voice.

THE POINT: ARGUMENTATION

The point is persuasion. Your written voice, your personal style, remember, is a part of your persuasiveness. But having a point to make is the real centre of persuasion, the likely goal of most of your writing and speaking in university and in contemporary life. Hence, the centre of your writing course is indeed argumentation. Even explaining the Battle of Batoche or the Oedipus complex invites an argumentative thrust as you persuade your readers of the most significant causes and crucial events. Argumentation thus ranges through the coolest explanation, or exposition, up to the burning issues you support. Argument, as we will see as we move along, absorbs for its ends every kind of writing you can think of. Narration, dialogue, anecdotes, exposition, description, newspaper headlines, statistical tables, and chemical formulas may all illustrate the point you are making in that written personality of yours that gives it life.

Plan to Rewrite

As you write your weekly assignments and find your voice, you will also be learning to groom your thoughts, to present them clearly and fully, to make sure you have said what you thought you said. This is the process of composition, of putting your thoughts together, beginning with jotted questions and tentative ideas, all to be mulled over, selected, rejected, expanded as you discover your ideas and write them into full expression. Ultimately, good writing comes only from *re*writing. Even your happy thoughts will need resetting, as you join them to the frequently happier ones that a second look seems to call up. Even the letter-perfect paper will improve almost of itself if you simply sit down to type it through again. You will find, almost unbidden, sharper words, better phrases, new figures of speech, and new illustrations and ideas to replace the weedy patches not noticed before. Indeed, this process of rewriting is what strengthens that instinctive editing you do as you speak extemporaneously or write impromptu essays and exams when revision is out of the question. Rewriting improves your fluency, making each rewrite less demanding.

So allow time for revision. After you have settled on something to write about, have turned your ideas over on paper for a while, have found a central idea, and feel ready to write the whole thing out, plan for at least three drafts—and try to manage four. Thinking of things to say is the hardest part at first. Even a short assignment of 500 words seems to stretch ahead like a Sahara. You have asserted your central idea in a sentence, and that leaves 490 words to go. But if you step off boldly, one foot after the other, you will make progress, find an oasis or two, and perhaps end at a run in green pastures. With longer papers, you will want some kind of outline to keep you from straying, and probably some jotted notes even for short ones, but the principle is the same: step ahead and keep moving until you've arrived. That is the first draft.

The second draft is a penciled correction of the first. Here you refine and polish, checking your dubious spellings in the dictionary, sharpening your punctuation, clarifying your meaning, pruning away the deadwood, adding a thought here, extending an illustration there—running in a whole new paragraph on an inserted page. You will also be tuning your sentences, carefully adjusting your tone until it is clearly that of an intelligent, reasonable person at ease with his knowledge and his audience. Your third draft, a typing and smoothing of your penciled version, will generate further improvements.

Here is a passage from a student's paper that has gone the full course. First you see the student's initial draft, with his own corrections on it. Next you see the passage after a second typing (and some further changes), as it was returned by the instructor with his marks on it. Then you see the final revision, handed in again, as this particular assignment required:

First Draft

In a university education, students should
be allowed to ~~make~~ ^{choose} their own course. ~~Too many~~ ^{All the}
requirements_, ~~are discouraging to~~ ^{they must take discourage} people's

creativity and they cannot learn anything
~~which is~~ ^{they are} not motivated ~~for him~~ to learn.
~~With~~ ^R ⟋requirements_, ^{restrict} their freedom to choose
~~what he is interested in is taken~~ ^{and their eagerness to learn. They are only discouraged} away by
having to study dull subjects like German_, ^{in which} ~~which~~
~~he is not interested in.~~ ^{they can see no relevance to their interests}.

The Paper, with Instructor's Markings

can you get rid of the passive?

redundant?

relevant?

true?

In a university education, students <u>should</u> <u>be allowed</u> to choose their own curricula and select their own courses. <u>All the require-</u> <u>ments they must take</u> stifle their <u>creativity</u>. Moreover, <u>they cannot</u> learn anything they are not motivated to learn. Requirements restrict their freedom to choose and their eagerness to explore the subjects they are

activate

interested in. <u>They are only discouraged</u> by having to study dull subjects like German, in which they can see no relevance.

Revised Paper

Students should choose their own education, their own curricula, their own
courses. Their education is really theirs
alone. Every university requirement threatens
to stifle the very enthusiasms upon which
true education depends. Students learn best
when motivated by their own interests, but,
in the midst of a dozen complicated require-

ments, they can hardly find time for the

courses they long to take. Requirements

therefore not only restrict their freedom

to choose but destroy their eagerness to

explore. Dull subjects like German, in

which they can see no relevance anyway,

take all their time and discourage them

completely.

AIMING FOR A STYLE OF YOUR OWN

By writing frequently, you will create a style of your own—and with it, a good bit of your future. But what is style? At its best, it is much like style in a car, a gown, a Greek temple—the ordinary materials of this world so poised and perfected as to stand out from the landscape and compel a second look, something that hangs in the reader's mind, like a vision. It is a writer's own voice, with the hems and haws chipped out, speaking the common language uncommonly well. It comes from a craftsman who has discovered the knots and potentials in his material, one who has learned to enjoy phrasing and syntax, and the very punctuation that keeps them straight. It is the labour of love, and like love it can bring pleasure and satisfaction.

But style is not for the gifted only. Quite the contrary. Indeed, as I have been suggesting, everyone already has a style, and a personality, and can develop both. The stylistic side of writing is, in fact, the only side that can be analyzed and learned. The stylistic approach is the practical approach: you learn some things to do and not to do, as you would learn strokes in tennis. Your ultimate game is up to you, but you can at least begin in good form. Naturally, it takes practice. You have to keep at it. Like the doctor and the lawyer and the golfer and the tennis player, you just keep practising—even to write a nearly perfect letter. But if you like the game, you can probably learn to play it well. You will at least be able to write a respectable sentence, and to express your thoughts clearly, without puffing and flailing.

In the essay, as in business, trying to get started and getting off on the wrong foot account for most of our lost motion. So we will next consider how to find a thesis, which will virtually organize your essay for you. Then we will study the relatively simple structure of the essay, and the structure of the paragraph—the architecture of spatial styling. Then we will experiment with various styles of sentence, playing with length and complexity to help you find the right mix to convey your personal rhythm. And finally we will get down to words themselves. Here again you will experiment to find those personal ranges of vocabulary, those blends of the breezy and the formal, that will empower your personal style. Here, in the word, is where writing tells; and here, as in ancient times, you will be in touch with the mystery. But again, there are things to do and things not to do, and these can be learned. So, to begin.

2
Making a Beginning
From Subject to Thesis

GETTING SET

Get set! Writing an essay isn't exactly a fifty-yard dash, but you
do need to get ready and get set before you can go to it. Writing
requires a time and place, an habitual environment to coax and
support those inspired moments that seem to flow spontaneously
into language. Your best scheme is to plan two or three sittings
for each assignment. Your place should be fixed. It should be
comfortable and convenient. Your times should be regular, varied in length from short to long, and set to fit your schedule and
your personal rhythm, as morning person or night owl, sprinter
or long-distance runner. Arrange your first period for a time as
soon as possible after assignments, perhaps only half an hour for
scribbling and thinking on paper. Your next two sessions should
be longer, the last with expandable time to get the job done.

WHAT SHALL I WRITE?

First you need a subject, and then you need a thesis. Yes, but *what
shall I write?* Here you are, an assignment before you and the
paper as blank as your mind, especially if your instructor has left
the subject up to you. Look for something that interests you,
something you know about, some hobby—something that shook
you up, left you perplexed, started you thinking.

Writing will help you discover that something. Don't stare at that blank page. Set yourself the task of writing for ten minutes, no matter what. Start your pencil moving and keep it going, even beginning with *Good grief, what shall I write? Write on anything, the big oaf said. OK, but what what what what what? Fishing? Baby-sitting? Skipping rope? Crime? Nuclear power? Oh no. Crime? Rape? How about the time I ripped off a candy bar and got caught? The shock of recognition. Everyone's done it at some time or other. Everyone's guilty. Everyone's tempted. Something for nothing. The universal temptation of crime.* . . . Keep it going until your watch tells you to stop. That's a good start. Take a break and let your thoughts sink in and accumulate.

Probe your own experiences and feelings for answers as to why people behave as they do, especially in times of crisis. Prestige? The admiration of peers? Fear of not going with the gang? Why is fishing (let us say) so appealing to you? Why more so than water skiing or swimming or sailing or tennis or painting? Why don't some people like it? What might they object to? Now have another bout on paper, perhaps just writing the questions down, perhaps discovering some answers as you go. You have found your subject—and indeed have already moved a good way toward a thesis. The more your subject matters to you, the more you can make it matter to your readers. It might be skiing. It might be dress. It might be roommates, the Peloponnesian War, a political protest, a personal discovery of racial tensions, an experience as a nurse's aide. But do not tackle a big philosophical abstraction, like Freedom, or a big subject, like the Supreme Court. They are too vast, your time and space and knowledge all too small. You would probably manage no more than a collection of platitudes. Start rather with something specific, like running, and let the ideas of freedom and justice and responsibility arise from there. An abstract idea is a poor beginning. To be sure, as you move ahead through your course in writing, you will work more directly with ideas, with problems posed by literature, with questions in the great civilizing debate about what we are doing in this strange world and universe. But again, look for something within your concern. The best subjects lie nearest at hand, and nearest the heart.

You can personalize almost any subject and cut it down to size, getting a manageable angle on it. On an assigned subject, particularly in courses like political science or anthropology or sociology, look for something that connects you with it. Suppose your instructor assigns a paper on social assistance. Think of a grandparent, a parent, a neighbor, a friend—or perhaps yourself as a student receiving benefits, and how reductions would or would not affect your life. You will have a vivid illustration as well as one corner of the huge problem to illuminate. Nuclear energy? Perhaps you have seen on television the appalling space suits and mechanical arms required to handle the radioactive stuff, along with something of its astounding problems. Perhaps you remember an article, or a sentence, that started you thinking. With subjects to find, keep an eye and an ear open as you read the newspaper or *Maclean's,* or watch TV, and talk with your friends. Your classes and textbooks will inevitably turn up subjects for your writing course, if you watch for them, which you can bring into your personal range. Deregulating petroleum? You have probably seen the price of gas soar, your pocketbook shrink, and have taken to the bus, or your bike, or your heels. You need to find a personal interest in your subject to have something to say and to interest others.

FROM SUBJECT TO THESIS

Suppose, for the present, we start simply with "Drugs." Certainly, most of us have been tempted, or had to resist, or to go along, have experimented, or gotten hooked, or have known someone who has—especially if we include cigarettes and alcohol. "Drugs" is a subject easily personalized. Taking a subject like this will also show how to generalize from your own experience, and how to cut your subject down to manageable size. Your first impulse will probably be to write in the first person, but your experience may remain merely personal and may not point your subject into a thesis. As I have said, a personal anecdote makes a lively *illustration,* but first you need to generate your thesis and establish it for your reader. You need to move out of that bright, self-centered spotlight of consciousness in which we live before we really grow up, in which the child assumes that all his or her experiences are unique. If you shift from "me" to "the beginner" or "the young adult," however, you will be stepping into maturity: acknowledging that others have gone through exactly the same thing, that your experiences have illustrated once again the general dynamics of the individual and the group. So instead of writing "I was afraid to refuse," you write:

> The *beginner* is afraid to refuse, and soon discovers the tremendous pressure of the group.

By generalizing your private feelings, you change your subject into a thesis—your argumentative proposition. You simply assume you are normal and fairly representative, and you then generalize with confidence, transposing your particular experiences, your particular thoughts and reactions, into statements about the general ways of the world. Put your proposition, your thesis, into one sentence. This will get you focussed. And now you are ready to begin.

WHERE ESSAYS FAIL

You can usually blame a bad essay on a bad beginning. If your essay falls apart, it probably has no primary idea, no thesis, to hold it together. "What's the big idea?" we used to ask. The phrase will serve as a reminder that you must find the "big idea" behind your several smaller thoughts and musings and drafts before you can start to shape your final essay. In the beginning was the *logos,* says the Bible—the idea, the plan, caught in a flash as if in a single word. Find your *logos,* and you are ready to round out your essay and set it spinning.

Suppose you had decided to write about a high-speed ride —another case of group dynamics. If you have not focussed your big idea in a thesis, you might begin something like this:

> Everyone thinks he is a good driver. There are more accidents caused by young drivers than any other group. Driver education is a good beginning, but further practice is very necessary. People who object to driver education do not realize that modern society, with its suburban pattern of growth, is built around the automobile. The car becomes a way of life and a status symbol. When teenagers go too fast they are probably only copying their own parents.

A little reconsideration, aimed at a good thesis-sentence, could turn this into a reasonably good opening paragraph, with your thesis, your big idea, asserted at the end to focus your reader's attention:

> **Modern society is built on the automobile. Children play with tiny cars; teenagers long to take out the car alone. Soon they are testing their skills at higher and higher speeds, especially with a group of friends along. One final test at extreme speeds usually suffices. It is usually a sobering experience, if survived, and can open one's eyes to the deadly dynamics of the group.**

Thus your thesis is your essay's life and spirit. If it is sufficiently firm, it may tell you immediately how to organize your supporting material. But if you do not find a thesis, your essay will be a tour through the miscellaneous, replete with scaffolds and catwalks—"We have just seen this; now let us turn to this" —an essay with no vital idea. A purely expository essay, one simply on "Cats," for instance, will have to rely on outer scaffolding alone (some orderly progression from Persia to Siam), since it really has no idea at all. It is all subject, all cats, instead of being based on an idea *about* cats, with a thesis *about* cats.

THE ARGUMENTATIVE EDGE

Find Your Thesis

The *about*-ness puts an argumentative edge on the subject. When you have something to say *about* cats, you have found your underlying idea. You have something to defend, something to fight about: not just "Cats," but "The cat is really a person's best friend." Now the hackles on all dog people are rising, and you have an argument on your hands. You have something to prove. You have a thesis.

"What's the big idea, Mac?" Let the impudence in that time-honoured demand remind you that the most dynamic thesis is a kind of affront to somebody. No one will be very much interested in listening to you deplete the thesis. "The dog is a person's best friend." Everyone knows that already. Even the dog lovers will be uninterested, convinced they know better than you. But the cat. . . .

So it is with any unpopular idea. The more unpopular the viewpoint and the stronger the push against convention, the stronger the thesis and the more energetic the essay. Compare the energy in "Democracy is good" with that in "Communism is good," for instance. The first is filled with platitudes, the second with plutonium. By the same token, if you can find the real energy in "Democracy is good," if you can get down through the sand to where the roots and water are, you will have a real essay, because the opposition against which you generate your energy is the heaviest in the world: boredom. Probably the most energetic thesis of all, the greatest inner organizer, is some tired old truth that you cause to spurt with new life, making the old ground green again.

To find a thesis and to put it into one sentence is to narrow and define your subject to workable size. Under "Cats" you must deal with all felinity from the jungle up, carefully partitioning the eons and areas, the tigers and tabbies. But proclaim the cat the friend of humanity, and you have pared away whole categories and chapters, and need only think up the arguments sufficient to overwhelm the opposition. So, put an argumentative edge on your subject—and you will have found your thesis.

Neutral exposition, to be sure, has its uses. You may want to tell someone how to build a doghouse, how to can asparagus, how to follow the outlines of relativity, or even how to write an essay. Performing a few exercises in simple exposition will no doubt sharpen your insight into the problems of finding orderly sequences, of considering how best to lead your readers through the hoops of writing clearly and accurately. It will also illustrate how much finer and surer an argument is.

You will see that picking an argument immediately simplifies the problems so troublesome in straight exposition: the defining, the partitioning, the narrowing of the subject. Not that you must be constantly pugnacious or aggressive. I have overstated my point to make it stick. Actually, you can put an argumentative edge on the flattest of expository subjects. "How to build a doghouse" might become "Building a doghouse is a thorough introduction to the building trades, including architecture and civil

engineering." "Canning asparagus" might become "An asparagus patch is a course in economics." "Relativity" might become
"Relativity is not so inscrutable as many suppose." Literary subjects take an argumentative edge almost by nature. You simply
assert what the essential point of a poem or play seems to be:
"*Hamlet* is essentially about a world that has lost its values." You
assume that your readers are in search of clarity, that you have
a loyal opposition consisting of the interested but uninformed.
You have given your subject its edge; you have limited and organized it at a single stroke. Pick an *argument,* then, and you will
automatically be defining and narrowing your subject, and all the
partitions that you don't need will fold up. Instead of dealing with
things, subjects, and pieces of subjects, you will be dealing with
an idea and its consequences.

Sharpen Your Thesis

Come out with your subject pointed. You have chosen something
that interests you, something you have thought about, read
about, something preferably of which you have also had some
experience—perhaps, let us say, seeing a friend loafing while
cashing welfare cheques. So take a stand. Make a judgment of
value, make a *thesis.* Be reasonable, but don't be timid. It is
helpful to think of your thesis, your main idea, as a debating
question—"Resolved: Welfare payments must go"—taking out
the "Resolved" when you actually write your thesis down. But
your resolution will be even stronger, your essay clearer and
tighter, if you can sharpen your thesis even further—"Resolved:
Welfare payments must go because _____." Fill in that blank,
and your worries are practically over. The main idea is to put
your whole argument into one sentence.

Try, for instance: "Welfare payments must go because they
are making people irresponsible." I don't know at all if that is
true, and neither will you until you write your way into it, considering probabilities and alternatives and objections, and especially
the underlying assumptions. In fact, no one, no master sociolo-
gist or future historian, can tell absolutely if it is true, so multi-
plex are the causes in human affairs, so endless and tangled the
consequences. The basic assumption—that irresponsibility is

growing—may be entirely false. No one, I repeat, can tell absolutely. But likewise, your guess may be as good as another's. At any rate, you are now ready to write. You have found your *logos*.

Now you can put your well-pointed thesis-sentence on a card on the wall in front of you to keep from drifting off target. But you will now want to dress it for the public, to burnish it and make it comely. Suppose you try:

> **Welfare payments, perhaps more than anything else, are eroding personal initiative.**

But is this fully true? Perhaps you had better try something like:

> **Despite their immediate benefits, welfare payments may actually be eroding personal initiative and depriving society of needed workers.**

This is your full thesis. You have acknowledged the opposition ("immediate benefits"); you have spelled out your *because* (erosion, deprivation). This is your opinion, stated as certainty. But how do you know, without all the facts? Well, no one knows everything. No one would write anything if he waited until he did. To a great extent, the writing of a thing is the learning of it—the discovery of truth. So make a desperate thesis and get into the arena. This is probably solution enough. If it becomes increasingly clear that your thesis is untrue, turn it around and use the other end. If your convictions have begun to falter with:

> **Despite their immediate benefits, welfare payments undermine initiative. . . .**

try it the other way around, with something like:

> **Although welfare payments may offend the rugged individualist, they relieve much want and anxiety, and they enable many a family to maintain its integrity.**

You will now have a beautiful command of the major objections to your new position. And you will have learned something about human fallibility and the nature of truth. You simply add enough evidence to persuade your reader that what you say is probably true, finding arguments that will stand up in the marketplace—public reasons for your private convictions.

Use Your Title

After your thesis, think of a title. A good title focusses your thinking even more sharply and catches your reader's thoughts on your finished paper. Your title is your opening opportunity. It is an integral part of your paper. Don't forget it.

Work up something from your thesis. It will be tentative, of course. Your thinking and your paper may change in the writing, and you will want to change your title to match. But a good title, like a good thesis, has a double advantage: (1) it helps you keep on track as you write; (2) it attracts and helps keep your reader on track as he reads. It is the first step in your persuasion. So try something attractive:

> **Welfare Not Warfare**
> **Farewell to Welfare**
> **Whom Does Welfare Benefit?**

You can probably do better. You will do better when you finish your paper. But don't make it sound like a newspaper headline, and don't make it a complete statement. Don't forget your title as a starter, both for your writing and for your written paper. Capitalize all significant words (see 243–45 for details). Titles do not take periods, but do take question and exclamation marks if you need them. Your title and your opening sentence should be independent of each other. With a title like "Polluted Streams," for instance, don't begin with *"This* is a serious problem."

SAMPLE: FROM SUBJECT TO THESIS

Now with the concepts in hand, we need a framework, a structure, to put them in. This we will look at in the next chapter. But let us close with a student's paper to illustrate the points of this chapter as it looks ahead to the structural points of the next. In it, you can see the mechanics of typing, spacing, quoting, and so forth. The author has made a few small last-minute corrections in pencil, which are perfectly acceptable. Her writing is a little wordy and awkward. She is a little uncertain of her language. Her *one*'s, for instance, seem far too stiff and insistent. This is her first paper, and she has not yet fully discovered her own written voice. But it is an excellent beginning. It shows well how a personal experience produces a publicly valid thesis, then turns around to give that thesis its most lively and specific illustration. The assignment had asked for a paper of about five hundred words on some book (or movie, or TV program) that had proved personally meaningful. Even a memorable experience would do—fixing a car, or building a boat, or being arrested. The aim of the assignment was to generalize from a personally valuable experience and to explain to others how such an experience can be valuable to them.

On Finding Oneself in New Guinea

Opposing
View

    Reading for pleasure is not considered to be popular. **Young adults prefer the "boob tube," the television set with which they have spent so many childhood hours. Too many attractions beckon them away from the books which the teacher recommended to the class for summer reading. One's friends come by in their automobiles to drive down for a coke. The kids go to the moving pictures, or to the beach, and the book one had intended to read remains on the shelf, or probably the library, where one has not yet been able**

Thesis

to find the time to go. Nevertheless, *a book can furnish real enjoyment.*

Generalized
Support

    The reader enjoys the experience of being in another world. **While one reads, one forgets that one is in one's own room. The book has served as a magic carpet to take one to India, or Africa, or Sweden, or even to the cities and areas of one's own country where one has never been. It has also transported one into the lives of people with different experiences and problems, from which one can learn to solve one's own problems of the future. The young person, in particular, can learn by the experience of reading what it is like to be a complete adult.**

    A book is able to help the young person to mature even

further, and change one's whole point of view. *Growing up in New Guinea* by **Margaret Mead is a valuable experience for this reason.** *I found the book on our shelf, after having seen Margaret Mead on TV.* **I was interested in her because the teacher had referred to her book entitled** *Coming of Age in Samoa.* **I was surprised to find this one about New Guinea. I thought it was a mistake. I opened it and read the first sentence:**

Personal Experience

> The way in which each human infant is trans-
> formed into the finished adult, into the compli-
> cated individual version of his city and his cen-
> tury, is one of the most fascinating studies open to
> the curious minded.

Quotation

The idea that the individual is a version of his city and his century was fascinating. I started reading and was surprised when I was called to dinner to learn that two hours had passed. I could hardly eat my dinner fast enough so that I could get back to New Guinea.

From this book I learned that different cultures have very different conceptions about what is right and wrong, in particular about the sex relations and the marriage cere-mony, but that people have the same problems all over the world, namely the problem of finding one's place in society. *I also learned that books can be more enjoyable than any other form of pleasure.* **Books fascinate the reader because while one is learning about other people and their problems, par-ticularly about the problem of becoming a full member of society, one is also learning about one's own problems.**

Thesis Restated

EXERCISES

1. *Put down quickly the first four or five subjects that come to mind—golf, cars, architecture, lipstick, tomatoes. These must have interested you sometime, somewhere. Now make each into an established one-sent-ence argumentative thesis on the pattern* Although _____, golf accom-plishes more because _____.

2. *Supply a thesis-statement and a title for each of the following subjects:*

1. Nuclear armament
2. The appearance of our campus
3. Jogging

4. A book you have read
5. Opportunities for native peoples

3. *Now expand one of your thesis-statements from the preceding exercises into a paper about the length of the preceding example. First, introduce your thesis with a few remarks to get your reader acquainted with your subject, then write your paper straight through to illustrate your thesis as fully as you can. Then go back over this draft and make it publicly presentable, revising until you know you have done your best.*

4. *Making a thesis can also help your reading, and in all your courses. Therefore, at the end of each chapter, or other reading, try to put down in one sentence (and right in your textbook) that chapter's point: not* This chapter discusses racial discrimination, *but* Racial discrimination arises from powerful biological drives to seek one's own kind and to shun aliens. *This practice strengthens your knowledge, aids your analysis— has your author said it anywhere as well as you have?—and develops your ability to generate theses for your own thoughts. It works equally well for poems, stories, and plays.*

3
Your Paper's Basic Structure

BEGINNING, MIDDLE, END

As Aristotle long ago pointed out, works that spin their way through time need a beginning, a middle, and an end to be complete. You need a clear beginning to give your essay character and direction so the reader can tell where he is going and can look forward with expectation. Your beginning, of course, will set forth your thesis. You need a middle to amplify and fulfill. This will be the body of your argument, the bulk of your essay. You need an end to let readers know that they have arrived. This will be your final paragraph, a summation and reassertion of your idea. So give your essay the three-part *feel* of completion, of beginning, middle, and end. Many a first-year student's essay has no structure and leaves no impression. It is all chaotic middle. It has no beginning, it just starts; it has no end, it just stops, burned out at two in the morning.

The beginning must feel like a beginning, not just like an accident. It should be at least a full paragraph that leads your reader into the subject and culminates with your thesis. The end, likewise, should be a full paragraph, one that drives the point home, pushes the implications wide, and brings the reader to rest, back on the fundamental thesis with a sense of completion. When we consider paragraphing in the next chapter, we will look more closely at beginning paragraphs and end paragraphs. The "middle" of your essay, which constitutes its bulk, needs further structural consideration now.

MIDDLE TACTICS

Arrange Your Points in Order of Increasing Interest

Once your thesis has sounded the challenge, your reader's interest is probably at its highest pitch. He wants to see how you can prove so outrageous a thing, or to see what the arguments are for this thing he has always believed but never tested. Each step of the way into your demonstration, he is learning more of what you have to say. But, unfortunately, his interest may be relaxing as it becomes satisfied: the reader's normal line of attention is a progressive decline, arching down like a wintry graph. Against this decline you must oppose your forces, making each successive point more interesting. And save your best till last. It is as simple as that.

Here, for example, is the middle of a short, three-paragraph essay on the thesis that "Working your way through university is valuable." The student's three points ascend in interest:

The student who works finds that the experience is worth more than the money. First, he learns to budget his time. He now supports himself by using time he would otherwise waste, and he studies harder in the time he has left because he knows it is limited. Second, he makes real and lasting friends on the job, as compared to the other casual acquaintances around the campus. He has shared rush hours, and nighttime cleanups with the dishes piled high, and conversation and jokes when business is slow. Finally, he gains confidence in his ability to get along with all kinds of people, and to make his own way. He sees how businesses operate, and how waitresses, for instance, can work cheerfully at a really tiring job without much hope for the future. He gains an insight into the real world, which is a good contrast to the more intellectual and idealistic world of the university student.

Again, each successive item should be more interesting than the last, or you will suddenly seem anticlimactic. Actually, minor regressions of interest make no difference so long as the whole tendency is uphill and your last item clearly the best. Suppose, for example, you were to try a thesis about cats. You decide that four points would make up the case, and that you might arrange them in the following order of increasing interest: (1) cats are affectionate but make few demands; (2) cats actually look out for themselves; (3) cats have, in fact, proved extremely useful to society throughout history in controlling mice and other plaguy rodents; (4) cats satisfy some human need for a touch of the jungle, savagery in repose, ferocity in silk, and have been worshiped for the exotic power they still seem to represent. It may be, as you write, that you will find Number 1 developing attractive or amusing instances, and perhaps even virtually usurping the whole essay. Numbers 2, 3, and 4 should then be moved ahead as interesting but brief preliminaries.

Interests vary, of course. This is the point. And various subjects will suggest different kinds of importance: from small physical details to large, from incidental thought to basic principles. Sometimes chronology will supply a naturally ascending order of interest: as a tennis match or hockey game reaches its climax; or as in any contest against natural hazards and time itself, like crossing a glacier with supplies and endurance dwindling. Space, too, may offer natural progressions of interest, as you move from portico to inner shrine. But usually interest ascends in ideas, and these quite naturally ascend from your own interest in your subject, in which, with a little thought, you can tell which points to handle first and which to arrange for more and more importance, saving best till last. In short, your middle structure should range from least important to most important, from simple to complex, from narrow to broad, from pleasant to hilarious, from mundane to metaphysical—whatever "leasts" and "mosts" your subject suggests.

ACKNOWLEDGING AND DISPOSING
OF THE OPPOSITION

Your cat essay, because it is moderately playful, can proceed rather directly, throwing only an occasional bone of concession to the dogs, and perhaps most of your essays, as you discuss the

Canadian Constitution or explain a poem, will have no opposition to worry about. But a serious controversial argument demands one organizational consideration beyond the simple structure of ascending interest. Although you have taken your stand firmly as a *pro,* you will have to allow scope to the *cons,* or you will seem not to have thought much about your subject. The more opposition you can manage as you carry your point, the more triumphant you will seem, like a high-wire artist daring the impossible.

This balancing of *pros* against *cons* is one of the most fundamental orders of thought: the dialectic order, which is the order of argument, one side pitted against the other. Our minds naturally swing from side to side as we think. In dialectics, we simply give one side an argumentative edge, producing a thesis that cuts a clear line through any subject: "This is better than that." The basic organizing principle here is to get rid of the opposition first, and to end on your own side. Probably you will have already organized your thesis-sentence in a perfect pattern for your *con-pro* argument:

> **Despite their many advantages, welfare payments. . . . Although dogs are fine pets, cats. . . .**

The subordinate clause (see 102–04) states the subordinate part of your argument, which is your concession to the *con* viewpoint; your main clause states your main argument. As the subordinate clause comes first in your thesis sentence, so does the subordinate argument in your essay. Sentence and essay both reflect a natural psychological principle. You want, and the reader wants, to get the opposition out of the way. And you want to end on your best foot. (You might try putting the opposition last, just to see how peculiarly the last word insists on seeming best, and how, when stated last by you, the opposition's case seems to be your own.)

Your opposition, of course, will vary. Some of your audience will agree with you but for different reasons. Others may disagree hotly. You need, then, to imagine what these varying objections might be, as if you were before a meeting in open discussion, giving the hottest as fair a hearing as possible. You probably would not persuade them, but you would ease the pressure and probably persuade the undecided by your reasonable stance. Asking what objections might arise will give you the opposing points that your essay must meet—and overcome.

GET RID OF THE OPPOSITION FIRST. This is the essential tactic of argumentation. You have introduced and stated your thesis in your beginning paragraph. Now start the middle with a paragraph of concession to the *cons:*

> **Dog lovers, of course, have tradition on their side. Dogs are indeed affectionate and faithful. . . .**

And with that paragraph out of the way, go to bat for the cats, showing their superiority to dogs in every point. In a very brief essay, you can use the opposition itself to introduce your thesis in the first paragraph, and dispose of your opponents at the same time:

> **Shakespeare begins *Romeo and Juliet* with ominous warnings about fate. His lovers are "star-crossed," he says: they are doomed from the first by their contrary stars, by the universe itself. They have sprung from "fatal loins." Fate has already determined their tragic end. The play then unfolds a succession of unlucky and presumably fated accidents. Nevertheless, we soon discover that Shakespeare really blames the tragedy not on fate but on human stupidity and error.**

But usually your beginning paragraph will lead down to your thesis somewhat neutrally, and you will attack your opposition head-on in paragraph two, as you launch into the middle.

If the opposing arguments seem relatively slight and brief, you can get rid of them neatly all together in one paragraph before you get down to your case. Immediately after your beginning, which has stated your thesis, you write a paragraph of concession: "Of course, security is a good thing. No one wants people begging." And so on to the end of the paragraph, deflating every conceivable objection. Then back to the main line: "But the price in moral decay is too great." The structure of the essay, paragraph by paragraph, might be diagrammed something like the scheme shown in Diagram I:

Diagram I

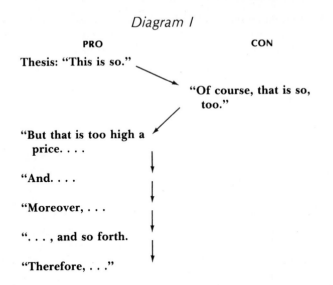

If the opposition is more considerable, demolish it point by point, using a series of *cons* and *pros,* in two or three paragraphs, before you steady down to your own side. Each paragraph can be a small argument that presents the opposition, then knocks it flat —a kind of Punch-and-Judy show: "We must admit that. . . . But. . . ." And down goes the poor old opposition again. Or you can swing your argument through a number of alternating paragraphs: first your beginning, the thesis, then a paragraph to the opposition *(con),* then one for your side *(pro),* then another paragraph of *con,* and so on. The main point, again, is this: *get rid of the opposition first.* One paragraph of concession right after your thesis will probably handle most of your adversaries, and the more complicated argumentative swingers, like the ones shown in Diagram II, will develop naturally as you need them.

You will notice that *But* and *however* are always guides for the *pros,* serving as switches back to the main line. Indeed, *But, however,* and *Nevertheless* are the basic *pros. But* always heads its turning sentence (not followed by a comma); *nevertheless* usually does (followed by a comma). I am sure, however, that *however* is always better buried in the sentence between commas. "However, . . ." at a sentence's beginning is the habit of heavy prose. *But* is for the quick turn; the inlaid *however* for the more elegant sweep.

The structural line of your arguments, then, might look like Diagram II:

Diagram II. Controlling Firearms—Pro and Con

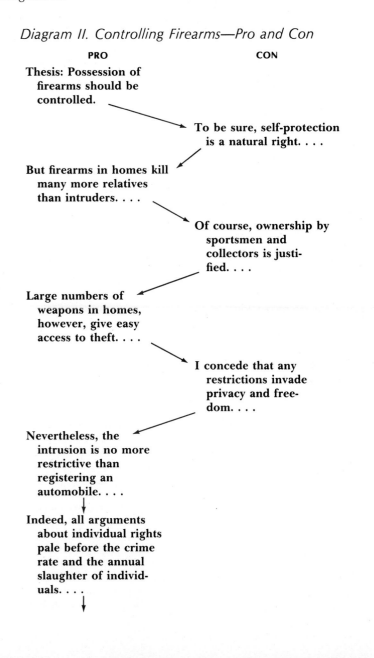

PRO   CON

Thesis: Possession of firearms should be controlled.

To be sure, self-protection is a natural right. . . .

But firearms in homes kill many more relatives than intruders. . . .

Of course, ownership by sportsmen and collectors is justified. . . .

Large numbers of weapons in homes, however, give easy access to theft. . . .

I concede that any restrictions invade privacy and freedom. . . .

Nevertheless, the intrusion is no more restrictive than registering an automobile. . . .

Indeed, all arguments about individual rights pale before the crime rate and the annual slaughter of individuals. . . .

↓

**In the United States, for
example, where controls
are inadequate, firearms
kill thousands more
than in any other
country.**

↓

**Therefore, controlling
firearms is reasonable
and necessary.**

Comparing and contrasting two poems, two stories, two ball players, are further instances of this essential process of thought, of this important way to understanding. You may wish simply to set two similars, or dissimilars, side by side to illustrate some larger point—that excellence may come in very different packages, for instance. Comparing and contrasting can illuminate the unfamiliar with the familiar, or it can help you discover and convey to your readers new perspectives on things well known—two popular singers, two of Shakespeare's sonnets, two nursery rhymes. But, whether or not you are presenting one side as superior to the other, the structural tactic is the same: compare point for point, so long as the comparison illuminates.

Here is a short *pro-con* essay that gets rid of the opposition early and in one paragraph.

Woman and Human Superiority

Woman has kept the home fire burning for eons, probably since the discovery of fire. Her place has been in the
home, and men have been all too happy to keep her in her
place. Men are usually taller, stronger, and more aggressive,
as war paths through forest and battlefield and stock market
have demonstrated. Women themselves tend to give men
the edge of superiority, if the men haven't already grabbed
it for themselves. But although the weaker sex has been
outshone and outshown in many ways, women are actually
superior in the most fundamental qualities.

Of course, men are more muscular, but both the actuar-
ial statistics and accounts of extended hardship, like that of
the Donner Party in the last century, show that women have
more physical endurance. Pictures of women runners at the
end of marathons like the annual Boston run show them still
in good shape while the men are collapsing, though both

have given their best. The men have run faster, but the women have outlasted just as they will in the race of life. Women are also immune to a number of sex-linked diseases, which, like hemophilia, they carry while the men succumb. Women have achieved less in the arts and sciences, but actually their brains are bigger in proportion to their weight. Clearly, they have had less time and motivation to compete.

Their achievement and motivation lie where their true superiority is: in the compassion that nurtures and holds together the human race that men seem bent on tearing apart. Compassion distinguishes humanity from inhumanity. Jane Goodall, who, *In the Shadow of Man* (1971), found chimpanzees so very human in many ways, saw their indifference toward their suffering fellows as the crucial distinction. Woman has nurtured the young and the aged from long before that first fire put her in her place. If, as some anthropologists believe, man learned to walk by carrying food back to the wife and kids, he learned this consideration from the mother who cared for him during the human infant's extended dependency. Woman's superiority lies in her instinctive sympathy, her caring, her loving. As Ashley Montagu says, *"It is the function of woman to teach men how to be human."** Women may well catch up in the arts and sciences, in business and government, but if we ever achieve a peace on earth in which humanity can fulfill itself, we will do so because men have at last caught up to woman's true superiority.

THE INDUCTIVE STRUCTURE

The natural dialectical swing of the way we think gives us the basic *pro-con* structure. Our two essential directions of thinking —induction and deduction—provide structures for organizing an essay. In fact, we have been talking about deductive structure all along: setting your Big Idea, your thesis, then demonstrating, illustrating, and arguing its validity in detail, showing the parts that support the whole. This is the essay's most useful structure.

---

*"The Natural Superiority of Women," *Saturday Review* (1 March 1952):35—to which I am indebted for the main point and several details.

But the inductive structure, though more infrequent, can give your essays variety. Inductive reasoning starts with details and, considering *pros* and *cons,* works up to their significance. An inductive essay follows this same pattern. The writer knows where he is going, but he leads the reader from detail to significant detail upward to his thesis, simulating an inductive search and taking the reader along. Both inductive and deductive structures thus follow an ascending order of interest, considering *pros* and *cons* along the way. The inductive saves the opening thesis, however, for the end. You lead your reader in—by successive questions and their dismissal, or partial answers—to your main and conclusive point. "Is it this? Well, no." "Then may it be this? No, not exactly this either." "Then how about this? Ah, yes, this is it." The deductive order, beginning with your thesis and then explaining it, is clearer. But the inductive order has suspense, an intellectual excitement, if you can keep your answer from slipping out.

Inductive order works best for short essays, since you must keep the cat in the bag, and you can't keep him in too long. You use a question for your thesis-sentence and then simulate your speculation. Here is an inductive paragraph from an interview with George Harris, a man reminiscing about the Depression:

Topic Question Answer 1	***What was the worst thing about the Depression?*** **Well, I don't know. I guess** *for some folks it was losing money they had put away.* **For us that wasn't so bad. I only had about $400 that I could lose, and, while I never got any of it back, I**
Answer 2	**know a lot of people who lost more. Then, too,** *being out of work was rough for a lot of people.* **But even that wasn't so bad for me. I lost my job with the foundry in 1931, but we lived on a farm. And with that and some odd jobs I picked up, I managed to keep pretty busy until I got a steady job again.**
Answer 3	**Of course, I know** *a lot of people didn't have enough to eat or enough to wear during the Depression.* **For us that wasn't too bad. We grew most of our own food, and my wife is pretty handy at sewing, so we got by. Nothing very fancy, you**
Main answer (thesis)	**understand, but we managed. No, I guess for us** *the worst thing about the Depression was we got to feeling after a while that times just weren't ever going to get better.* **It just went on too long. For us, things got a little rough in 1931 and they stayed pretty rough until I got a job with Ontario Transport in 1938. Seven years is a long time to keep hoping. It just went on so long.**

This will give you an idea of inductive order. You may well use a short inductive section in a longer essay, especially for dismissing the opposition's arguments by putting them as questions ("Do we want unlimited freedom?") and then reducing them to absurdities. But a wholly inductive essay is usually short, and you won't find many of these, because your answer, your thesis, keeps slipping out of the bag and spoiling your surprise.

THE DEDUCTIVE STRUCTURE

Hang Your Essay from Your Big Idea

The deductive structure is basic, much more widely used, and useful, than the inductive one, because it sustains itself page after page, even through chapters in a whole book. You set down your thesis, your general proposition, then *explain* it in detail and at length, presenting *pros* and *cons* as needed. The mode of induction is question and partial answer; the mode of deduction is assertion and explanation. As we have seen, however, the usual deductive order does not simply begin with your Big Idea and then dwindle down to nothing. You match some of the inductive's suspense by saving your best for last. You can even include a short inductive paragraph or two for more suspense and variety. You start with your thesis, then jump down to your smallest small and work progressively uphill until you again reach your thesis, which is now restated as your conclusion and rounded off in a concluding paragraph. Again, the deductive order is the normal one we have been talking about all along.

To change Mr. Harris's inductive rumination about the Depression into a deductive structure, we make his opening question a thesis to be demonstrated: not "What was the worst thing about the Depression?" but "The worst thing about the Depression was its hopeless duration." In the following example, notice how deduction expands the inductive structure in detail, thought, and explanation. Notice how it uses first-person statement, which fell into an inductive pattern, as a piece of evidence in the more ample deductive structure, still giving the facts as Harris stated them.

Topic   *For most Canadians, the stock-market crash was not the worst thing about the Depression.* True, it carried away billions of dollars of investors' money, but relatively few of us felt directly affected. Few of us owned stock, and for most of us the market collapse was something that happened to other people, not to us. Of course, as we found out, the stock-market collapse was only the trigger, and soon more and more Canadians found their lives directly affected. By 1932, twenty-five percent of the work force was without jobs. Yet, for many Canadians, the worst thing about the Depression was not the financial loss, or being out of work, or even shortages of food and clothing. For many of us, *the worst*

Thesis   *thing about the Depression was that it lasted so long we almost gave up hoping that times would ever get better.* George Harris of Galt, Ontario, is a good example of how the Depression hit most of us.

Demon-   *In 1931, Mr. Harris had a job with a foundry that manu-*
stration   *factured boilers and other pieces of heavy equipment for indus-try.* His income was generally pretty good, and Mr. Harris had managed to buy a small farm just outside town. *But cutbacks in industrial production,* particularly in the produc-tion of steel, *soon forced cutbacks in the foundry as well.* And in August of 1931, *Mr. Harris was laid off.* The next year, in 1932, the Harrises learned that *the $400 they had invested in a small processing plant was lost* because the plant had gone bankrupt. And so *for the next seven years, Mr. Harris bounced from job to job,* whatever he could get: a few days here, a few days there. *He was thus able to hold onto his small farm,* and on it he raised most of the food for the Harris family for the next seven years. *Mrs. Harris, too, helped to cut cor-ners* by making most of the family's clothes, and by repair-ing things when they wore out. In this way, taking it one day at a time, and living as simply and as frugally as possi-ble, *the Harrises managed to get by until, in 1938, Mr. Harris once again got a secure and well-paying job with Ontario Trans-port.*

Restatement   *So the Harrises are a good example of how the Depression hit many Canadians.* They lost some savings, they lost their jobs, they had to tighten their belts, but they managed to get by. *For them, the worst thing about the Depression was not the depri-vation; it was simply that the Depression went on year after year.* As Mr. Harris says, "Seven years is a long time to keep hoping. It just went on so long."

THE HYBRID STRUCTURE

Halfway between, many essayists blend deduction with induction. They trim a fully assertive thesis about welfare to "We need some system to help those in need." They ask, "How should one plan a vacation?" They have the answers, as we know, and they feed them to us in successive steps of significance: "First, decide where you want to go." But the essential mode is deductive. The essayist knows, or discovers, what he believes, and persuades with successively convincing points. His thesis is open-ended, merely implied by a leading question, or suggested indirectly in the first two paragraphs or so, as in the opening of Margaret Atwood's "Canadians: What Do They Want?":

> **Last month, during a poetry reading, I tried out a short prose poem called "How to Like Men." It began by suggesting that one start with the feet. Unfortunately, the question of jackboots soon arose, and things went on from there. After the reading I had a conversation with a young man who thought I had been unfair to men. He wanted men to be liked totally, not just from the heels to the knees, and not just as individuals but as a group; and he thought it negative and inegalitarian of me to have alluded to war and rape. I pointed out that as far as any of us knew these were two activities not widely engaged in by women, but he was still upset. "We're both in this together," he protested. I admitted that this was so; but could he, maybe, see that our relative positions might be a little different.**
>
> **This is the conversation one has with Americans, even, uh, *good* Americans, when the dinner-table conversation veers round to Canadian-American relations. "We're in this together," they like to say, especially when it comes to continental energy reserves. How do you *explain* to them, as delicately as possible, why they are not categorically beloved? It gets like the old Lifebuoy ads: even their best friends won't tell them. And Canadians are supposed to be their best friends, right? Members of the family?***

A fully inductive essay might have posed the question "What causes anti-American feelings in Canada?" A deductive thesis

---

* Originally published in *Mother Jones*, January 1982. ©1982, Margaret Atwood.

might have been "Anti-American feelings in Canada stem from the fact that Canadians are not really treated as 'members of the family.' " We get Atwood's point indirectly, but it is clearly there, by the end of the second paragraph, setting the deductive frame for her essay.

EXERCISES

1. *Write three con-and-pro thesis-sentences beginning "Although. . . ."*
2. *For the following assertions, write one argument against and one argument for. Now combine your statements into one thesis-sentence:*

   EXAMPLE *Assertion: Movies should not be censored.*

   Con: *Children should not be exposed to obscene and explicitly sexual images on the screen.*

   Pro: *Obscenity is far too subjective a thing for any person to define for anyone else.*

   Thesis-Statement: *Although young people probably should not be exposed to explicit sex in films, movies still should not be censored because obscenity is so subjective that no one can legitimately serve as censor for the rest of us.*

   1. Assertion: Discussion classes are superior to lectures.
   2. Assertion: Rapid and convenient transit systems must be built in our cities.
   3. Assertion: The federal government should subsidize large companies forced near bankruptcy.
   4. Assertion: Medical schools should reduce the time required for a degree in general medicine from four years to two.
   5. Assertion: Provincial governments should sell all their liquor stores to private businesses.

3. *Trim three of these into open-ended "hybrid" theses, like "We need some system to help those in need" or the question "How should one plan a vacation?"*
4. *Write a dialectical swinger, an essay following Diagrams I or II (32–34).*

4
Paragraphs: Beginning, Middle, End

THE STANDARD PARAGRAPH

A paragraph is a structural convenience—a building block to get firmly in mind. I mean the standard, central paragraph, setting aside for the moment the peculiarly shaped beginning paragraph and ending paragraph. You build the bulk of your essay with standard paragraphs, with blocks of concrete ideas, and they must fit smoothly. But they must also remain as perceptible parts, to rest your reader's eye and mind. Indeed, the paragraph originated, among the Greeks, as a resting place and place-finder, being first a mere mark *(graphos)* in the margin alongside *(para)* an unbroken sheet of handwriting—the proofreader's familiar ¶. You have heard that a paragraph is a single idea, and this is true. But so is a word, usually; and so is a sentence, sometimes. It seems best, after all, to think of a paragraph as something you use for your reader's convenience, rather than as some granitic form laid down by molten logic.

The medium determines the size of the paragraph. Your average longhand paragraph may look the same size as a typewritten one, much like a paragraph in a book. But the printed page would show your handwritten paragraph a short embarrassment, and your typewritten one barely long enough for decency. The beginner's insecurity produces inadequate paragraphs, often only a sentence each. Journalists, of course, are one-sentence paragraphers. The narrow newspaper column makes a sentence look like a paragraph, and narrow columns and short paragraphs serve the newspaper's rapid transit. A paragraph from a book might fill a whole newspaper column with solid lead. It would have to be broken—paragraphed—for the reader's convenience. A news story on the page of a book would look like a gap-toothed comb, and would have to be consolidated for the reader's comfort. So make your paragraphs ample.

Plan for the Big Paragraph

Imagine yourself writing for a book. Force yourself to four or five sentences at least, visualizing your paragraphs as identical rectangular frames to be filled. This will allow you to build with orderly blocks, to strengthen your feel for structure. Since the beginner's problem is usually one of thinking of things to say rather than of trimming the overgrowth, you can do your filling out a unit at a time, always thinking up one or two sentences more to fill the customary space. You will probably be repetitive and wordy at first—this is our universal failing—but you will soon learn to fill your paragraph with interesting details. You will develop a constructional rhythm, coming to rest at the end of each paragraphic frame.

Once accustomed to a five-sentence frame, say, you can then begin to vary the length for emphasis, letting a good idea swell out beyond the norm, or bringing a particular point home in a paragraph short and sharp—even in one sentence, like this.

The paragraph's structure, then, has its own rhetorical message. It tells the reader visually whether or not you are in charge of your subject. Tiny, ragged paragraphs display your hidden uncertainty, unless clearly placed among big ones for emphasis. Brief opening and closing paragraphs sometimes can emphasize your thesis effectively, but usually they make your beginning seem hasty and your ending perfunctory. So aim for the big paragraph all the way, and vary it only occasionally and knowingly, for rhetorical emphasis.

Find a Topic Sentence

Looked at as a convenient structural frame, the paragraph reveals a further advantage. Like the essay itself, it has a beginning, a middle, and an end. The beginning and the end are usually each one sentence long, and the middle gets you smoothly from one to the other. Since, like the essay, the paragraph flows through time, its last sentence is the most emphatic. This is your home punch. The first sentence holds the next most emphatic place. It will normally be your *topic sentence,* stating the paragraph's point, like a small thesis of a miniature essay, something like this:

> **The *Attitude* [toward Toronto] *of the outsider is compounded of envy, malice and pity in about equal quantities.* It is admitted that Torontonians make large sums of money but not much else; certainly they never have any fun. There is none of the leisurely Gracious Living that is to be found in Montreal, say, or Halifax or Okotoks, Alberta. When a young man sets out for Toronto (and, sooner or later, all young men set out for Toronto) he is surrounded by a covey of friends—all loudly commiserating with him and whispering to him to look about for a job for them in the big city. It is generally acknowledged that the bereaved young man will return, but he rarely does. If he sees his friends again, he sees them in Toronto where they all have a good cry, and talk over the grand old days when they were poor in Pelvis or West Webfoot.***

If your topic sentence covers everything within your paragraph, your paragraph is coherent, and you are using your paragraphs with maximum effect, leading your reader into your community block by block. If your end sentences bring him briefly to rest, he will know where he is and appreciate it.

This is the basic frame. As you write, you will discover your own variations, a paragraph that illustrates its topic sentence with parallel items and no home punch at the end at all, or one beginning with a hint and ending with its topical idea in the most emphatic place, like the best beginning paragraphs.

BEGINNING PARAGRAPHS: THE FUNNEL

State Your Thesis at the END of Your Beginning Paragraph

Your beginning paragraph should contain your main idea, and present it to best advantage. Its topic sentence is also the *thesis*

---

*From Pierre Berton's introduction to Henri Rossier's collection of photographs entitled *The New City, a Prejudiced View of Toronto,* as quoted in *Profile of a Nation,* ed. Alan Dawe (Toronto: The Macmillan Co. of Canada, Ltd., 1969), p. 81.

sentence of your entire essay. The clearest and most emphatic place for your thesis sentence is at the *end*—not at the beginning—of the beginning paragraph. Of course, many an essay begins with a subject-statement, a kind of open topic sentence for the whole essay, and unfolds amiably from there. But these are usually the more personal meditations of seasoned writers and established authorities. Bacon, for instance, usually steps off from a topical first sentence: "Studies serve for delight, for ornament, and for ability." Similarly, A. A. Milne begins with "Of the fruits of the earth, I give my vote to the orange"—and just keeps going.

But for the less assured and the more structurally minded, the funnel is the reliable form, as the thesis-sentence brings the reader to rest for a moment at the end of the opening paragraph, with his bearings established. If you put your thesis-sentence first, you may have to repeat some version of it as you bring your beginning paragraph to a close. If you put it in the middle, the reader will very likely take something else as your main point, probably whatever the last sentence contains. The inevitable psychology of interest, as you move your reader through your first paragraph and into your essay, urges you to put your thesis last —in the last sentence of your beginning paragraph.

Think of your beginning paragraph, then, not as the middle paragraph's frame to be filled, but as a funnel. Start wide and end narrow:

OPENING   INVITATION

THESIS

If, for instance, you wished to show that "Learning to play the guitar pays off in friendship"—your thesis—you would start somewhere back from that thesis-idea with something more general—about music, about learning, about the pleasures of achievement, about guitars: "Playing the guitar looks easy," "Music can speak more directly than words," "Learning anything is a course in frustration." You can even open with something quite specific, *as long as it is more general than your thesis:* "Pick up a guitar, and you bump into people." A handy way to find an opener is to take one word from your thesis—*learning, play,* or *guitar,* for instance—and make a sentence out of it. Say something about it, and you are well on your way to your thesis, three or four sentences later.* Your opening line, in other words, should look forward to your thesis, should be something to engage interest easily, something to which most readers would assent without a rise in blood pressure. (Antagonize and startle if you wish, but beware of having the door slammed before you have a chance and of making your thesis an anticlimax.) Therefore: broad and genial. From your opening geniality, you move progressively down to smaller particulars. You narrow down: from learning the guitar, to its musical and social complications, to its rewards in friendship (your thesis). Your paragraph might run, from broad to narrow, like this:

> **Learning anything has unexpected rocks in its path, but the guitar seems particularly rocky. Playing it looks so simple. A few chords, you think, and you are on your way. Then you discover not only the musical and technical difficulties, but a whole unexpected crowd of human complications. Your friends think you are showing off; the people you meet think you are a fake. Then the frustrations drive you to achievement. You learn to face the music and the people honestly. You finally learn to play a little, but you also discover something better. You have learned to make and keep some real friends, because you have discovered a kind of ultimate friendship with yourself.**

Now, that paragraph turned out a little different from what I anticipated. I used the informal *you,* and it seemed to suit the subject. I also overshot my original thesis, discovering, as I wrote, a thesis one step farther—an underlying cause—about coming to friendly terms with oneself. But it illustrates the funnel, from the broad and general to the one particular point that will be your essay's main idea, your thesis. Here is another example:

---

*I am grateful to James C. Raymond, of the University of Alabama, for this helpful idea.

> The environment is the world around us, and everyone agrees it needs a cleaning. Big corporations gobble up the countryside and disgorge what's left into the breeze and streams. Big trucks rumble by, trailing their fumes. A jet roars into the air, and its soot drifts over the trees. Everyone calls for massive action, and then tosses away his cigarette butt or gum wrapper. The world around us is also a sidewalk, a lawn, a lounge, a hallway, a room right here. Cleaning the environment can begin by reaching for the scrap of paper at your feet.

In a more argumentative paper, you can sometimes set up your thesis effectively by opening with the opposition, as we have already noted (31):

> Science is the twentieth century's answer to everything. We want the facts. We conduct statistical polls to measure the Prime Minister's monthly popularity. We send spaceships to bring back pieces of the moon and send back data from the planets. We make babies in test tubes. We believe that eventually we will discover the chemical formula for life itself, creating a human being from the basic elements. Nevertheless, one basic element, what has been called the soul, or spirit, may be beyond science and all human planning, as Gore Vidal's recent novel *Kalki* suggests.

MIDDLE PARAGRAPHS

Make Your Middle Paragraphs Full, with Transitions

The middle paragraph is the standard paragraph, the little essay in itself, with its own little beginning and little end. But it must also declare its allegiance to the paragraphs immediately before and after it. Each topic sentence must somehow hook onto the paragraph above it, must include some word or phrase to ease the reader's path: a transition. (1) You may simply repeat a word from the sentence that ended the paragraph just above. (2) You may bring down a thought generally developed or left slightly hanging in air: "Smith's idea is different" might be a tremendously economical topic sentence with automatic transition. (3) Or you may get from one paragraph to the next by the usual steppingstones, like *But, however* (within the sentence), *Nevertheless, Therefore, Indeed, Of course.* One brief transitional touch in your topic sentence, or opening sentence, is usually sufficient.

The topic sentences in each of the following three paragraphs by David Suzuki contain neat transitions, here shown in italics. I have just used an old standby myself: repeating the words *topic sentence* from the close of my preceding paragraph. Suzuki has just explained the nature and development of genetic experimentation, in particular in Canada, and its implications for the future. He begins his next paragraph with a transitional sentence, reinforced by the reference to *genetic knowledge,* to introduce a discussion of the problems inherent in genetic experimentation. In the next paragraph, he uses the transitional word *however* to introduce examples of dangerous policies aimed at genetically controlling society. The paragraphs are nearly the same length, all cogent, clear, and full. Notice how Suzuki develops his thought with smooth transitions from sentence to sentence. No one-sentence paragraphing here, no gaps, but all a vivid, orderly progression:

> *As with all scientific discoveries,* **the application of genetic knowledge can be used for the benefit or detriment of society, and decisions for its use require considerable foresight and wisdom. Techniques permitting the detection and prevention or correction of inherited defects can help to eliminate suffering and expense to society and afflicted individuals. But who will make the decisions—the pregnant woman, doctors, members of Parliament? What risks of a defect will be accepted? What will be decided against—diabetes, shortsightedness, albinism, harelip? There is no question in my mind that society can benefit greatly from foetal analysis (analyzing unborn young) and abortion of genetic defects. If the present trend towards restriction of family size continues, pregnancy will be a more serious condition that we will want to ensure will result in a healthy child.**
>
> *However,* **we are still haunted by the spectre of Hitler's infamous pseudogenetic extermination of Jews to produce a superior race. There is no shortage of superstitions, old wives' tales, and just plain prejudice which could be used to justify discriminatory biological programs. The most recent example was the statement by the newly elected President**

of the Canadian Medical Association. He suggested that educated, higher-income groups are restricting family size and therefore being outbred by lower-class groups, and that recipients of welfare should be sterilized.

It is highly questionable whether *social position* has a genetic basis or that *upper-class people* have greater wisdom or better human qualities. Others suggest that greater intelligence is highly desirable and should be selected for by incentives for college graduates to have lots of children. Again, as a university teacher, I find it hard to believe that a college degree is a good indicator of intellectual ability or that it indicates a "better" person. I doubt that we have sufficient knowledge or wisdom to apply genetics to man on a large scale.*

Check Your Paragraphs for Clarity and Coherence

Suzuki's paragraphs run smoothly from first sentence to last. They are coherent. The *topic sentence* is the key. It assures that the subsequent sentences will fall into line, and it is the first point to check when you look back to see if they really do. Many a jumbled paragraph can be unifed by writing a broader topic sentence. Consider this disjointed specimen:

> Swimming is healthful. The first dive into the pool is always cold. Tennis takes a great deal of energy, especially under a hot sun. Team sports, like soccer, hockey, and volleyball, always make the awkward player miserable. Character and health go hand in hand.

What is all that about? From the last sentence, we can surmise what the writer intended. But the first sentence about swimming in no way covers the paragraph, which treats several sports not in the least like swimming, and seems to be driving at something other than health. The primary remedy is to find the paragraph's thesis and to devise a topic sentence that will state it, thus covering everything in the paragraph. Think of your topic sentence as a roof —covering your paragraph and pulling its contents together.

---

*"Genetics: Will the Science Save Us or Kill Us," *Canada and the World,* 37 (February 1972), quoted in *Modern Canadian Essays,* ed. William H. New (Toronto: Macmillan of Canada Ltd, 1976), 174–175. © 1972, David Suzuki.

POOR COVERAGE   GOOD COVERAGE

The first dive. Tennis.   *Swimming. The first dive.*
Soccer, hockey,   *Tennis. Soccer, hockey,*
volleyball. Character   *volleyball. Character and*
and health.   *health.*

Suppose we add only a topic sentence, suggested by our right-hand diagram. It will indeed pull things together:

> *Sports demand an effort of will and muscle that is healthful for the soul as well as the body.* Swimming is healthful. The first dive into the pool is always cold. Tennis takes a great deal of energy, especially under a hot sun. Team sports, like soccer, hockey, and volleyball, always make the awkward player miserable. Character and health go hand in hand.

Topic Sentence

But the paragraph is still far from an agreeable coherence. The islands of thought still need some bridges. Gaining coherence is primarily a filling in, or a spelling out, of submerged connections. You may fill in with (1) thought and (2) specific illustrative detail; you may spell out by tying your sentences together with (3) transitional tags and (4) repeated words or syntactical patterns. Let us see what we can do with our sample paragraph.

From the first, you probably noticed that the writer was thinking in pairs: the pleasure of sports is balanced off against their difficulty; the difficulty is physical as well as moral; character and health go hand in hand. We have already indicated this doubleness of idea in our topic sentence. Now to fill out the thought, we need merely expand each sentence so as to give each half of the double idea its due expression. We need also to qualify the thought here and there with *perhaps, often, some, sometimes, frequently, all in all,* and the like. As we work through the possibilities, more specific detail will come to mind. We have already made the general ideas of *character* and *health* more specific with *will, muscle, soul,* and *body* in our topic sentence, and we shall add a touch or two more of illustration, almost automatically, as our imagination becomes more stimulated by the subject. We shall add a number of transitional ties like *but, and, of course, nevertheless,* and *similarly.* We shall look for chances to repeat key words, like *will,* if we can do so gracefully; and to repeat syntactical patterns, if we can emphasize similar thoughts by doing so, as with *no matter how patient his teammates . . . no matter how heavy his heart,* toward the end of our revision below (the original phrases are in italics):

Topic Sentence	*Sports demand an effort of will and muscle that is healthful for the soul as well as the body.* Swimming is **physically health-**
Illustrative Sentences with Transitions	**ful,** of course, **although it may seem undemanding and highly conducive to lying for hours inert on a deck chair in the sun.** But *the first dive into the pool is always cold:* **taking the plunge always requires some effort of will. And the swimmer soon summons his will to compete, against himself or others, for greater distances and greater speed, doing twenty laps where he used to do one.** Similarly, *tennis takes* **quantities** *of energy,* **physical and moral,** *especially* **when the competition stiffens** *under a hot sun.* **Team** *sports, like soccer, hockey, and volleyball,* **perhaps demand even more of the amateur.** *The awkward player* **is** *miserable* **when he kicks and misses, loses the puck, or falls on the ice, no matter how patient his teammates. He must drive himself to keep on trying, no matter how heavy his heart. Whatever the**
End Sentence: The Point	**sport, a little determination can eventually conquer one's awkwardness and timidity, and the reward will be more than physical.** *Character and health frequently go hand in hand.*

Here we can see the essence of coherence: REPETITION, (1) repeating parallel examples, like *swimming, tennis, team sports,* as if stacking them up to support your topic sentence; or (2) stringing them along by idea and word, sentence by sentence, as in *sports, swimming, dive, tennis, team sports,* and so forth, as one thought suggests the next. Finally, transitions *within* a paragraph contribute importantly to its coherence. Since beginners usually do not think of transitions, try to include a helpful *of course, But, And, similarly, perhaps, consequently, still,* and the like.

Here are the five points to remember about middle paragraphs. First, think of the middle paragraph as a miniature essay, with a beginning, a middle, and an end. Its beginning will normally be its topic sentence, the thesis of this miniature essay. Its middle will develop, explain, and illustrate your topic sentence. Its last sentence will drive home the idea. Second, remember that this kind of paragraph is the norm, which you may instinctively vary when your topic sentence requires only a series of parallel illustrations *(swimming, tennis, golf, soccer, hockey)*, or when you open your paragraph with some hint to be fulfilled in a topical conclusive sentence *(Sports build body and soul)*. Third, see that your paragraph is coherent, not only flowing smoothly but with nothing in it not covered by the topic sentence. Fourth, make your paragraphs full and well developed, with plenty of details, examples, and full explanations, or you will end up with a skeletal paper with very little meat on its bones. Fifth, remember transitions. Though each paragraph is a kind of miniature essay, it is also a part of a larger essay. Therefore, hook each paragraph smoothly to the paragraph preceding it, with some transitional touch in each opening sentence.

END PARAGRAPHS: THE INVERTED FUNNEL

Reassert Your Thesis

If the beginning paragraph is a funnel, the end paragraph is a funnel upside down: the thought starts moderately narrow—it is more or less the thesis you have had all the time—and then pours out broader and broader implications and finer emphases. The end paragraph reiterates, summarizes, and emphasizes with decorous fervour. This is your last chance. This is what your reader will carry away—and if you can carry *him* away, so much the better. All within decent intellectual bounds, of course. You are the person of reason still, but the person of reason supercharged with conviction, sure of your idea and sure of its importance.

    If your essay is anecdotal, however, largely narrative and descriptive, your ending may be no more than a sentence, or it may be a ruminative paragraph generalizing upward and outward from the particulars to mirror your beginning paragraph, as in a more argumentative essay. The dramatic curve of your illustrative incident will tell you what to do. An essay illustrating how folly may lead to catastrophe—a friend dead from an overdose, or drowned by daring too far on thin ice—might end when the story has told itself out and made its point starkly: "The three of us walked numbly up the street toward home."

But the usual final paragraph conveys a sense of assurance and repose, of business completed. Its topic sentence is usually some version of the original thesis sentence, since the end paragraph is the exact structural opposite and complement of the beginning one. Its transitional word or phrase is often one of finality or summary—*then, finally, thus,* and *so:*

> **So, the guitar is a means to a finer end.**
> **The environment, then, is in our lungs and at our fingertips.**

The paragraph would then proceed to expand and elaborate this revived thesis. We would get a confident assertion that both the music and the friendships are really by-products of an inner alliance; we would get an urgent plea to clean up our personal environs and strengthen our convictions. One rule of thumb: the longer the paper, the more specific the summary of the points you have made. A short paper will need no specific summary of your points at all; the renewed thesis and its widening of implications are sufficient.

Here is an end paragraph by Sir James Jeans. His transitional phrase is *for a similar reason.* His thesis was that previous concepts of physical reality had mistaken surfaces for depths:

> **The purely mechanical picture of visible nature fails for a similar reason. It proclaims that the ripples themselves direct the workings of the universe instead of being mere symptoms of occurrences below; in brief, it makes the mistake of thinking that the weather-vane determines the direction from which the wind shall blow, or that the thermometer keeps the room hot.***

Here is an end paragraph of Professor Richard Hofstadter's. His transitional word is *intellectuals,* carried over from the preceding paragraphs. His thesis was that intellectuals should not abandon their defense of intellectual and spiritual freedom, as they have tended to do, under pressure to conform:

---

* The New Background of Science (Cambridge: Cambridge University Press, 1933): 261.

> **This world will never be governed by intellectuals—it may rest assured.** But *we* **must be assured, too, that intellectuals will not be altogether governed by this world, that they maintain their piety, their longstanding allegiance to the world of spiritual values to which they should belong. Otherwise there will be no intellectuals, at least not above ground. And societies in which the intellectuals have been driven underground, as we have had occasion to see in our own time, are societies in which even the anti-intellectuals are unhappy.***

Remember a conclusion when you have used up all your points and had your say. You and your argument are both exhausted. You will be tempted to stop, but don't stop. You need an end, or the whole thing will unravel in your reader's mind. You need to buttonhole him in a final paragraph, to imply "I told you so" without saying it, to hint at the whole round experience he has just had, and to leave him convinced, satisfied, and admiring. One more paragraph will do it: beginning, middle, *and* end.

THE WHOLE ESSAY

You have now discovered the main ingredients of a good essay. You have learned to find and to sharpen your thesis in one sentence, to give your essay that all-important argumentative edge. You have learned to arrange your points in order of increasing interest, and you have practised disposing of the opposition in a *pro-con* structure. You have seen that your beginning paragraph should seem like a funnel, working from broad generalization to thesis. You have tried your hand at middle paragraphs, which are almost like little essays with their own beginnings and ends. And finally, you have learned that your last paragraph should work like an inverted funnel, broadening and embellishing your thesis.

Some students have pictured the essay as a Greek column, with a narrowing beginning paragraph as its top, or capital, and a broadening end paragraph as its base. Others have seen it as

*"Democracy and Anti-intellectualism in America," *Michigan Alumnus Quarterly Review*, 59 (1953): 295.

a keyhole (see the keyhole diagram).* Picturing your structure like this is very handy. This is the basic pattern. Keeping it in mind helps as you write. Checking your drafts against it will show you where you might amplify, or rearrange. As you write more and more, you will discover new variations as each new subject pushes its way to fulfillment, like a tree growing toward full light. But every tree is a tree. Each follows the general pattern, as if fulfilling some heavenly arboreal keyhole. Similarly, this essayistic one works out in convenient detail the inevitability of Aristotle's Beginning, Middle, and End.

The student's essay that follows illustrates this basic structure fairly well. He has clearly thought about, and talked about, his subject, picking up facts from the daily news, and evidently, as he sat down to put his thoughts on paper, has looked to see what *The Encyclopaedia Britannica* had to say about "Conscription."

The Need for a Democratic Draft

Broad Subject, Illustration

Armies make wars. **The bigger the army, the greater the threat, as we saw twice in 1982, when Argentinian generals with a large army of conscripts thought invading the Falkland Islands would establish their regime, and when Israel's tanks rumbled into southern Lebanon and just kept going to Beirut.**

Narrowing

Now, the United States faces the question of expanding its army by conscription, and against considerable resistance both from a distrust of militarism and from a championship of democratic rights.

Thesis

Nevertheless, that country needs conscription, including, for effectiveness and fairness, the conscription of women.

Topic Sentence, Opposition 1

Of course, *the draft creates military and philosophical problems.* **Militarily,** *it forces men into a trade, or an apprenticeship, they do not choose, and forces them to fight and die. Ideally, a volunteer army is the best army,* **fired by patriotism, resentment, or even despair, to defend home and country, like the**

Middle: Specific Evidence

Athenians at Marathon or the Spartans at Thermopylae. In times of war, when patriotism rises, a drafted army approaches the spirit of a voluntary one, as farm boys, like Henry Fleming in Stephan Crane's *The Red Badge of Courage,* **rush off to enlist in the Civil War, or a fraternity class,**

---

*Mrs. Fran Measley of Santa Barbara, California, has devised for her students a mimeographed sheet to accompany my discussion of structure and paragraphing —to help them to visualize my points, through a keyhole, as it were. I am grateful to Mrs. Measley to be able to include it here.

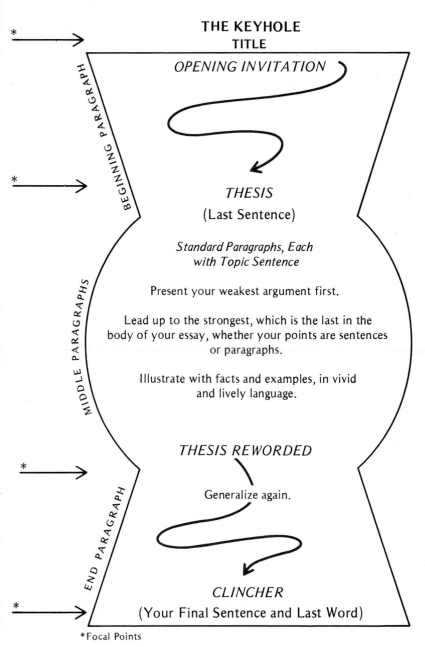

THE KEYHOLE
TITLE

OPENING INVITATION

BEGINNING PARAGRAPH

THESIS
(Last Sentence)

*Standard Paragraphs, Each
with Topic Sentence*

Present your weakest argument first.

Lead up to the strongest, which is the last in the
body of your essay, whether your points are sentences
or paragraphs.

Illustrate with facts and examples, in vivid
and lively language.

MIDDLE PARAGRAPHS

THESIS REWORDED

Generalize again.

END PARAGRAPH

CLINCHER
(Your Final Sentence and Last Word)

*Focal Points

at Princeton, I believe, volunteers as a group in World War I. Even draftees are fired up for sacrifice to save the world for democracy, or at least for freedom from Hitler. But a draft in peacetime requires the military's severest indoctrination and punishment to keep it going and to prevent desertion. An individual's freedom is out of the question.

Topic Sentence, Opposition 2

The philosophical problem of the draft concerns that freedom, which is at the heart of democracy. Does one's elected government have the right to take him out of college or off his chosen job and force him into an endurance contest designed for killing his fellow man? Those who resist the draft say an emphatic "No." They also argue on the grounds of sexual discrimination, picking only men from their careers and leaving women free.

Topic Sentence, *Pro*

Middle: Authoritative Evidence

Specific Allusions

But harsh necessity sets aside most of the military and philosophical objections. *The volunteer system in the United States, set up after the Vietnamese War, has not worked.* The army has tried it and failed. Only the poorest and marginally educated have volunteered, and not in sufficient numbers, according to a recent report in *Time.* The army's call for a draft and the registration enacted for it by the U.S. Congress under President Carter prove that the volunteer army is inadequate in a world blazing with wars from *Cambodia* to the *Falkland Islands.*

Topic Sentence

Middle: Authoritative Evidence

Contemporary Examples

The idea of a peacetime draft, which the protesters resist, is unreal. The world is not at peace, and has not been for a single day since Hitler invaded Poland in 1939. Almost every nation maintains an army through conscription, according to *The Encyclopaedia Brittanica,* with required training and service varying from several months to several years. Both *Israel* and *China* require service of both men and women, on the old democratic principle of everyone's sharing responsibility, and this evidently contributes to reducing resentment and increasing willingness to serve. Japan is a notable exception, with no army at all. But the United States is pledged to defend her, just as Canada is pledged to defend its NATO allies, confronted by Russia's tremendous conscripted army. The United States must wake up to the warlike realities and generate some spirit of necessity to counteract the draft's built-in defect: the lack of the professionalism and patriotism that makes a good voluntary army.

Thesis Restated

In short, the United States needs a draft of both men and women to face the necessities of an armed world around it, and with a system democratically fair and effective, as Israel has shown. No one would think of a draft if volunteers, with squirrel rifles from the cabin, could bring the army up to

strength in numbers and intelligence. But the volunteer system has failed. *A draft, or at least a registration of both sexes to be ready for a draft when dire reality hits, is necessary now.*

The Clincher

EXERCISES

1. *Below is a list of thesis-sentences. Choose one (or its opposite), or make one of your own on the same pattern. Then back off from it at least four or five sentences, and write a funnel-like beginning paragraph leading your reader down to it: your thesis, the last sentence of your beginning funnel.*

> **EXAMPLE** *with thesis italicized as follows:*

> The coal operators will tell you that stripping is cheaper and more efficient than conventional mining. Their 250-cubic-yard drag-lines, their 200-cubic-yard shovels, their 50-ton trucks, can rip the top off a mountain and expose a whole seam of coal in a fraction of the time it takes to sink a shaft. "It is cheaper," they will say, "to bring the surface to the coal than to bring the coal to the surface." And of course they are right; in a sense it is cheaper. But visit Eastern Kentucky and look at the real price we pay for stripped coal. Visit a stripped area and you will see that, no matter how low the price for a truckload of stripped coal, *the real price for strip-mining has to be reckoned in terms of blighted land, poisoned streams, and stunted human lives.*

1. Although motivated by proper concern for the public welfare, the government's student assistance program is inadequate and discriminatory.
2. The computer has contributed to the modern sense of alienation.
3. If parliamentary debates are supposed to guarantee respect for minority opinion, they usually turn out to be flagrant wastes of time.
4. The new sense of French Canadian pride comes from our increasing awareness of Quebec's cultural heritage.
5. If women are discriminated against in schools and in industry, they are far more discriminated against in politics.

2. *Now try the inverted funnel, in which your topic sentence is some version of the thesis with which you began and your final paragraph broadens its implications outward to leave the reader fully convinced and satisfied. Using the thesis-sentences in Exercise 1, write two ending paragraphs for imaginary papers.*

EXAMPLE with the rephrased thesis (its topic sentence) italicized, and some of the evidence from the paper's middle summarized for emphasis:

> *So, at last, we should add up the real costs of strip-mining; we should admit that the ultimate price of coal is far too high if we must rape the land, poison the streams, and wreck human lives to mine it.* For after the drag-lines have gone, even after the coal itself has been burned, the bills for strip-mining will keep coming in. So far, following the expedient path, we have laid bare more than 2,600 square miles of land, and we show no signs of stopping. Every year we strip an additional 50,000 acres. Just as we cut down our forests in the nineteenth century and fouled our air in the twentieth, we still blunder along toward ecological and social disaster. Isn't it time to stop?

3. *Staying with the same topic sentence, develop a full middle paragraph, remembering the four points: (1) the miniature essay, with beginning, middle, and end; (2) coherence; (3) fullness; (4) transition.*

EXAMPLE with transitional touches italicized:

> The streams tell the story *as drearily as* the *eroded land.* In winter, *they* are red with running silt, and sometimes black with *coal* dust. *In summer, many* are no *streams* at all, merely gullies through which the *winter* rains have rushed. Before *the drag-lines stripped* the earth of its skin, the massed roots of grasses, shrubs, and trees held the soil in place and soaked up the *water,* easing it into the *streams* for a full year's run. Fish fed in pools below *grassy* banks and among the weeds that slowed the *water* to a leisurely pace. Now the *water* is soon gone, if not *poisoned* with *industrial waste,* and the *land* is *gone* with it.

Now you will have a three-paragraph essay that should convey a thorough sense of beginning, middle, end.

4. *Now, to make an even richer, fuller essay, add two or more middle paragraphs, with good transitions, to give a stronger impetus to the implications of your end paragraph. If you had developed the sample paragraphs in these exercises, for example, you could develop separate paragraphs, each with several illustrations, on ruined land, streams, and lives.*

5
Middle Tactics: Description, Narration, Exposition

With the whole essay in mind, we will now look more closely at the possibilities in arranging those middle points, the descriptive, narrative, and expository orders that illustrate your argument and carry your ideas. Description talks about what we see; narration, about what we do. Exposition, which may include both, essentially follows modes of thought, the ancient *topoi* of comparison and contrast, cause and effect, classification, definition. All are tactics for arrangement and persuasion.

DESCRIPTION

Description is essentially *spatial*. Arranging details in some kind of tour through space is as natural as walking. When your subject dwells in and upon physical space—the layout of a campus, for instance—you literally take your reader with you. You organize your paragraphs virtually as units of space, one for the gate, one for the first building, conducting your reader in an orderly progress down the mall or around the quadrangle. Or you show him a rooming house floor by floor, from the apartment by the entry to the garret four flights up, where the graduate student lives on books and cheese. Within the paragraph, you similarly take your reader from one detail to the next in spatial order. Your topic sentence summarizes the total effect: "The Whistler Building was once elegant, three classic stories of brick with carved stone pediments." Then your paragraph proceeds with noteworthy details in any convenient spatial order: first the sagging front door, then the windows to the left, then those to the right, then the second-floor windows, with their suggestion of dingy apartments, then those of the third, which suggest only emptiness.

A city's slum or its crowded parking, a river's pollution, a mountain's trees from valley to timberline—any spatial subject will offer a convenient route, from bottom to top, or top to bottom, left to right, east to west, centre to periphery. You will instinctively use a series of spatial signals: *on the right, above, next, across, down the slope.* Your concern is to keep your progress orderly, to help your reader see what you are talking about. This is exactly the way Oliver Statler, in his *Japanese Inn,* takes us to the place he loves:

> On this day, I have already progressed along the old Tokaido Road to the village of Yui. A new highway has been built a few hundred yards inland to avoid the congested main street of the village, but leaving Yui it swings back to the shore and runs between the sea wall on my left and the sheer face of Satta Mountain on my right.
>
> It is here, as I drive almost into the sea, that my spirits always quicken, for only Satta Mountain divides Yui from Okitsu, the next village, where my inn lies. . . . I notice men and women diving around the off-shore rocks, sharp knives in hand, hunting for abalone. Beyond them, fishing boats dot Suruga Bay. . . .
>
> At the highest point of the pass, where the path breaks out of the pines and into the open, there is a breath-taking view, and anyone who finds himself there must turn to drink it in. He faces the great sweep of Suruga Bay and the open Pacific beyond, while waves break into flowers on the rocks far beneath his feet. Yui lies on the shore to his left and Okitsu at his right. Beyond Yui, bathed in mist far off on the left, looms the mountainous coast of Izu. Beyond Okitsu, on the right, is one of the loveliest sights in Japan, for the harbor that lies there is protected by a long arm of curving black sand, covered with ancient and twisted pines. This is the fabled beach of Miho. . . .*

*Oliver Statler, *Japanese Inn* (New York: Pyramid Books, Random House, 1962): 14–16. Copyright © 1961, Oliver Statler.

As you can *see,* literally, the best spatial description follows the perceptions of a person looking at or entering the space described, reporting the impressions, the colours, textures, sights, or sounds as they come, as again with the imaginary visitor in this description by R. Prawer Jhabvala of a modern house in India:

> Our foreign visitor stands agape at the wonderful residence his second host has built for himself. No expense has been spared here, no decoration suggested by a vivid taste omitted. There are little Moorish balconies and Indian domes and squiggly lattice work and an air-conditioner in every window. Inside, all is marble flooring, and in the entrance hall there is a fountain lit up with green, yellow, and red bulbs. The curtains on the windows and in the doorways are of silk, the vast sofa-suites are upholstered in velvet, the telephone is red, and huge vases are filled with plastic flowers.*

Some novels proceed like this paragraph after paragraph, as in the beginning of Thomas Hardy's *The Return of the Native,* for instance, in which we are moved into the setting from a great distance, as if, years before moving pictures, we are riding a cameraman's dolly.

Description frequently blends time and space, picking out striking features then moving along. This is the usual way of describing people, as in this paragraph about an actual Englishman whose odd occupation is mending the broken eggs brought to him by bird's-egg collectors:

> Colonel Prynne, who is sixty-seven, lives and carries on his singular pursuit in a rambling, thatch-roofed, five-hundred-year-old cottage in the tiny village of Spaxton, Somerset, and there, on a recent sunny afternoon, he received us. A man of medium build who retains a military carriage, he was sprucely turned out in a brown suit, a tan jersey vest, a green shirt and tie, and tan oxfords. He has a bald, distinctly egg-shaped head, wears a close-cropped mustache and black shell-rimmed glasses, and seems always to have his nose tilted slightly upward and the nostrils faintly distended, as if he were sniffing the air. After taking us on a

Encounter 22 (1964): 42–43.

**rather cursory tour of his garden, which is as neat and well
tended as its owner, he remarked crisply that it was time to
get cracking, and we followed him indoors, past an enor-
mous fireplace, which burns five-foot logs, and up a flight
of stairs to a room that he calls his studio.***

NARRATION

In contrast with description, narration is essentially *temporal.* Like
space, time is a natural organizer. Hour follows hour, day follows
day, year follows year, life follows life. Again, you simply take
your reader along the natural sequence of what happens—to us,
or to nations, or to any items in experience or experiment. We
understand processes most clearly by tracking the way they move
through time, even processes complicated by other, simultaneous events:

> **And when this wheel turns, that lever tips the food into the
> trough.**
> **While this conveyor moves into the oven, the other one is
> bringing the chassis to point B.**
> **And all the time he talked, his hands were moving the shells
> and flicking the invisible pea.**

Any event, whether a football game or the inauguration of a
mayor, can be best perceived as you have perceived it—through
time—and you can bring your reader to perceive it by following
the sequence of things as they happened, stepping aside as necessary to explain background and simultaneous events, guiding
your reader along with temporal signposts: *at the same time, now,
when, while, then, before, after, next, all the time.*

As Audubon, the nineteenth-century naturalist, describes in
his *Ornithological Biography* the passenger pigeon and its astounding flights in masses a mile wide and 180 long, he naturally gives
us his observations through the order of time. I have italicized the
temporal words in one of his paragraphs:

---

*"Talk of the Town," *The New Yorker* (23 May 1964): 37. © 1964, The New Yorker
Magazine, Inc. Reprinted by permission.

As soon as the pigeons discover a sufficiency of food to entice them to alight, they fly round in circles, reviewing the country below. *During* their evolutions, *on such occasions,* the dense mass which they form exhibits a beautiful appearance, *as* it changes direction, *now* displaying a glistening sheet of azure, *when* the backs of the birds come *simultaneously* into view, *and anon, suddenly* presenting a mass of rich deep purple. They *then* pass lower, over the woods, and *for a moment* are lost among the foliage, *but again* emerge, and are seen gliding aloft. They *now* alight, but *the next moment,* as if *suddenly* alarmed, they take to wing, producing by the flappings of their wings a noise like the roar of distant thunder, and sweep through the forests to see if danger is near. Hunger, however, *soon* brings them to the ground. *When* alighted, they are seen industriously throwing up the withered leaves. . . .

You can most clearly explain any kind of development or decline—the civil rights movement, the decay of a neighbourhood—by taking your reader up or down the path of time. But you will do your reader a favour by keeping to your order, whether forward or backward, and not reversing it inadvertently somewhere along the way. Any event invites chronological narration, and such narration naturally includes a rich infusion of description, often alive with pictorial metaphors to convey the writer's impressions. Frank A. Worsley does this surpassingly well as he describes his sailing journey, with Sir Ernest Shackleton and four others, in a small boat through grotesquely melting Antarctic icebergs:

They rose and fell on the heaving sea, drawing deceptively apart, then closing with a thud that would have smashed our boat like a gas-mantle between thumb and finger. Castles, towers, and churches swayed unsteadily around us. Small pieces gathered and rattled against the boat. Swans of weird shape pecked at our planks; a gondola steered by a giraffe ran foul of us, which much amused a duck sitting on a crocodile's head. Just then a bear, leaning over the top of a mosque, nearly clawed our sail. An elephant, about to spring from a Swiss chalet on to a battleship's deck, took no notice at all; but a hyena, pulling a lion's teeth, laughed so much that he fell into the sea, whereupon a sea-boot and three real penguins sailed lazily

through a lovely archway to see what was to do, by the shores of a floe littered with the ruins of a beautiful white city and surrounded by huge mushrooms with thick stalks. All the strange, fantastic shapes rose and fell in stately cadence, with a rustling, whispering sound and hollow echoes to the thudding seas, clear green at the water-line, shading to a deep blue far below, all snowy purity and cool blue shadows above.*

Sometimes an argumentative essay will give over its entire middle to a narrative of some event that illustrates its thesis. Of this kind is George Orwell's great "Shooting an Elephant." Orwell's thesis is that imperialism tyrannizes over the rulers as well as the ruled. To illustrate it, he tells of an incident during his career as a young police officer in Burma, when he was compelled, by the expectations of the crowd, to shoot a renegade elephant. Here is a narrative paragraph in which Orwell reports a crucial moment; notice how he mixes external events and snippets of conversation with his inner thoughts, pegging all perfectly with a topic sentence:

But I did not want to shoot the elephant. I watched him beating his bunch of grass against his knees, with that preoccupied grandmotherly air that elephants have. It seemed to me that it would be murder to shoot him. At that age I was not squeamish about killing animals, but I had never shot an elephant and never wanted to. (Somehow it always seems worse to kill a *large* animal.) Besides, there was the beast's owner to be considered. Alive, the elephant was worth at least a hundred pounds; dead, he would only be worth the value of his tusks, five pounds, possibly. But I had got to act quickly. I turned to some experienced-looking Burmans who had been there when we arrived, and asked them how the elephant had been behaving. They all said the same thing: he took no notice of you if you left him alone, but he might charge if you went too close to him.†

---

*Commander F. A. Worsley, *Shackleton's Boat Journey,* Introduction and Notes by Duncan Carse (London: The Folio Society, 1974): 66–67.
†From "Shooting an Elephant" in *Shooting an Elephant and Other Essays* by George Orwell, copyright 1950 by Sonia Brownell Orwell; renewed 1978 by Sonia Pitt-Rivers. Reprinted by permission of Harcourt Brace Jovanovich, Inc.

Orwell is simply recounting events, and his thoughts, as they happened, one after the other. Almost any kind of essay could use a similar paragraph of narrative to illustrate a point.

EXPOSITION

Exposition is a setting forth, an explaining, which naturally may include both description and narration. But it also includes some essential modes of thought: comparison and contrast, cause and effect, classification, and definition. Good exposition depends on specific details to illustrate its general point.

Loren Eisley, for instance, illustrates his generalization "these apes are not similar" not only with comparative contrasts but with particularized specifics. He has been writing about Alfred Russel Wallace's and Charles Darwin's conflicting views as to the evolution of man's brain from that of the humanoid ape:

> **These apes are not all similar in type or appearance. They are men and yet not men. Some are frailer-bodied, some have great, bone-cracking jaws and massive gorilloid crests atop their skulls. This fact leads us to another of Wallace's remarkable perceptions of long ago. With the rise of the truly human brain, Wallace saw that man had transferred to his machines and tools many of the alterations of parts that in animals take place through evolution of the body. Unwittingly, man had assigned to his machines the selective evolution which in the animal changes the nature of its bodily structure through the ages. Man of today, the atomic manipulator, the aeronaut who flies faster than sound, has precisely the same brain and body as his ancestors of twenty thousand years ago who painted the last Ice Age mammoths on the walls of caves in France.***

Notice how he spells out the specifics of bodies, jaws, and skulls. He does not say *aeronauts,* plural, but *the* single and specific *aeronaut,* adding the further specific *who flies faster than sound,*

---

*"The Real Secret of Piltdown," in *The Immense Journey* (New York: Random House, Inc., 1955). © Copyright 1955 by Loren C. Eiseley.

letting that single specific person illustrate the whole general range of what man can do with machines. He does not say merely "ancestors," but ancestors of specifically *twenty thousand years ago;* not merely "lived," but *who painted,* and not merely "pictures," but *the last Ice Age mammoths,* and specifically on *walls* in specific *caves* in one specific country, *France.* The point is to try to extend each of your generalizations by adding some specific detail to illustrate it. Don't stop with *awkward player:* go on to *when he strikes out, or misses an easy fly, or an easy basket.*

Your illustration may also be hypothetical, as it frequently is in scientific explanation. "Suppose you are riding along in a car," the scientist will say, as he tries to convey the idea of relative motion. "You drop a baseball straight down from your hand to the floor between your feet." And he continues by explaining that this vertical drop describes a long line slanting downward in relation to the line of the rapidly receding highway beneath the car, illustrating each new aspect of relativity, by the same dropped ball in its relation to curves in the road, the earth itself, the sun, and to whatever hypothetical platforms he may wish to put into orbit.

Comparison and Contrast: Run Contrasts Side by Side

Comparison and contrast is a natural mode of thought, a natural organizer of exposition, making two specifics vivid by bringing them side by side. It may be the very basis of thought itself. All knowledge involves comparing things for their similarities and noticing their contrasting differences. We group all people as people, and then tell them apart as individuals.

We instinctively know our friends in this way, for instance. Two of them drift side by side in our thoughts. We are comparing them. They are both boys; they are the same age and stature; we like them both. But one bubbles up like a mountain spring, and the other runs deep. Their appearances, mannerisms, and tastes match their contrasting personalities. One's room is messy; the other's is neat. One races his car; the other collects stamps. We compare the similar categories—looks, habits, hobbies, goals— and contrast the differences.

Your topic sentence sets the comparison and makes the contrast:

> **Opposites seem to attract.** *My father is tall, blond, and*   Contrast
> *outgoing. My mother is small, and even her dark brown hair,*
> *which is naturally wavy, has a certain quiet repose about it.* My
> **dad does everything at a cheerful run,** whether he is off to a
> **sales conference or off to the golf course with his foursome**
> **on Saturday mornings.** *My mother never seems to hurry.* She
> **hums at her work, and the house seems to slip into order**
> **without effort. She plays bridge with a few friends, and**
> **belongs to a number of organizations, but she is just as**
> **happy with a book. When dad bursts in at the end of the day,**
> **her face lights up. They grin at each other. They obviously**
> **still find each other attractive.**

Comparison and Contrast: Illustrate by Analogy

An analogy points up similarities between things otherwise dissimilar. With an analogy, you help your reader grasp your subject by showing how it is like something familiar. Your topic sentence asserts the comparison, and then your paragraph unfolds the comparison in detail:

> **School spirit is like patriotism. Students take their**
> **school's fortunes as their own, defending and promoting**
> **them against those of another school, as citizens champion**
> **their country, right or wrong. Their school is not only their**
> **alma mater but their fatherland as well. Like soldiers, they**
> **will give their utmost strength in field games and intellec-**
> **tual contests for both personal glory and the greater glory**
> **of the domain they represent. And, in defeat, they will**
> **mourn as if dragged in chains through the streets of Rome.**

Here is Farley Mowat describing an Innuit "house." His comparison shows that analogy is really a form of extended metaphor:

> **The tent and the igloo are really only auxiliary shelters.**   Topic
> **The real home of the Ihalmio is much like that of the turtle,**   Sentence
> **for it is what he carries about on his back. In truth it is the** with Analogy
> **only house that can enable men to survive on the merciless**

> **plains of the Barrens. It has central heating from the fat furnace of the body, its walls are insulated to a degree of perfection that we white men have not been able to surpass, or even emulate. It is complete, light in weight, easy to make and easy to keep in repair. It costs nothing, for it is a gift of the land, through the deer. When I consider that house, my opinion of the astuteness of the Ihalmiut is no longer clouded.***

That is probably as long as an analogy can effectively run. One paragraph is about the limit. Beyond that, the reader may tire of it.

Comparison and Contrast: Develop Differences Point by Point

Your *comparisons* present helpful illustrations of your subject by emphasizing similarities. Contrasts, on the other hand, compare similar things to emphasize their differences—West Germany as against East Germany, for example—usually to persuade your reader that one is in some or most ways better than the other.

The danger lies in losing your contrastive advantage, writing about one side of your contrast and forgetting the other. Make your comparisons point for point. Don't write all about sheep for three pages, for instance, then all about goats. Every time you say something about a sheep, say something comparable about a goat, pelt for pelt, horn for horn, beard for beard. Otherwise your essay will fall in two, your reader will be surprised when the goats come along, and you will need to repeat all your sheep points when you at last begin the comparison. So keep your contrasts vivid, point for point.

Keep both sides before the reader. You may do this in one of two ways: (1) by making a topic sentence to cover one point —agriculture, let us say—and then continuing your paragraph in paired sentences, one for the West, one for the East, another for the West, another for the East, and so on; or (2) by writing your

---

*From *People of the Deer* (Toronto: McClelland and Stewart Ltd., 1952).

paragraphs in pairs, one paragraph for the West, one for the East, using the topic sentence of the first paragraph to govern the second, something like this:

> *West Germany's agriculture is far ahead of the East's.* **Every-** Topic
> **where about the countryside, one sees signs of prosperity.** Sentence
> **Trucks and tractors are shiny. Fences are mended and in** West
> **order. Buildings all seem newly painted, as if on exhibit for**
> **a fair. New Volkswagens buzz along the country roads. The**
> **annual statistics spell out the prosperous details. . . .**
>
> *East Germany, on the other hand, seems to be dropping* Contrast
> *progressively behind.* **The countryside is drab and empty. On**
> **one huge commune, everything from buildings to equip-**
> **ment seems to be creaking from rusty hinges. . . . The an-**
> **nual statistics are equally depressing. . . .**

In an extended contrast, you will probably want to contrast some things sentence against sentence, within single paragraphs, and to contrast others by giving a paragraph to each. Remember only to keep your reader sufficiently in touch with both sides.

Here are two paragraphs from a student's paper neatly contrasted without losing touch:

> **In fact,** *in some respects the commercials are really better* Topic
> *than the shows they sponsor.* **The** *commericals are carefully* Sentence
> *rehearsed, expertly photographed, highly edited and polished.* First Subject
> **They are made with absolute attention to detail and to the**
> **clock. One split-second over time, one bad note, one**
> **slightly wrinkled dress, and they are done over again.**
> **Weeks, even months, go into the production of a single**
> **sixty-second commerical.**
>
> *The shows, on the other hand, are slapped together hastily by* The Contrast
> *writers and performers who have less than a week to put together*
> *an hour show.* **Actors have little time to rehearse, and often**
> **the pieces of a show are put together for the first time in**
> **front of the camera. Lighting, sound reproduction, and ed-**
> **iting are workmanlike, but unpolished; a shadow from an**
> **overhead microphone on an actor's face causes no real con-**
> **cern in the control room. A blown line or a muffed cue is**
> **"just one of those things that happen." In all, it often takes**
> **less time and money to do an hour show than to do the four**
> **sixty-second commercials that sponsor it.**

Contrasts done sentence by sentence, or by clauses hinged on a semicolon, are also effective:

> **The most essential distinction between athletics and education lies in the institution's own interest in the athlete as distinguished from its interest in its other students. Universities attract students in order to teach them what they do not already know; they recruit athletes only when they are already proficient. Students are educated for something which will be useful to them and to society after graduation; athletes are required to spend their time on activities the usefulness of which disappears upon graduation or soon thereafter. Universities exist to do what they can for students; athletes are recruited for what they can do for the universities. This makes the operation of the athletic program in which recruited players are used basically different from any educational interest of colleges and universities.***

Cause and Effect: Trace Back or Look Ahead

Because is the impulse here: "Such and such is so *because.* . . ." You think back through a train of causes, each one the effect of something prior; or you think your way into the future, speculating about the possible effects of some present cause. In other words, you organize your paragraph in one of two ways:

1. You state a general effect, then deal with its several causes.
2. You state a general cause, then deal with its possible effects.

In Arrangement 1, you know the effect (a lost football game, or the solar system, let us say), and you speculate as to causes. In Arrangement 2, you know the cause (a new restriction, or abolishing nuclear weapons, let us say), and you speculate as to the effects.

---

*Harold W. Stoke, "College Athletics: Education or Show Business?" *Atlantic Monthly* (March 1954): 46–50. Copyright © 1954 by Harold W. Stoke. Reprinted by permission.

Arrangement 1: Effect Followed by Causes

> **An unusual cluster of bad luck lost the game.** Many blamed Fraser's failure to block the tackler who caused the fumble that produced the winning touchdown. But even here, bad weather and bad luck shared the blame. Both teams faced a slippery field, of course. But Fraser was standing in a virtual bog when he lunged for the block and slipped. Moreover, the storm had delayed the bus for hours, tiring and frustrating the team, leaving them short of sleep and with no chance to practice. Furthermore, Hunter's throwing arm was still not back in shape from his early injury. Finally, one must admit, the Acorns were simply heavier and stronger, which is the real luck of the game.

You will probably notice, as you try to explain causes and effects, that they do not always run in a simple linear sequence, one thing following another, like a row of falling dominoes. Indeed, mere sequence is so famously untrustworthy in tracing causes that one of the classical errors of thought is named *post hoc, ergo propter hoc* ("after this, therefore because of this"). In other words, we cannot reasonably suppose that *A* caused *B* simply because *A* preceded *B*. The two may have been entirely unrelated. But the greatest danger in identifying causes is to fasten upon a single cause while ignoring others of equal significance. Both your paragraph and your persuasiveness will be better if you do not insist, as some did, that only Fraser's failure to block the tackler lost the game.

In the lost ball game, you were interested in explaining causes, but sometimes your interest will lie with effects. When describing a slum problem, for instance, your topic sentence might be *The downtown slum is a screaming disgrace* (the effect), and you might then in a single sentence set aside the causes as irrelevant, as water over the dam, as so much spilt milk: "perhaps caused by inefficiency, perhaps by avarice, perhaps by the indifference of Mayor Richman." Your interests will dictate your proportions of cause and effect. You might well write an entire essay that balances the slum's causes and effects in equal proportions: a paragraph each on inefficiency, avarice, and the mayor's indifference, then a paragraph each on ill health, poor education, and hopelessness.

Here is how a brief essay, in three paragraphs, can deal with cause and effect alone. I have begun and ended with the *effect* (the peculiar layout of a town). First, I located the *immediate cause* (cattle) as my thesis, and then, in the middle paragraph, I moved through the cause and its *conditions* up to the *effect* again—the town as it stands today:

North of the Tracks

Effect   **If you drive out west from Chicago, you will notice something happening to the towns.** *After the country levels into Nebraska, the smaller towns are built only on one side of the road.* **When you stop for a rest, and look south across the broad main street, you will see the railroad immediately**

Effect   **beyond.** *All of these towns spread northward from the tracks.* **Why? As you munch your hamburger and look at the restau-**

Thesis   **rant's murals,** *you will realize that the answer is cattle.*

Cause   *These towns were the destinations of the great cattle drives*
Conditions *from Texas.* **They probably had begun at the scattered watering places in the dry land.** **Then** *the wagon trails and, finally,*

Causes   *the transcontinental railroad had strung them together.* **Once the railroad came, the whole Southwest could raise cattle for the slaughterhouses of Chicago. The droves of cattle came**

Effect   **up from the south, and** *all of these towns reflect the traffic:* **corrals beside the tracks to the south, the road for passengers and wagons paralleling the tracks on the northern side, then, along the road, the row of hotels, saloons, and businesses, with the town spreading northward behind the businesses.**

Cause   *The cattle-business itself shaped these one-sided Nebraska towns.* **The conditions in which this immediate cause took root were the growing population in the East and the railroad that connected the plains of the West, and Southwest, with the tables of New York. The towns took their hopeful being north of the rails, on the leeward side of the vast cattle drives from the south. The trade in cattle has now changed, all the way from Miami to Sacramento. But** *the great herds of*

Effect   *the old Southwest, together with the transcontinental railroad and man's need to make a living, plotted these Western towns north of the tracks.*

Arrangement 2: Cause Followed by Probable Effects

Arrangement 2 is the staple of deliberative rhetoric, of all political and economic forecasting, for instance. Your order of presenting cause and effect is reversed. You are looking to the future. You state a known cause (a new restriction on residence hours) or a hypothetical cause ("If this restriction is passed"), and then you speculate about the possible, or probable, effects. Your procedure will then be much the same as before. But for maximum persuasiveness, try to keep your supposed effects, which no one can really foresee, as nearly probable as you can. Occasionally, of course, you may put an improbable hypothetical cause to good use in a satiric essay, reducing some proposal to absurdity: "If all restrictions were abolished. . . ." "If no one wore clothes. . . ." Or the improbable *if* may even help clarify a straightforward explanation of real relationships, as in the following excerpt from *Time* magazine's report on Fred Hoyle, the British astronomer and mathematician who has been modifying Newton's gravity and Einstein's relativity. The paragraph states the general condition, proposes its hypothetical cause with an *if,* then moves to the effects, first in temporal order and then in order of human interest:

> **The masses, and therefore the gravity, of the sun and the earth are partly due to each other, partly to more distant objects such as the stars and galaxies. According to Hoyle, if the universe were to be cut in half, local solar-system gravitation would double, drawing the earth closer to the sun. The pressure in the sun's center would increase, thus raising its temperature, its generation of energy, and its brightness. Before being seared into a lump of charcoal, a man on earth would find his weight increasing from 150 to 300 lbs.**

Classification: Use the Natural Divisions

Many subjects fall into natural or customary classifications, as if they were blandly jointed, like a good roast of pork ready for carving, contrasting one joint with the next: freshman, sophomore, junior, senior; Liberal, Conservative, NDP; right, middle, left; municipal, provincial, federal. You can easily follow these divisions in organizing a paragraph, or you can write one paragraph for each division, and attain a nicely coherent essay. Similarly, any manufacturing process, or any machine, will already have distinct steps and parts. These customary divisions will help your reader, since he knows something of them already. Describe the Conservative position on foreign investment, and he will naturally expect your description of the Liberal position to follow. If no other divisions suggest themselves, you can often organize your paragraph—or your essay—into a consistent series of parallel answers, or "reasons for," or "reasons against," something like this:

A broad liberal education is best:
1. It prepares you for a world of changing employment.
2. It enables you to function well as a citizen.
3. It enables you to make the most of your life.

Many problems present natural classifying joints. Take the Panama Canal, for instance. Its construction divides into three nicely jointed problems, political, geological, and biological, each with its solutions, as the following paragraph shows:

	Building the Panama Canal posed problems of politics, geology, and human survival from the beginning. *A French*
Problem 1	*company, organized in 1880 to dig the canal, repeatedly had to extend its treaties at higher and higher prices as the work dragged*
Solution 1	*on.* **Uneasy about the French,** *the United States made treaties with Nicaragua and Costa Rica* **to dig along the other most feasible route.** *This political threat,* **together with the failure of the French and the revolt of Panama from Colombia,** *finally enabled the United States to buy the French rights and negotiate new treaties,* **which, nevertheless, continue to cause**
Problem(s) 2	**political trouble to this day.** *Geology also posed its ancient problems:* **how to manage torrential rivers and inland lakes; whether to build a longer but more enduring canal at sea**
Solution to 2	**level, or** *a shorter, cheaper, and safer canal with locks.* **Economy**
Problem 3	**eventually won, but the problem of** *yellow fever and malaria,* **which had plagued the French, remained.** *By detecting and*
Solution to 3	*combating the fever-carrying mosquito, William Gorgas solved these ancient tropical problems.* **Without him, the political and geological solutions would have come to nothing.**

You could easily organize this into three paragraphs of problem and solution, with topic sentences like these:

> The Panama Canal posed three major problems, the first of
> which was political.
> The second problem was geological, a massive problem of
> engineering.
> The third problem, that of human survival, proved the most
> stubborn of all.

Any problem and its solution can produce a neatly ordered paragraph—or essay, for that matter: choosing a university, or something to wear (if you want to be lighthearted), making an apartment or a commune work, building the Eiffel Tower or the
pyramids. You can often similarly classify sets of comparisons
and contrasts, causes and effects, combining your tactics with
magnified force.

Describing Processes: Follow the Natural Steps

Describing a process combines description and narration with
classification. This is probably exposition at its most basic intent:
explaining how to assemble the Christmas toy, the new hibachi
or deck chair, how to build a sun dial or plant a vegetable garden
or write an essay. Your subject will again offer natural sequences
in space and time and natural divisions in classification. As always, you will find a topic sentence to govern the job. Then you
proceed through those steps that will most clearly help your
reader to do the job:

> Growing the iris, the poor man's orchid, is easy. Irises
> grow almost like weeds in well-drained soil, but a little care
> pays glorious dividends. Plant your rhizomes—the iris root
> —in early fall. First, enrich your soil with an organic fertili-
> zer low in nitrogen, at about one ounce to the square foot,
> three weeks before planting. Then plant the rhizomes al-
> most even with the surface. Spruce up each plant in the
> spring with a quarter of a cup of superphosphate. In the
> fourth or fifth year, dig them up in late July or early Septem-
> ber. Cut off the old tubers with a sharp knife. Let the hardy
> tubers harden in the sun for a day. Then replant them. They
> bloom long in the spring, and their attractive fans of leaves
> stand green until fall.

In the following paper, a student has nicely amalgamated description, narration, and the classification implied in a problem and its solution to analyze a fascinating process.

Nothing Primitive About It

Stonehenge, the gigantic prehistoric construction on Salisbury Plain in England, cannot fail to fascinate us with a number of nearly unanswerable questions. How long has it been there? Who built it? Why? But of all the questions Stonehenge raises, none is more intriguing than *"How was it built?"* *How did these primitive people,* whose only tools were rock, bone, or crudely fashioned sticks, who had not yet even discovered the wheel, *manage to transport* the *huge rocks,* most of them more than twenty feet in length and weighing over thirty tons, *more than twenty miles overland?*

And by what ingenuity did they manage, having transported the rocks, *to stand them on end and support them so that now,* thousands of years later, *most* of them *still stand?* What primitive engineering geniuses were these?

Transporting the stones from their original site at Marlborough Downs, some twenty miles to the north of Stonehenge, must have been, by any of the possible means, a very slow process. One possibility is that *hundreds of men,* some pulling on the rock, some cutting down trees and filling in holes as they went, *simply dragged the stones over the bare ground. Or perhaps they used snow or mud to "grease" the path.* Foot by foot, and day by day, they may have dragged the rocks all the way from Marlborough Downs to Stonehenge. *Another guess is that these primitive men,* even though they had not yet invented the wheel, *knew about using logs as rollers.* If so, perhaps they mounted each stone on a sledge, and rolled the sledge slowly forward, workmen placing logs in its path as it moved. Such a method, while a good deal easier than dragging the rock along the ground, would still have required as many as seven or eight hundred men, and perhaps as much as a decade to move all the stones. *A third possibility is that the stones were moved along riverbeds,* the shallow water helping to buoy the weight, and the muddy banks helping to slide the weight along. Though much less direct than the overland route, the riverbed route would have provided these primitive men with a relatively clear path that ran approximately halfway from the stones' point of origin to their final location. Of course, the point is that any of these three means of transporting the stones must have been an

The marginal notes read:

Thesis
Problem 1
Description
and Narration

Problem 2

Narrating the
Process

Solutions to 1
First
Classification

Second
Classification
Narrating and
Describing
the Process

Third
Classification

incredibly laborious task, occupying as many as a thousand men, year after year after year.

Lifting the stones into an upright position, once they had been transported, *was another triumph of ingenuity and brute strength.* Apparently, the workmen dug closely fitted holes where they wanted the stones eventually to stand. Probably they cut away one side of the hole, the side nearest the stone, to form a ramp. Perhaps they also lined the hole with wooden skids. Then gradually they eased the stone down the ramp until it rested in a tilted position at the bottom of the hole. Next, they used brute strength, some men pushing, some pulling on primitive ropes, to raise the rock into a vertical position. If we suppose each man lifted only his own weight, say 150 pounds, it might have taken as many as 400 men to stand the stones upright. Finally, while some workers held the rock in position, others quickly filled in the excavation left by the ramp. For many months afterward they probably refilled and pounded the dirt until it was completely firm. They probably placed the huge transverse pieces across the tops of columns by similarly dragging them up long earthern ramps. The fact that most of the rocks are still standing after thousands of years is testimony of their planning and workmanship.

Solutions to 2 Describing and Narrating the Process

We may never know quite why these primitive men chose to build Stonehenge, or who the men were. We may never know where they came from, or where they went. *In Stonehenge, however, they have left a testament to their perseverance and their ingenuity. Clearly, they rivaled any of the builders of the ancient world.*

Thesis Restated

Definition: Clear Up Your Terms

Definition is another mode of classification, in which we clear away hidden assumptions, along with unwanted categories. What the Russians and Chinese call a People's Democracy is the very opposite of what the Canadians and British call democracy, assumed also to be of and for and by the people. Ideally, your running prose should make your terms clear to your reader, avoiding those definitions that seem too stiff and stuffy, and especially avoid quoting the dictionary: "As *Webster's* says. . . ." Nevertheless, what we mean by *egotism, superiority, education,* or *character* may need laying on the table.

Richard Hofstadter, for instance, found it necessary in his essay "Democracy and Anti-Intellectualism in America" to devote a number of paragraphs to defining both *democracy* and *intellectual,* each paragraph examining the evidence and clarifying one aspect of his term. Coming early in his essay, after he has set his thesis and surveyed his subject, his section of definition begins with the following paragraph:

Topic Sentence as Question	*But what is an intellectual, really?* **This is a problem of definition that I found, when I came to it, far more elusive than I had anticipated.** *A great deal of what might be called the*
What It Is *Not*	*journeyman's work of our culture—*the work of engineers, physicians, newspapermen, and indeed of most professors*—does not strike me as distinctively intellectual,* although it is certainly work based in an important sense on ideas.
What It *Is*	*The distinction that we must recognize,* then, *is one* originally made by Max Weber *between living* for *ideas and living* off *ideas. The intellectual lives for ideas;* the journeyman lives off
Con: Examples	them. *The engineer or the physician—*I don't mean here to be invidious*—needs to have a pretty considerable capital stock in frozen ideas* to do his work; but they *serve for him a purely*
Pro: Examples	*instrumental purpose: he lives off them, not for them.* Of course he may also be, in his private role and his personal ways of thought, an intellectual, but it is not necessary for him to be in order to work at his profession. There is in fact no profes-
Con: Detailed Opposition	sion which demands that one be an intellectual. *There do seem to be vocations, however, which almost demand that one be an anti-intellectual,* in which those who live off ideas seem to have implacable hatred for those who live for them. The marginal intellectual workers and the unfrocked intellectuals who work in journalism, advertising, and mass communication are the bitterest and most powerful among those who work at such vocations.*

Your subject will prompt you in one of two ways, toward inclusiveness or toward exclusiveness. Hofstadter found that he needed to be inclusive about the several essentials in *democracy* and *intellectual—*terms used commonly, and often loosely. Inclusiveness is the usual need, as you will find in trying to define *love* or *loyalty* or *education.* But you may sometimes need to move

---

*The Michigan Alumnus Quarterly Review 59 (1953): 282. Copyright © 1953 by the University of Michigan.

in the opposite direction, toward exclusiveness, as in sociological, philosophical, or scientific discussion, when you need to nail your terms firmly to single meanings: "By *reality*, I mean only that which exists in the physical world excluding our ideas about it."

Such exclusive defining is called *stipulative*, since you stipulate the precise meaning you want. But you should avoid the danger of trying to exclude more than the word will allow. If you try to limit the meaning of the term *course* to "three hours a week per term," your discussion will soon encounter courses with different hours; or you may find yourself inadvertently drifting to another meaning, as you mention something about graduating from an "engineering course." At any rate, if you can avoid the sound of dogmatism in your stipulation, so much the better. You may well practice some disguise, as with *properly speaking* and *only* in the following stipulative definition: "Properly speaking, the *structure* of any literary work is only that framelike quality we can picture in two, or three, dimensions."

Definitions frequently seem to develop into paragraphs, almost by second nature. A sentence of definition is usually short and crisp, seeming to demand some explanation, some illustration and sociability. The definition, in other words, is a natural topic sentence. Here are three classic single-sentence kinds of definitions that will serve well as topics for your paragraphs:

1. DEFINITION BY SYNONYM. A quick way to stipulate the single meaning you want: "Virtue means moral rectitude."
2. DEFINITION BY FUNCTION. "A barometer measures atmospheric pressure"—"A social barometer measures human pressures"—"A good quarterback calls the signals and sparks the whole team's spirits."
3. DEFINITION BY SYNTHESIS. A placing of your term in striking (and not necessarily logical) relationship to its whole class, usually for the purposes of wit: "The fox is the craftiest of beasts"—"A sheep is a friendlier form of goat" —"A lexicographer is a harmless drudge"—"A sophomore is a sophisticated moron."

Three more of the classic kinds of definition follow, of broader dimensions than the single-sentence kinds above, but also ready-made for a paragraph apiece, or for several. Actually, in making paragraphs from your single-sentence definitions, you have undoubtedly used at least one of these three kinds, or a mixture of them all. They are no more than the natural ways we define our meanings.

4. DEFINITION BY EXAMPLE. The opposite of *definition by synthesis*. You start with the class ("crafty beasts") and then name a member or two ("fox"—plus monkey and raccoon). But of course you would go on to give further examples or illustrations—accounts of how the bacon was snitched through the screen—that broaden your definition beyond the mere naming of class and members.

5. DEFINITION BY COMPARISON. You just use a paragraph of comparison to expand and explain your definition. Begin with a topic sentence something like: "Love is like the sun." Then extend your comparison on to the end of the paragraph (or even separate it, if your cup runneth over, into several paragraphs), as you develop the idea: love is like the sun because it too gives out warmth, makes everything bright, shines even when it is not seen, and is indeed the centre of our lives.

6. DEFINITION BY ANALYSIS. This is Hofstader's way, a searching out and explaining of the essentials in terms used generally, loosely, and often in ways that emphasize incidentals for biased reasons, as when it is said that an *intellectual* is a manipulator of ideas.

Here are four good steps to take in reaching a thorough definition of something, assuring that you have covered all the angles. Consider:

1. What it *is not like*
2. What it *is like.*
3. What it *is not.*
4. What it *is.*

This program can produce a good paragraph of definition:

> **Love may be many things to many people, but, all in all,**
> 1 **we agree on its essentials.** *Love is not like a rummage sale,* **in**
> 2 **which everyone tries to grab what he wants.** *It is more like a Christmas,* **in which gifts and thoughtfulness come just a little unexpectedly, even from routine directions.** *Love, in*

short, is not a matter of seeking self-satisfaction; it is first a matter 3
of giving and then discovering, **as an unexpected gift,** *the deep-* 4
est satisfaction one can know.

The four steps above can also furnish four effective paragraphs, which you would present in the same order of ascending
interest and climax. The same tactics also work well in reverse
order:

> ***Black Power means, for example, that in Lowndes County,*** What It *Is*
> ***Alabama, a black sheriff can end police brutality.*** **A black tax** Definition by
> **assessor and tax collector and county board of revenue can** Example
> **lay, collect, and channel tax monies for the building of**
> **better roads and schools serving black people. In such areas**
> **as Lowndes, where black people have a majority, they will**
> **attempt to use power to exercise control. This is what**
> **they seek: control. When black people lack a majority, Black** Definition by
> **Power means proper representation and sharing of control.** Analysis
> **It means the creation of power bases, of strength, from**
> **which black people can press to change local or nation-wide**
> **patterns of oppression—instead of from weakness.**
> **It does not mean** *merely* **putting black faces into office.**
> ***Black visibility is not Black Power.*** **Most of the black politi-** What It *Is*
> **cians around the country today are not examples of Black** *Not*
> **Power.** *The power must be that of a community, and emanate from* What It *Is*
> *there.* **The black politicians must start from there. The black**
> **politicians must stop being representatives of "downtown"**
> **machines, whatever the cost might be in terms of patronage**
> **and holiday handouts.*****

Avoid the Pitfalls

1. Avoid echoing the term you are defining. Do not write
   "Courtesy is being courteous" or "Freedom is feeling
   free." Look around for synonyms: "Courtesy is being polite, being attentive to others' needs, making them feel at
   ease, using what society accepts as good manners." You
   can go against this rule to great advantage, however, if
   you repeat the *root* of the word meaningfully: "Courtesy
   is treating your girl like a princess in her *court.*"

*Stokely Carmichael and Charles V. Hamilton, *Black Power, the Politics of Liberation
in America* (New York: Random House, 1967): 15.

2. Don't make your definitions too narrow—except for humour ("Professors are only disappointed students"). Do not write: "Communism is subversive totalitarianism." Obviously, your definition needs more breadth, something about sharing property, and so forth.
3. Don't make your definition too broad. Do not go uphill in your terms, as in "Vanity is pride" or "Affection is love." Bring the definers down to the same level: "Vanity is a kind of frivolous personal pride"—"Affection is a mild and chronic case of love."

EXERCISES

1. *Write a paragraph describing a unit of space, taking your reader from the outside to the inside of your own home, for instance, or dealing with some interesting spatial unit as in the following paragraph from a student's paper.*

The courtyard of the hotel at Uxmal was a wonderfully cool and welcome surprise after the sweaty bus trip out from Mérida. Surrounding the whole yard was a large *galería,* its ceiling blocking out the few rays of the sun that managed to filter through the heavy plantings that filled the yard. Overhead, along the *galería,* ceiling fans quietly turned, and underfoot the glazed tile floors felt smooth and delightfully cool even though the temperature on the road had pushed up past 100 degrees. Airy wicker chairs lined the railing, and just a few feet away, flowering jungle plants rose almost to the top of the stone arches on the second floor. Under the branches of a tall tree in the middle of the courtyard, out beyond the rail and the thick plantings, raised tile walkways crisscrossed the yard, bordered all along by neatly cultivated jungle flowers. And right in the middle of the yard, at the base of the big tree, a small waterfall splashed down over mossy rocks into a tiny bathing pool. The splashing water, the shade, the cool tile, all made the road outside seem very far off indeed.

2. *Write a narrative paragraph in which you blend the incidents and thoughts of a crucial moment, as in Orwell's paragraph on 64.*
3. *Write a paragraph comparing two people—like the one on 67.*
4. **(a)** *Write a paragraph developed by contrasts, running them point by point, as in the paragraph contrasting "students" and "athletes" on 70.*

(b) *Write two paragraphs contrasting something like high school and university, small town and city, football and hockey, men and women —the first paragraph describing one, the second the other, and the two using parallel contrasting terms, as in the example contrasting the two Germanys or the television commercials and shows on 69.*

5. *Write a paragraph of* effect *followed by* causes *like that on 71, Arrangement 1.*
6. *Write a paragraph about some* cause *followed by its probable* effects, *Arrangement 2. See 72–73. Work in a hypothetical effect if you can.*
7. *Here are some topics that fall conveniently into natural divisions. For each topic, list the divisions that occur to you.*

   1. Causes affecting the rate at which a population grows.
   2. Levels of government.
   3. Undersea exploration.
   4. Geological eras.
   5. Mathematics in the schools.

8. *Write a paragraph using one of the topics and the divisions you have worked out in Exercise 7.*
9. *Write a paragraph describing a process you know well—how to make a bracelet, a belt, a cake, how an internal combustion engine works.*
10. *Now find a thesis that will change this described process into an argument making some statement about the subject: making a cake is no child's play; what's under the hood is really no mystery. Rewrite your descriptive-narrative paragraph into a brief three-paragraph essay, using everything you said before and expanding your points with comments rising from your thesis, and with further descriptive and narrative details. Hand in your original paragraph with your essay.*
11. *Using the classifications of problem and solution, write a three- or four-paragraph paper in which you describe the process behind some particularly interesting architectural or engineering accomplishment. Choose any topic you wish. For example, how did architects design the high-rise buildings in San Francisco so that they would withstand the shock of the severe earthquakes of 1971? Or how did medieval man make a suit of armour? Or how do you plan to convert your van into a camper that will sleep four people? In the first paragraph, state the problem as your thesis sentence. Then go on to describe how the problem could be, or was, solved.*
12. *Work out a paragraph defining some term like barometer, computer, class, humanities, intelligence. Avoid the scent of the dictionary. Consider, and use if possible: (1) what it is not like, (2) what it is like, (3) what it is not, and, finally, (4) what it is. See 80–81.*

6
Straight and Crooked Thinking: Working with Evidence

All along, you have been working to support your thesis and persuade your reader with evidence. Evidence is an example, or several examples. Your thesis has, in fact, emerged from the evidence, from thinking about the specific things you have experienced, seen, heard, in person, in reading, or on TV. To support that thesis, you have simply turned the process around, bringing in those same specific things, and others, as evidence—descriptive, narrative, and expository. You have been deciding logically on the weight and shape of that evidence, comparing, working out causes and effects, classifying, defining. But your evidence and its connections are always liable to certain logical fallacies that may defeat its persuasiveness.

DEGREES OF EVIDENCE

Write as Close to the Facts as Possible

Facts are the firmest kind of thought, but they are *thoughts* nevertheless—verifiable thoughts about the coal and wheat and other

entities of our experience. The whole question of fact comes
down to verifiability: things not susceptible of verification leave
the realm of factuality. Fact is limited, therefore, to the kinds of
things that can be tested by the senses (verified empirically, as the
philosophers say) or by inferences from physical data so strong
as to allow no other explanation. "Statements of fact" are assertions of a kind provable by referring to experience. The simplest
physical facts—that a stone is a stone and that it exists—are so
bound into our elementary perceptions of the world that we
never think to verify them, and indeed could not verify them
beyond gathering testimonials from the group. With less tangible
facts, verification is simply doing enough to persuade any reasonable person that the assertion of fact is true, beginning with what
our senses can in some way check.

Measuring, weighing, and counting are the strongest empirical verifiers; assertions capable of such verification are the most
firmly and quickly demonstrated as factual:

> **Smith is five feet high and four feet wide.**
> **The car weighs 2300 pounds.**
> **Three members voted for beer.**

In the last assertion, we have moved from what we call physical
fact to historical fact—that which can be verified by its signs: we
have the ballots. Events in history are verified in the same way,
although the evidence is scarcer the farther back we go.

Believe What You Write—But Learn the Nature of Belief

Facts, then, are things established by verification. Belief presents
an entirely different kind of knowledge: things believed true but
yet beyond the reach of sensory verification—a belief in God, for
instance. We may infer a Creator from the creation, a Beginning
from the beginnings we see around us. But a doubting Thomas
will have nothing to touch or see; judging our inferences wrongly
drawn, he may prefer to believe in a physical accident, or in a flux
with neither beginning nor end. The point is that although beliefs are unprovable, they are not necessarily untrue, and they are
not unusable as you discourse with your reader. Many beliefs, of

course, have proved false as new evidence turns up. Nevertheless, you can certainly assert beliefs in your writing, establishing their validity in a tentative and probable way, so long as you do not assume you have *proved* them. State your convictions; support them with the best reasons you can find; and don't apologize. But you may wish to qualify your least demonstrable convictions with "I believe," "we may reasonably suppose," "perhaps," "from one point of view," and the like.

Don't Mistake Opinion for Fact

Halfway between fact and belief is *opinion,* a candidate for fact or belief, something you believe true but about whose verification or support you are still uncertain. The difference between fact and opinion is simply a difference in verifiableness. One opinion may eventually prove true, and another false; an opinion may strengthen into belief and then, through verifying tests, into accepted fact, as with Galileo's opinion that the earth moved.

The testing of opinions to discover the facts is, indeed, the central business of argumentation. When you assert something as fact, you indicate (1) that you assume it true and easily verified, and (2) that its truth is generally acknowledged. When you assert something as opinion, you imply some uncertainty about both these things. Here are two common opinions that will probably remain opinions exactly because of such uncertainty:

> **Girls are brighter than boys.**
> **Men are superior to women.**

We know that the terms *brighter* and *superior* have a range of meaning hard to pin down. Even when agreeing upon the tests for numerical and verbal abilities, and for memory and ingenuity, we cannot be sure that we will not miss other kinds of brightness and superiority, or that our tests will measure these things in any thorough way. The range of meaning in our four other terms, moreover, is so wide as virtually to defy verification. We need only ask "At what age?" to illustrate how broad they are. So in these slippery regions of opinion, keep your assertions tentative with *may* and *might* and *perhaps*.

Dispute Your Preferences with Care

Preferences are something else again. They are farther from proof than opinions—indeed, beyond the pale of proof. And yet they are more firmly held than opinions, because they are primarily subjective, sweetening our palates and warming our hearts. *De gustibus non est disputandum:* tastes are not to be disputed. So goes the medieval epigram, from the age that refined the arts of logic. You can't argue successfully about tastes, empirical though they be, because they are beyond empirical demonstration. Are peaches better than pears? Whichever you choose, your choice is probably neither logically defensible nor logically vulnerable. The writer's responsibility is to recognize the logical immunity of preferences, and to qualify them politely with "I think," "many believe," "some may prefer," and so forth.

So go ahead, dispute over tastes, and you may find some solid grounds for them. Shakespeare is greater than Ben Jonson. Subjective tastes have moved all the way up beside fact: the grounds for Shakespeare's margin of greatness have been exhibited, argued, and explored over the centuries, until we accept his superiority, as if empirically verified. Actually, the questions that most commonly concern us are beyond scientific verification. But you can frequently establish your preferences as testable opinions by asserting them reasonably and without unwholesome prejudice, and by using the secondary evidence that other reasonable people agree with you in persuasive strength and number.

ASSESSING THE EVIDENCE

Logical Fallacies: Trust Your Common Sense

From the first, in talking about a valid thesis, about proof, about assumptions and implications and definition, we have been facing logical fallacies—that is, flaws in thought, things that do not add up. Evidence itself raises the biggest question of logic. Presenting any evidence at all faces a logical fallacy that can never be surmounted: no amount of evidence can *logically* prove an assertion because *one* and *some* can never equal *all*. Because the sun has gotten up on time every morning so far is—the logicians tell us —no logical assurance that it will do so tomorrow. Actually, we can take comfort in that fallacy. Since we can never *logically* produce enough evidence for certitude, we can settle for a reasonable amount and call it quits. One piece of evidence all by itself tempts us to cry, "Fallacy! *One* isn't *all* or *every*." But three or four pieces will probably suit our common sense and calm us into agreement.

Cite Authorities Reasonably

An appeal to some authority to prove your point is really an appeal beyond logic, but not necessarily beyond reason. We naturally turn to authorities to confirm our ideas. "Einstein said" can silence many an objection. But appeals to authority risk four common fallacies. The first is in appealing to the authority outside of his field, even if his field is the universe. After all, the good doctor, of the wispy hair and frayed sweater, was little known for understanding money too.

The second fallacy is in misunderstanding or misrepresenting what the authority really says. Sir Arthur Eddington, if I may appeal to an authority myself, puts the case: "It is a common mistake to suppose that Einstein's theory of relativity asserts that everything is relative. Actually it says, 'There are absolute things in the world but you must look deeply for them. The things that first present themselves to your notice are for the most part relative.' "* If you appeal loosely to Einstein to authenticate an assertion that everything is "relative," you may appeal in vain— since *relative* means relative *to* something else, eventually to some absolute.

The third fallacy is in assuming that one instance from an authority represents him accurately. Arguments for admitting the split infinitive (see 212, 285) to equal status with the unsplit, for instance, often present split constructions from prominent writers. But they do not tell us how many splits a writer avoided, or

---

***The Nature of the Physical World* (Ann Arbor: University of Michigan Press, 1958): 23.

how he himself feels about the construction. A friend once showed me a split infinitive in the late Walter Lippmann's column after I had boldly asserted that careful writers like Lippmann never split them. Out of curiosity, I wrote Mr. Lippmann: after all, he might have changed his tune. He wrote back that he had slipped, that he disliked the thing and tried to revise it out whenever it crept in.

The fourth fallacy is deepest: the authority may have faded. New facts have generated new ideas. Einstein has limited Newton's authority. Geology and radioactive carbon have challenged the literal authority of Genesis. Jung has challenged Freud; and Keynes, Marx.

The more eminent the authority, the easier the fallacy. Ask these four questions:

1. Am I citing him outside his field?
2. Am I presenting him accurately?
3. Is this instance really representative?
4. Is he still fully authoritative?

Do not claim too much for your authority, and add other kinds of proof, or other authorities. In short, don't put all your eggs in one basket.

Handle Persistences as You Would Authorities

That an idea's persistence constitutes a kind of unwritten or cumulative authority is also open to logical challenge. Because a belief has persisted, the appeal goes, it must be true. Since earliest times, for example, man has believed in some kind of supernatural beings or Being. Something must be there, the persistence seems to suggest. But the appeal is not logical; the belief could have persisted from causes other than the actuality of divine existence, perhaps only from man's psychological need. As with authority, new facts may vanquish persistent beliefs. The belief that the world was a pancake, persistent though it had been, simply had to give way to Columbus and Magellan. For all this, however, persistence does have considerable strength as an *indication* of validity, to be supported by other reasons.

Inspect Your Documentary Evidence
Before Using

Documents are both authoritative and persistent. They provide the only evidence, aside from oral testimony, for all that we know beyond the immediate presence of our physical universe, with its physical remains of the past. Documents point to what has happened, as long ago as Nineveh and Egypt and as recently as the tracings on last hour's blackboard. But documents vary in reliability. You must consider a document's historical context, since factuality may have been of little concern, as with stories of heroes and saints, or with propaganda. You must allow, as with newspapers, for the effects of haste and limited facts. You should consider a document's author, his background, his range of knowledge and belief, his assumptions, his prejudices, his probable motives, his possible tendencies to suppress or slant the facts.

Finally, you should consider the document's data. Are the facts of a kind easily verifiable or easily collected? Indeed, can you present other verification? For example, numerical reports of population can be no more than approximations, and they are hazier the farther back you go in history, as statistical methods slacken. Since the data must have been selected from almost infinite possibilities, does the selection seem reasonably representative? Are your source's conclusions right for the data? Might not the data produce other conclusions? Your own data and conclusions, of course, must also face questioning.

Statistics are particularly persuasive evidence, and because of their psychological appeal, they can be devilishly misleading. To reduce things to numbers seems scientific, incontrovertible, final. But each "1" represents a slightly different quantity, as one glance around a class of 20 students will make clear. Each student is the same, yet entirely different. The "20" is a broad generalization convenient for certain kinds of information: how many seats the instructor will need, how many people are absent, how much the instruction costs per head, and so forth. But clearly the "20" will tell nothing about the varying characteristics of the students or the education. So present your statistics with some caution so that they will honestly show what you want them to show and will not mislead your readers. Averages and percentages can be especially misleading, carrying the numerical generalization one step farther from the physical facts. The truth behind a statement that the average student earns $10 a week could be that nine students earn nothing and one earns $100.

SOME INDUCTIVE TRAPS

Keep Your Hypothesis Hypothetical

Induction and deduction are the two paths of reasoning. Induction is "leading into" (*in ducere,* "to lead in"), thinking through the evidence to some general conclusion. Deduction is "leading away from" some general precept to its particular parts and consequences. All along, you have been *thinking inductively* to find your thesis, and then you have turned the process around, *writing deductively* when you present your thesis and support it with your evidence. Both modes have their uses, and their fallacies.

Induction is the way of science: one collects the facts and sees what they come to. Sir Francis Bacon laid down in 1620 the inductive program in his famous *Novum Organum, sive indicia vera de interpretatione naturae* ("The New Instrument, or true evidence concerning the interpretation of nature"). Bacon was at war with the syllogism; its abstract deductions seemed too rigid to measure nature's subtlety. His new instrument changed the entire course of thought. Before Bacon, the world had deduced the consequences of its general ideas; after Bacon, the world looked around and induced new generalizations from what it saw. Observed facts called the old ideas into question, and theories replaced "truths." As you may know, Bacon died from a cold caught while stuffing a chicken's carcass with snow for an inductive test of refrigeration.

Induction has great strength, but it also has a basic fallacy. The strength is in taking nothing on faith, in having no ideas at all until the facts have suggested them. The fallacy is in assuming that the mind can start blank. Theoretically, Bacon had no previous ideas about refrigeration. Theoretically, he would experiment aimlessly until he noticed consistencies that would lead to the icebox. Actually, from experience, one would already have a hunch, a half-formed theory, that would suggest the experimental tests. Induction, in other words, is always well mixed with deduction. The major difference is in the tentative frame of mind: in making an hypothesis instead of merely borrowing an honored assumption, and in keeping the hypothesis hypothetical, even after the facts seem to have supported it.

Use Analogies to Clarify, Not to Prove

The simplest kind of induction is analogy: because this tree is much like that oak, it too must be some kind of oak. You identify the unknown by its analogy to the known. You inductively look over the similarities until you conclude that the trees are very similar, and therefore the same kind. Analogies are tremendously useful indications of likeness; analogy is virtually our only means of classification, our means of putting things into groups and handling them by naming them. Analogy also illustrates the logical weakness of induction: assuming that *all* characteristics are analogous after finding one or two analogous. We check a few symptoms against what we know of colds and flu, and conclude that we have a cold and flu; but the doctor will add to these a few more symptoms and conclude that we have a virulent pneumonia.

Similarity does not mean total identity, and analogies must always make that shaky assumption, or clearly demonstrate that the mismatching details are unimportant. In your writing, you may use analogy with tremendous effect. But watch out for the logical gap between *some* and *all.* Make sure that:

1. A reasonably large number of details agree.
2. These details are salient and typical.
3. The misfitting details are insignificant and not typical.

If the brain seems in some ways like a computer, be careful not to assume it is in all ways like a computer. Keep the analogy figurative: it can serve you well, as any metaphor serves, to illustrate the unknown with the known, but not to prove.

Look Before You Leap

The hypothetical frame of mind is the essence of the inductive method, because it acknowledges the logical flaw of induction, namely, the *inductive leap.* No matter how many the facts, or how carefully weighed, a time comes when thought must abandon the details and leap to the conclusion. We leap from the knowledge that *some* apples are good to the conclusion: "[All] apples are good." This leap, say the logicians, crosses an abyss no logic can bridge, because *some* can never guarantee *all*—except as a general *probability.* The major lesson of induction is that *nothing* can be proved, except as a probability. The best we can manage is an *hypothesis,* while maintaining a perpetual hospitality to new facts that might change our theory. This is the scientific frame of mind; it gets as close to substantive truth as we can come, and it keeps us healthily humble before the facts.

Probability is the great limit and guarantee of the generalizations to which we must eventually leap. You know that bad apples are neither so numerous nor so strongly typical that you must conclude: "Apples are unfit for human consumption." You also know what causes the bad ones. Therefore, to justify your leap and certify your generalization, you base your induction on the following three conditions:

1. Your samples are reasonably numerous.
2. Your samples are truly typical.
3. Your exceptions are explainable, and demonstrably not typical.

The inductive leap is always risky because all the data cannot be known. The leap might also be in the wrong direction: more than one conclusion may be drawn from the same evidence. Here, then, is where the inductive frame of mind can help you. It can teach you always to check your conclusions by asking if another answer might not do just as well. Some linguists have concluded that speech is superior to writing because speech has many more "signals" than writing. But from the same facts one might declare writing superior: it conveys the same message with fewer signals.

The shortcomings of induction are many. The very data of sensory observation may be indistinct. Ask any three people to tell how an accident happened, and the feebleness of human observation becomes painfully apparent. If the facts are slippery, the final leap is uncertain. Furthermore, your hypothesis, which must come early to give your investigation some purpose, immediately becomes a *deductive* proposition that not only will guide your selection of facts, but may well distort slightly the facts you select. Finally, as we have seen with statistics and averages, scientific induction relies heavily on mathematics, which requires that qualities be translated into quantities. Neither numbers nor words, those two essential generalizers of our experience, can adequately grasp all our particular diversities. The lesson of induction, therefore, is the lesson of caution. Logically, induction is shot full of holes. But it makes as firm a statement as we can expect about the physical universe and our experience in it. The ultimate beauty of science is perhaps not that it is efficient (and it is), but that it is hypothetical. It keeps our minds open for new hypotheses. The danger lies in thinking it absolute.

The Classic Fallacies

All in all, most fallacies in writing—our own and others'—we can uncover simply by knowing they are lurking and using our heads. We must constantly ask if our words are meaning what they say, and saying what we mean. We must check our assumptions. Then we must ask if we are inadvertently taking *some* for *all,* or making that inductive leap too soon or in an errant direction. But logicians have identified six classic fallacies that sum up most of our muddles:

1. EITHER-OR. You assume only two opposing possibilities: "Either we abolish requirements or education is finished." Education will probably amble on, somewhere in between. Similarly, IF-THEN: "If I work harder on the next paper, then I'll get a better mark." You have overlooked differences in subject, knowledge, involvement, inspiration.
2. OVERSIMPLIFICATION. As with *either-or,* you ignore alternatives. "A student learns only what he wants to learn" ignores all the pressures from parents and society, which in fact account for a good deal of learning.

3. BEGGING THE QUESTION. A somewhat unhandy term: you assume as proved something that really needs proving. "Free all political prisoners" assumes that none of those concerned has committed an actual crime.
4. IGNORING THE QUESTION. The question of whether it is right for a neighbourhood to organize against a newcomer shifts to prices of property and taxes.
5. NON SEQUITUR ("IT DOES NOT FOLLOW"). "He's certainly sincere; he must be right." "He's the most popular; he should be president." The conclusions do not reasonably follow from sincerity and popularity.
6. POST HOC, ERGO PROPTER HOC. ("AFTER THIS, THEREFORE BECAUSE OF THIS.") The non sequitur of events: "He stayed up late and therefore won the race." He probably won in spite of late hours, and for other reasons.

EXERCISES

1. *After each of the following assertions, write two or three short questions that will challenge its assumptions, questions like "Good for what? Throwing? Fertilizer?" For example: Girls are brighter than boys. "At what age? In chess? In physics?" In the questions, probe and distinguish among your facts, opinions, beliefs, and preferences.*

   1. Men are superior to women.
   2. The backfield made some mistakes.
   3. Communism means violent repression.
   4. Don't trust anyone over thirty.
   5. All men are equal.
   6. The big companies are ruining the environment.
   7. Travel is educational.
   8. Our brand of cigarette is free of tar.
   9. The right will prevail.
   10. A long run is good for you.

2. *Each of the following statements contains at least one fallacious citation of authority. Identify it, and explain how it involves one or several of these reasons: "Outside Field," "Not Accurately Presented," "Not Representative," "Out of Date."*

   1. According to Charles Morton, a distinguished seventeenth-century theologian and schoolmaster, the swallows of England disappear to the dark side of the moon in winter.

2. Einstein states that everything is relative.
3. "Nucular" is an acceptable pronunciation of "nuclear." John Diefenbaker himself pronounced it this way.
4. War between capitalists and communists is inevitable, as Karl Marx shows.
5. The Canadian economy should be controlled in every detail; after all, economist John Kenneth Galbraith comes out for control.
6. "Fluff is Canada's finest bubble bath," says Bobby Clarke.

3. *Each of the following statistical statements is fallacious in one or several ways, either omitting something necessary for full understanding or generalizing in unsupported ways. Identify and explain the statistical fallacies.*

1. This car gets fifteen kilometres per litre.
2. Fifty percent of his snapshots are poor.
3. Twenty-nine persons were injured when a local bus skidded on an icy road near Weston and overturned. Two were hospitalized. Twenty-seven were treated and released.
4. Women support this book one hundred percent, but fifty percent of American males are still antifeminist. (In a class of five girls and ten boys, all the girls and five of the boys vote to write about a book entitled *The Stereotyped Female.*)

4. *If hockey is in season, go to the sports page and write a brief explanation of the statistics on goals for and against, and so forth. Can you find any fallacies—things the statistics do not tell? Or do the same with another sport or subject where statistics are common.*

5. *Explain the following fallacious analogies and inductive leaps.*

1. The brain is like a computer. Scientists have demonstrated that it, like the computer, works through electrical impulses.
2. This girl has ten sweaters; that girl has ten sweaters. They are equally rich in sweaters.
3. At sixty, Kirk retires with investments and savings worth more than $500,000. He has nothing to worry about for the rest of his life.
4. Every time the Boilers play a post-season game, they lose. They will lose this one.
5. English majors are poor mathematicians.
6. I studied hard. I answered every question. None of my answers was wrong. I have read my exam over again and again and can still see no reason for getting only a C.

6. *Name and explain the fallacy in each of the following:*

1. Jones is rich. He must be dishonest.
2. He either worked hard for his money, or he is just plain lucky.

3. The best things in life are free, like free love.
4. Sunshine breeds flies, because when the sun shines the flies come out.
5. If they have no bread, let them eat cake. Cake is both tastier and richer in calories.
6. This is another example of American imperialism.
7. Smith's canned-soup empire reaches farther than the Roman empire.
8. *Chips* is Canada's most popular soap. It is clearly the best.
9. The draft is illegal. It takes young men away from their education and careers at the most crucial period of their lives. They lose thousands of dollars' worth of their time.
10. Women are the most exploited people in the history of the world.

7
Writing Good Sentences

All this time you have been writing sentences, as naturally as breathing, and perhaps with as little variation. Now for a close look at the varieties of the sentence. Some varieties can be shaggy and tangled indeed. But they are all offshoots of the simple active sentence, the basic English genus *John hits Joe,* with action moving straight from subject through verb to object.

This subject-verb-object sentence can be infinitely grafted and contorted, but there are really only two general varieties of it: (1) the "loose, or strung-along," in Aristotle's phrase, and (2) the periodic. English naturally runs "loose," or "cumulative." Our thoughts are by nature strung along from subject through verb to object, with whatever comes to mind simply added as it comes. The loose sentence puts its subject and verb early. But we can also use the periodic sentence characteristic of our Latin and Germanic ancestry, where ideas hang in the air like girders until all interconnections are locked by the final word, at the period: *John, the best student in the class, the tallest and most handsome, hits Joe.* A periodic sentence, in other words, is one that suspends its meaning until the end, usually with subject and verb widely separated, and the verb as near the end as possible.

So we have two varieties of the English sentence. The piece-by-piece and the periodic species simply represent two ways of thought: the first, the natural stringing of thoughts as they come; the second, the more careful contrivance of emphasis and suspense.

THE SIMPLE SENTENCE

Use the Simple Active Sentence, Loosely Periodic

Your best sentences will be hybrids of the loose and the periodic. First, learn to use active verbs *(John* HITS *Joe),* which will keep you within the simple active pattern with all parts showing (subject-verb-object), as opposed to a verb in the passive voice *(Joe* IS HIT *by John),* which puts everything backwards and uses more words. Then learn to give your native strung-along sentence a touch of periodicity and suspense.

Any change in normal order can give you unusual emphasis, as when you move the object ahead of the subject:

> **That I like.**
> **The house itself she hated, but the yard was grand.**
> **Nature I loved; and next to Nature, Art.**

Most often, we expect our ideas one at a time, in normal succession—*John hits Joe*—and with anything further added, in proper sequence, at the end—*a real haymaker.* Change this fixed way of thinking, and you immediately put your reader on the alert for something unusual. Consequently, some of your best sentences will be simple active ones sprung wide with phrases colouring subject, verb, object, or all three, in various ways. You may, for instance, effectively complicate the subject:

> **King Lear, proud, old, and childish, probably aware that his grip on the kingdom is beginning to slip, devises a foolish plan.**

Or the verb:

> **A good speech usually begins quietly, proceeds sensibly, gathers momentum, and finally moves even the most indifferent audience.**

Or the object:

**Her notebooks contain marvelous comments on the turtle
in the back yard, the flowers and weeds, the great elm by the
drive, the road, the earth, the stars, and the men and women
of the village.**

COMPOUND AND COMPLEX SENTENCES

Learn the Difference Between Compound and Complex Sentences

You make a compound sentence by linking together simple sentences with a coordinating conjunction (*and, but, or, nor, yet, still, for, so*) or with a colon or a semicolon. You make a complex one by hooking lesser sentences onto the main sentence with *that, which, who,* or one of the many other subordinating connectives like *although, because, where, when, after, if.* The compound sentence *coordinates,* treating everything on the same level; the complex *subordinates,* putting everything else somewhere below its one main self-sufficient idea. The compound links ideas one after the other, as in the basic simple sentence; the complex is a simple sentence elaborated by clauses instead of merely by phrases. The compound represents the strung-along way of thinking; the complex usually represents the periodic.

Avoid Simple-Minded Compounds

Essentially the compound sentence *is* simple-minded, a set of clauses on a string—a child's description of a birthday party, for instance: "We got paper hats and we pinned the tail on the donkey and we had chocolate ice cream and Randy sat on a piece of cake and I won third prize." *And . . . and . . . and.*

But this way of thinking is always useful for pacing off related thoughts, and for breaking the staccato of simple statement. It often briskly connects cause and effect: "The clock struck one, and down he run." "The solipsist relates all knowledge to his own being, and the demonstrable commonwealth of human nature dissolves before his dogged timidity." The compound sentence is built on the most enduring of colloquial patterns—the simple sequence of things said as they occur to the mind—it has the pace, the immediacy, and the dramatic effect of talk. Hemingway, for instance, often gets all the numb tension of a shell-shocked mind by reducing his character's thoughts all to one level, in sentences something like this: "It was a good night and I sat at a table and . . . and . . . and. . . ."

Think of the compound sentence in terms of its conjunctions—the words that yoke its clauses—and of the accompanying punctuation. Here are three basic groups of conjunctions that will help you sort out and punctuate your compound thoughts.

Group I. *The three common coordinating conjunctions:* and, but, *and* or (nor). *Put a comma before each.*

> **I like her, and I don't mind saying so.**
> **Art is long, but life is short.**
> **Win this point, or the game is lost.**

Group II. *Conjunctive adverbs:* therefore, moreover, however, nevertheless, consequently, furthermore. *Put a semicolon before, and a comma after each.*

> **Nations indeed seem to have a kind of biological span like human life, from rebellious youth, through caution, to decay; consequently, predictions of doom are not uncommon.**

Group III. *Some in-betweeners*—yet, still, so—*which sometimes take a comma, sometimes a semicolon, depending on your pace and emphasis.*

> **We long for the good old days, yet we never include the disadvantages.**
> **People long for the good old days; yet they rarely take into account the inaccuracy of human memory.**
> **The preparation had been halfhearted and hasty, so the meeting was wretched.**
> **Rome declined into the pleasures of its circuses and couches; so the tough barbarians conquered.**

Try Compounding Without Conjunctions

Though the conjunction usually governs its compound sentence, two powerful coordinators remain—the semicolon and the colon alone. For contrasts, the semicolon is the prince of coordinators:

Semicolon   **The dress accents the feminine; the pants suit speaks for freedom.**
              Golf demands the best of time and space; tennis, the best of personal energy.
              The government tries to get the most out of taxes; the individual tries to get out of the most taxes.

The colon similarly pulls two "sentences" together without blessing of conjunction, period, or capital. But it signals amplification, not contrast: the second clause explains the first.

Colon   **A house with an aging furnace costs more than the asking price suggests: twenty dollars more a month in fuel means about one hundred sixty dollars more a year.**
          A growing population means more business: more business will exhaust our supply of ores in less than half a century.
          Sports at any age are beneficial: they keep your pulses hopping.

Learn to Subordinate

You probably write compound sentences almost without thinking. But the subordinations of the complex usually require some thought. Indeed, you are ranking closely related thoughts, arranging the lesser ones so that they bear effectively on your main thought. You must first pick your most important idea. You must then change mere sequence into subordination—ordering your lesser thoughts "sub," or below, the main idea. The childish birthday sentence, then, might come out something like this:

> **After we got paper hats and ate chocolate ice cream, after Randy sat on a piece of cake and everyone pinned the tail on the donkey, I WON THIRD PRIZE.**

You do the trick with connectives—with any word, like *after* in the sentence above, indicating time, place, cause, or other qualification.

> *If* they try, *if* they fail, THEY ARE STILL GREAT *because* their spirit is unbeaten.

You daily achieve subtler levels of subordination with the three relative pronouns *that, which, who,* and with the conjunction *that. That, which,* and *who* connect thoughts so closely related as to seem almost equal, but actually each tucks a clause (subject-and-verb) into some larger idea:

> The car, *which* runs perfectly, is not worth selling. Relative
> The car *that* runs perfectly is worth keeping. Pronoun
> He thought *that* the car would run forever. Subordinating
> He thought [*that* omitted but understood] the car would run Conjunction
> forever.

But the subordinating conjunctions and adverbs *(although, if, because, since, until, where, when, as if, so that)* really put subordinates in their places. Look at *when* in this sentence of E. B. White's from *Charlotte's Web:*

> Next morning *when* the first light came into the sky and the Adverbs
> sparrows stirred in the trees, *when* the cows rattled their
> chains and the rooster crowed and the early automobiles
> went whispering along the road, Wilbur awoke and looked
> for Charlotte.

Here the simple *when,* used only twice, has regimented five subordinate clauses, all of equal rank, into their proper station below that of the main clause, "Wilbur awoke and looked for Charlotte." You can vary the ranking intricately and still keep it straight:

> *Although* some claim *that* time is an illusion, *because* we have Subordinating
> no absolute chronometer, *although* the mind cannot effec- Conjunctions
> tively grasp time, *because* the mind itself is a kind of timeless
> presence almost oblivious to seconds and hours, *al-
> though* the time of our solar system may be only an instant
> in the universe at large, WE STILL CANNOT QUITE DENY *that*

some progression of universal time is passing over us, *if* **only we could measure it.**

Complex sentences are, at their best, really simple sentences gloriously delayed and elaborated with subordinate thoughts. The following beautiful and elaborate sentence from the Book of Common Prayer is all built on the simple sentence "draw near":

> **Ye who do truly and earnestly repent you of your sins, and are in love and charity with your neighbors, and intend to lead a new life, following the commandments of God, and walking from henceforth in his holy ways, draw near with faith, and take this holy sacrament to your comfort, and make your humble confession to Almighty God, devoutly kneeling.**

Even a short sentence may be complex, attaining a remarkably varied suspense. Notice how the simple statement "I allowed myself" is skillfully elaborated in this sentence by the late Wolcott Gibbs of *The New Yorker:*

> **Twice in my life, for reasons that escape me now, though I'm sure they were discreditable, I allowed myself to be persuaded that I ought to take a hand in turning out a musical comedy.**

Try for Still Closer Connections: Modify

Your subordinating *if*'s and *when*'s have really been modifying— that is, limiting—the things you have attached them to. But there is a smoother way. It is an adjectival sort of thing, a shoulder-to-shoulder operation, a neat trick with no need for shouting, a stone to a stone with no need for mortar. You simply put clauses and phrases up against a noun, instead of attaching them with a subordinator. This sort of modification includes the following constructions, all using the same close masonry: (1) appositives, (2) relatives understood, (3) adjectives-with-phrase, (4) participles, (5) absolutes.

Appositives. Those phrases about shoulders and tricks and stones, above, are all in apposition with *sort of thing,* and they are grammatically subordinate to it. *Apposition* means "put to" or "add to"—putting an equivalent beside, like two peas in a pod —hence these phrases are nearly coordinate and interchangeable. They are compressions of a series of sentences ("It is an adjectival sort of thing. It is a neat trick . . . ," and so forth) set side by side, "stone to stone." Mere contact does the work of the verb *is* and its subject *it.* English often does the same with subordinate clauses, omitting the *who is* or *that is* and putting the rest directly into apposition. "The William who is the Conqueror" becomes "William the Conqueror." "The Jack who is the heavy hitter" becomes "Jack the heavy hitter." These, incidentally, are called "restrictive" appositions, because they restrict to a particular designation the nouns they modify, setting this William and this Jack apart from all others (with no separating commas). Similarly, you can make nonrestrictive appositives from nonrestrictive clauses, clauses that simply add information (between commas). "Smith, who is a man to be reckoned with, . . ." becomes "Smith, a man to be reckoned with, . . ." "Jones, who is our man in Liverpool, . . ." becomes "Jones, our man in Liverpool, . . ." Restrictive or nonrestrictive, close contact neatly makes your point.

Relatives Understood. You can often achieve the same economy, as I have already hinted, by omitting the relative pronouns *that, which,* and *who* with their verbs, thus gaining a compression both colloquial and classic:

> **A comprehension [that is] both colloquial and classic. . . .**
> **The house, [which was] facing north, had a superb view.**
> **The specimens [that] he had collected. . . .**
> **The girl [whom] he [had] left behind. . . .**

Adjectives-with-Phrase. This construction is also appositive and adjectival. It is neat and useful:

> **The law was passed,** *thick with provisions and codicils, heavy with implications.*
> **There was the lake,** *smooth in the early-morning air.*

Participles. Participles—when acting as adjectives—are extremely supple subordinates. Consider this sequence of six simple sentences:

> **He had been thrown.**
> **He had accepted.**
> **He felt a need.**
> **He demanded money.**
> **He failed.**
> **He chose not to struggle.**

Now see how Richard Wright, in *Native Son,* subordinates the first five of these to the sixth with participles. He elaborates the complete thought into a forceful sentence that runs for eighty-nine words with perfect clarity:

> *Having been thrown* by an accidental murder into a position where he had sensed a possible order and meaning in his relations with the people about him; *having accepted* the moral guilt and responsibility for that murder because it had made him feel free for the first time in his life; *having felt* in his heart some obscure need to be at home with people and *having demanded* ransom money to enable him to do it—*having* done all this and *failed,* he chose not to struggle any more.

These participles have the same adjectival force:

> **Dead to the world, *wrapped* in sweet dreams, *untroubled* by bills, he slept till noon.**

Notice that the participles operate exactly as the adjective *dead* does.

Beware of dangling participles. They may trip you, as they have tripped others. The participle, with its adjectival urge, may grab the first noun that comes along, with shocking results:

> **Bowing to the crowd, the bull caught him unawares.**
> **Observing quietly from the bank, the beavers made several**
>   **errors in judgment.**
> **Squandering everything at the track, the money was never**
>   **repaid.**

> **What we need is a list of teachers broken down alphabeti-
> cally.**

Move the participle next to its intended noun or pronoun; you
will have to supply this word if inadvertence or the passive voice
has omitted it entirely. Recast the sentence for good alignment
when necessary. You may also save the day by changing a present
participle to a past, as in the third example below, or, perhaps
better, by activating the sentence, as in the fourth example:

> **The bull caught him unawares as he bowed to the crowd.**
> **Observing quietly from the bank, they saw the beavers make
> several errors in judgment.**
> **Squandered at the track, the money was never repaid.**
> **Having squandered everything at the track, he never repaid
> the money.**
> **What we need is an alphabetical list of teachers.**

Gerunds, which look like present participles but act as nouns,
are also good economizers. The two sentences "He had been
thrown" and "It was unpleasant" can become one, with a gerund
as subject: *"Having been thrown* was unpleasant." Gerunds also
serve as objects of verbs and prepositions:

> **She hated** *going* **home.**
> **By** *driving* **carefully, they increased their mileage.**

Absolutes.   The absolute phrase has a great potential of polished economy. It stands grammatically "absolute" or alone,
modifying only through proximity, like an apposition. Many an
absolute is simply a prepositional phrase with the preposition
dropped:

> **He ran up the stairs, [with]** *a bouquet of roses under his
> arm,* **and rang the bell.**
> **She walked slowly, [with]** *her camera ready.*

But the ablative absolute (*ablative* means "removed") is absolutely removed from the main clause, modifying only by proximity. If you have had some Latin, you will probably remember this
construction as some kind of brusque condensation, something
like *"The road completed,* Caesar moved his camp." But it survives

in the best of circles. Somewhere E. B. White admits to feeling particularly good one morning, just having brought off an especially fine ablative absolute. And it is actually more common than you may suppose. A recent newspaper article stated that "the Prince had fled the country, *his hopes of a negotiated peace shattered.*" The *hopes shattered* pattern (noun plus participle) marks the ablative absolute (also called, because of the noun, a "nominative absolute"). The idea might have been more conventionally subordinated: "since his hopes were shattered" or "with his hopes shattered." But the ablative absolute accomplishes the subordination with economy and style.

Take a regular subordinate clause: *"When* the road *was* completed." Cut the subordinator and reduce the verb. You now have an ablative absolute, a phrase that stands absolutely alone, shorn of both its connective *when* and its full predication *was:* *"The road completed,* Caesar moved his camp." Basically a noun and a participle, or noun and adjective, it is a kind of grammatical shorthand, a telegram: *ROAD COMPLETED CAESAR MOVED—* most said in fewest words, speed with high compression. This is its appeal and its power.

> **The cat stopped,** *its back arched, its eyes frantic.*
> *All things considered,* **the plan would work.**
> **The** *dishes washed,* **the** *baby bathed* **and** *asleep,* **the last** *ashtray emptied,* **they could at last relax.**

PARALLEL CONSTRUCTION

Use Parallels to Strengthen Equivalent Ideas

No long complex sentence will hold up without parallel construction. Paralleling can be very simple. Any word will seek its own kind, noun to noun, adjective to adjective, infinitive to infinitive. The simplest series of things automatically runs parallel:

> **shoes and ships and sealing wax**
> **I came, I saw, I conquered**

to be or not to be
a dull, dark, and soundless day
mediocre work, cowardly work, disastrous work

But they very easily run out of parallel too, and this you must learn to prevent. The last item especially may slip out of line, as in this series: "friendly, kind, unobtrusive, and *a bore*" (boring). The noun *bore* has jumped off the track laid by the preceding parallel adjectives. Your train of equivalent ideas should all be of the same grammatical kind to carry their equivalence clearly—to strengthen it: either parallel adjectives, *friendly, kind, unobtrusive,* and *boring,* or all nouns, *a friend, a saint, a diplomat,* and *a bore.* Your paralleling articles and prepositions should govern a series as a whole, or should accompany *every* item:

a hat, cane, pair of gloves, and mustache
a hat, a cane, a pair of gloves, and a mustache
by land, sea, or air
by land, by sea, or by air

Verbs also frequently intrude to throw a series of adjectives (or nouns) out of parallel:

FAULTY: **He thought the girl was** *attractive, intelligent,* **and** *knew* **how to make him feel needed.**
IMPROVED: **He thought the girl was** *attractive, intelligent,* **and** *sympathetic,* **knowing how to make him feel needed.**

Watch the Paralleling of Pairs

Pairs should be pairs, not odds and ends. Notice how the faulty pairs in these sentences have been corrected:

She liked *the lawn and gardening* **(the lawn and the garden).**
They were *all athletic or big men on campus* **(athletes or big men on campus).**
They wanted *peace without being disgraced* **(peace without dishonour).**
He was *shy but a creative boy* **(shy but creative).**

Check your terms on both sides of your coordinating conjunctions *(and, but, or)* and see that they match:

> **Orientation week seems both worthwhile [adjective] and a**
> **necessary [adj.]**
> ~~**necessity**~~ **[noun].**
>
>   **that**
> **He prayed that they would leave and ^ the telephone would**
> **not ring.**

Learn to Use Paralleling Coordinators

The sentence above about "Orientation week" has used one of a number of useful (and tricky) parallel constructions: *both-and; either-or; not only-but also; not-but; first-second-third; as well as.* This last one is similar to *and,* a simple link between two equivalents, but it often causes trouble:

> **One should take care of one's physical self [noun]** *as well as* **being [participle] able to read and write.**

Again, the pair should be matched: "one's *physical self* as well as one's *intellectual self,*" or "one's physical *self* as well as one's *ability* to read and write"—though this second is still slightly unbalanced, in rhetoric if not in grammar. The best cure would probably extend the underlying antithesis, the basic parallel:

> **One should take care of one's physical self as well as one's intellectual self, of one's ability to survive as well as to read and write.**

With the *either-or*'s and the *not only-but also*'s, you continue the principle of pairing. The *either* and the *not only* are merely signposts of what is coming: two equivalents linked by a coordinating conjunction *(or* or *but).* Beware of putting the signs in the wrong place—too soon for the turn:

> **He ⟨either⟩ is an absolute piker or a fool!**
> **⟨Neither⟩ in time nor space. . . .**
> **He ⟨not only⟩ likes the girl but the family, too.**

In these examples, the thought got ahead of itself, as in talk. Just make sure that the word following each of the two coordinators is of the same kind, preposition for preposition, article for article, adjective for adjective—for even with signs well placed, the parallel can skid:

> **The students are not only organizing [present participle]**
> **discussing**
> **social activities, but also are ~~interested~~ [passive construction] ~~in~~ political questions.**

Put identical parts in parallel places; fill in the blanks with the same parts of speech: "not only ———, but also ———."

Beginning with *Not only,* a common habit, always takes more words as it duplicates subject and verb, inviting a comma splice and frequently misaligning a parallel:

> POOR: *Not only* is man limited in his mind and in his position in the universe, he is also limited in his physical powers.
> IMPROVED: Man is limited *not only* in his mind and in his position in the universe, *but also* in his physical powers. [*21 words for 23*]

The following sentence avoids the comma splice but still must duplicate subject and verb:

> POOR: *Not only* are the names similar, but the two men share some similarities of character.
> IMPROVED: The two men share similarities *not only* in name *but* in character. [*12 words for 15*]

The following experienced writer avoids the usual comma splice with a semicolon but makes a dubious parallel:

> POOR: *Not only* was the right badly splintered into traditional conservatives, economic liberals, and several other factions; the Communists were the weakest they had been in half a century.
> IMPROVED: The right was badly splintered . . . , and the Communists. . . .

You similarly parallel the words following numerical coordinators:

However variously he expressed himself, he unquestionably thought, first, *that* everyone could get ahead; second,
that workers generally were paid more than they earned;
and, third, *that* laws enforcing a minimum wage were
positively undemocratic.

For a number of reasons, he decided (1) *that* he did not like
it, (2) *that* she would not like it, (3) *that* they would be
better off without it. [Note that the parentheses around
the numbers operate exactly as any parentheses, and
need no additional punctuation.]

My objections are obvious: (1) *it* is unnecessary, (2) *it* costs
too much, and (3) *it* won't work.

In parallels of this kind, *that* is usually the problem, since you may
easily, and properly, omit it when there is only one clause and no
confusion:

. . . he unquestionably thought everyone could get ahead.

If second and third clauses occur, as your thought moves along,
you may have to go back and put up the first signpost:

                          that
. . . he unquestionably thought ∧ everyone could get ahead,
that workers . . . , and that laws. . . .

Enough of *that.* Remember simply that equivalent thoughts
demand parallel constructions. Notice the clear and massive
strategy in the following sentence from the concluding chapter
of Freud's last book, *An Outline of Psychoanalysis.* Freud is not only
summing up the previous discussion, but also expressing the
quintessence of his life's work. He is pulling everything together
in a single sentence. Each of the parallel *which* clauses gathers up,
in proper order, an entire chapter of his book (notice the parallel
force in repeating *picture,* and the summarizing dash):

The picture of an ego which mediates between the id and
the external world, which takes over the instinctual demands of the former in order to bring them to satisfaction,
which perceives things in the latter and uses them as memo-
ries, which, intent upon its self-preservation, is on guard
against excessive claims from both directions, and which is
governed in all its decisions by the injunctions of a modified

**pleasure principle—this picture actually applies to the ego
only up to the end of the first period of childhood, till about
the age of five.**

Such precision is hard to match. This is what parallel thinking brings—balance and control and an eye for sentences that
seem intellectual totalities, as if struck out all at once from the
uncut rock. Francis Bacon's sentences can seem like this (notice
how he drops the verb after establishing his pattern):

> **For a crowd is not company, and faces are but a gallery of
> pictures, and talk but a tinkling cymbal, where there is
> no love.**
> **Reading maketh a full man; conference a ready man; and
> writing an exact man.**

Commas would work well in the second example (see 228–29):

> **Reading maketh a full man; conference, a ready man; and
> writing, an exact man.**

THE LONG AND SHORT OF IT

Your style will emerge once you can manage some length of
sentence, some intricacy of subordination, some vigour of parallel, and some play of long against short, of amplitude against
brevity. Try the very long sentence, and the very short. Short
sentences are meatiest:

> **Money talks.**
> **The mass of men lead lives of quiet desperation.**
> **The more selfish the man, the more anguished the failure.**

Experiment with the Fragment

The fragment is close to conversation. It is the laconic reply, the
pointed afterthought, the quiet exclamation, the telling question.
Try to cut and place it clearly (usually at beginnings and ends of

paragraphs) so as not to lead your reader to expect a full sentence, or to suspect a poor writer:

> **But no more.**   **No, not really.**
> **First, a look behind the scenes.**   **Enough of that.**

The fragment, of course, usually counts as an error. The reader expects a sentence and gets only a fragment of one: you leave him hanging in air, waiting for the second shoe to fall, or the voice to drop, with the thought completed, at the period. The *rhetorical* fragment—the effective and persuasive one—leaves him satisfied: *Of course.* The *grammatical* fragment leaves him unsatisfied: *When the vote was counted.* A question hangs in the air: *what* happened? who won? who got mad? But the point here about rhetorical fragments is to use their short, conversational staccato as one of your means to vary the rhythm of your long and longer sentences, playing long against short.

Develop a Rhythm of Long and Short

The conversational flow between long and short makes a passage move. Study the subordinations, the parallels, and the play of short and long in this elegant passage of Virginia Woolf's—after you have read it once for sheer enjoyment. She is writing of Lord Chesterfield's famous letters to Philip Stanhope, his illegitimate son:

Subordinate, Long | **But while we amuse ourselves with this brilliant nobleman and his views on life we are aware, and the letters owe much of their fascination to this consciousness, of a dumb yet**

Short, Long | **substantial figure on the farther side of the page. Philip Stanhope is always there. It is true that he says nothing, but we feel his presence in Dresden, in Berlin, in Paris, opening the letters and pouring over them and looking dolefully at the thick packets which have been accumulating year after year since he was a child of seven. He had grown into a**

Short, Shorter; Longer, Long | **rather serious, rather stout, rather short young man. He had a taste for foreign politics. A little serious reading was rather to his liking. And by every post the letters came— urbane, polished, brilliant, imploring and commanding him**

to learn to dance, to learn to carve, to consider the
management of his legs, and to seduce a lady of fashion. He
did his best. He worked very hard in the school of the
Graces, but their service was too exacting. He sat down
halfway up the steep stairs which lead to the glittering hall
with all the mirrors. He could not do it. He failed in the
House of Commons; he subsided into some small post in
Ratisbon; he died untimely. He left it to his widow to break
the news which he had lacked the heart or the courage to
tell his father—that he had been married all these years to
a lady of low birth, who had borne him children.

    The Earl took the blow like a gentleman. His letter to
his daughter-in-law is a model of urbanity. He began the
education of his grandsons. . . .*

Side notes:
Short; Longer

Short
Parallels Long

Short; Longer

Those are some sentences to copy. We immediately feel the
rhythmic play of periodic and loose, parallel and simple, long and
short. Such orchestration takes years of practice, but you can
always begin.

EXERCISES

1. *Give each of the following sentences a touch of periodicity (that is,
suspense) by changing the normal word order, by adding interruptive
words or phrases, or by complicating one of the three principal elements of the sentence: the subject, the verb, the object.*

    EXAMPLE *She made her way along the smouldering roof.*

    *Carefully at first, then with reckless steps, she made her way
along the peak of the smouldering roof.*

1. Commune residents are often escapees from solidly middle-class fami-
lies.
2. Old friends are often shocked and embarrassed when they meet after
years of separation and find they now have little in common.
3. Some firemen began carrying guns when they were frightened by the
  chaos of the riots.
4. The bottleneck in education is that the teacher can listen and respond
to no more than one student at a time.
5. The car wheezed to a stop.

---

*From *The Second Common Reader* by Virginia Woolf, copyright 1932 by Harcourt
Brace Jovanovich, Inc.; renewed 1960 by Leonard Woolf. Reprinted by permission of the publisher.

2. *Write six compound sentences, two with* and, *two with* but, *two with* or (nor). *Try to get as grand a feeling of consequence as possible with your* and's: "Empires fall, and the saints come marching in."

3. *Write three compound sentences using conjunctive adverbs, on the pattern:* "———; therefore, ———." *Punctuate carefully with semicolon and comma.*

4. *Write three compound sentences in which the link is the semicolon alone. Try for meaningful contrasts.*

   EXAMPLE *The county wants the new expressway; the city wants to renew its streets.*

5. *Write three compound sentences in which the link is a colon. Try to make the second half of the compound explain the first.*

   EXAMPLE *His game was ragged: he went into sand traps four times, and into the trees five.*

6. *Here are some pairs of sentences. Convert them into complex sentences, trying to use a variety of subordinators.*

   1. He couldn't go on. He was just too tired.
   2. The crime commission recommended a number of such programs. Federal funds have been made available for putting them into operation.
   3. We can probably never perfect the process beyond its present state. We should still try.
   4. Most schools are now offering courses in computers. To evaluate those programs will take several years.
   5. On small farms, labour was not specialized. On medium farms, labour was partially specialized. But large farms carefully divided their workers into teams of specialists.

7. *Streamline the following sentences by using appositives:*

   1. The security guard, who must have been a very frightened man, fired point-blank into the crowd.
   2. Professor Stanley, who is now associate vice-president and director of business operations, has been named a vice-president at the University of Manitoba.
   3. The book, which has been a best-seller for several months, will be made into a movie.
   4. Canadian social mores have undergone staggering changes since the early 1950's. These changes are so great in quality and number as to constitute a virtual revolution.
   5. The Globe Theatre, which was immediately acclaimed the best designed and appointed playhouse in London, was completed in 1599.

8. *Consolidate the following sentences, using adjectival phrases and absolutes rather than subordinate clauses.*

1. The young girl cowered in the corner. There was pure terror in her eyes.
2. This construction is also appositional and adjectival. It is a neat trick for the beginning writer to remember.
3. Its deck was splintered and peeling. Its rigging was nearly all frayed and rotted. The boat obviously hadn't been cared for at all.
4. Griswell had neither eaten nor slept, and when he stumbled into the bar he was trembling with fatigue.
5. The ladder was sagging with his weight, and at last it collapsed.

9. *Keeping an eye out for dangling participles, revise the following sentences by transforming as many verbs as reasonably possible into participles.*

1. Apparently the boxer thought the bell had sounded. He dropped his guard, and he was immediately knocked out.
2. He settled into a Bohemian life in Vancouver. He started publishing in all the appropriate little magazines. And at last he found himself presiding over a colony of artists and writers.
3. The prisoners were obviously angered by the news that no guards were fired. They felt cheated and betrayed. And so on August 4 they seized three guards as hostages to force the warden to reconsider.
4. Dalton Trumbo was blacklisted in Hollywood; he was vilified in the press; and he was forced to write scripts under an assumed name until nearly 1960.
5. The student-designed rocket functioned perfectly. It rose one hundred miles above the earth, flew for ten minutes, traveled some fifty miles down range, and splashed down precisely on target.

10. *Try turning the phrases and subordinate clauses in the following sentences into absolutes.*

1. With examinations coming and with the temperature dropping, students are beginning to show up at the health service with all sorts of nebulous ailments, most of them purely imagined.
2. Ted left the room, leaving his things still scattered over the floor.
3. Even though the tank was filled with gas and the ignition was working perfectly, the engine still wouldn't start.
4. Even though the stock market had collapsed, and fifteen percent of the workers were jobless, Mackenzie King nonetheless felt the economy would eventually right itself without tinkering.
5. When his three minutes were up, he deposited another quarter.

11. *Correct the faulty parallelism in the following sentences from students' papers, and clean up any wordiness you find.*

1. A student follows not only a special course of training, but among his studies and social activities finds a liberal education.
2. Either the critics attacked the book for its triteness, or it was criticized for its lack of organization.
3. This is not only the case with the young voters of Canada but also of the adult ones.
4. Certain things are not actually taught in the classroom. They are learning how to get along with others, to depend on oneself, and managing one's own affairs.
5. Knowing Greek and Roman antiquity is not just learning to speak their language but also their culture.

12. *Write an imitation of the passage from Virginia Woolf on 114–15, choosing your own subject but matching the pattern, lengths, and rhythms of her sentences, sentence for sentence, if you can. At any rate, aim toward effective rhythms of long and short.*

8
Correcting Wordy Sentences

Now let us contemplate evil—or at least the innocently awful, the bad habits that waste our words, fog our thoughts, and wreck our delivery. Our thoughts are naturally roundabout, our phrases naturally secondhand. Our satisfaction in merely getting something down on paper naturally blinds us to our errors and ineptitudes. It hypnotizes us into believing we have said what we meant, when our words actually say something else: "Every seat in the house was filled to capacity." Two ways of expressing your thought, two clichés, have collided: *every seat was taken* and *the house was filled to capacity.* Cut the excess wordage, and the absurd accident vanishes: "Every seat was taken." Good sentences come from constant practice in correcting the bad.

Count Your Words

Writing is devilish; the general sin is wordiness. We put down the first thought that comes, we miss the best order, and we then need lengths of *is*'s, *of*'s, *by*'s, and *which*'s—words virtually meaningless in themselves—to wire our meaningful words together again. Look for the two or three words that carry your meaning; then see if you can rearrange them to speak for themselves, cutting out all the little useless wirings:

> **This is the young man who was elected to be president by the class. [This is the young man the class elected president.**

Or: **The class elected this young man president.** *9 words, or 7 words, for 14*]

See if you can't promote a noun into a verb, and cut overlaps in meaning:

> **Last week, the gold stampede in Europe reached near panic proportions.** [Last week, Europe's gold speculators almost *stampeded.* *7 words for 11*]

Frequently you can reduce tautologies (285):

each separate incident	**each incident**
many different ways	**many ways**
dash quickly	**dash**

As these examples show, the basic cure for wordiness is to count the words in any suspected sentence or phrase—and to make each word count. If you can rephrase to save even one word, your sentence will be clearer. And seek the active verb: *John* HITS *Joe.*

Shun the Passive Voice

The passive voice is more wordy and deadly than most people imagine, or it would not be so persistent.

> **It was voted that there would be a drive for the cleaning up of the people's park.** [*passive voice—17 words*]
> **We** [the town, the council] **voted a drive to clean up the people's park.** [*active voice—10 or 11 words, depending on subject*]

The passive voice puts the cart before the horse: the object of the action first, then the harnessing verb, running backwards, then the driver forgotten, and the whole contraption at a standstill. The passive voice is simply "passive" action, the normal action backwards: object-verb-subject (with the true subject usually forgotten) instead of subject-verb-object—*Joe is hit by John* instead of *John hits Joe.*

The passive voice liquidates and buries the active individual, along with most of the awful truth. Our massed, scientific, and bureaucratic society is so addicted to it that you must constantly alert yourself against its drowsy, impersonal pomp. The simple English sentence is active; it *moves* from subject through verb to object: "The dean's office has turned down your proposal." But the impersonal bureau emits instead a passive smokescreen, and the student sees no one at all to help him:

It has been decided that your proposal for independent study is not sufficiently in line with the prescribed qualifications as outlined by the regulations of the Faculty.

Committees always write this way, and the effect on academic writing, as the professor goes from committee to desk to classroom, is astounding. "It was moved that a meeting would be held," the secretary writes, to avoid pinning the rap on anybody. So writes the professor, so writes the student.

I reluctantly admit that the passive voice has certain uses. In fact, your meaning sometimes demands the passive voice; the agent may be better under cover—insignificant, or unknown, or mysterious. The active "Shrapnel hit him" seems to belie the uncanny impersonality of "He was hit by shrapnel." The broad forces of history similarly demand the passive: "The West was opened in 1870." Moreover, you may sometimes need the passive voice to place your true subject, the hero of the piece, where you can modify him conveniently: "Joe was hit by John, who, in spite of all. . . ." And sometimes it simply is more convenient: "This subject-verb-object sentence can be infinitely contorted." You can, of course, find a number of passive constructions in this book, which preaches against them, because they can also space out a thought that comes too fast and thick. In trying to describe periodic sentences, for instance (98), I changed "until all interconnections lock in the final word" (active) to ". . . are locked by the final word" (passive). The *lock* seemed too tight, especially with *in,* and the locking seemed contrary to the ways buildings *are built.* Yes, the passive has its uses.

But it is wordy. It puts useless words in a sentence. Its dullness derives as much from its extra wordage as from its impersonality. The best way to prune is with the active voice, cutting the passive and its fungus as you go. Notice the effect on these typical and real samples:

PASSIVE: Public concern *has* also *been given* a tremendous impetus *by* the findings of the Hoover Commission on the federal government, and "little Hoover" commissions to survey the organizational structure and functions of many state governments *have been established.*

ACTIVE: The findings of the Hoover Commission on federal government *have* also greatly stimulated public concern, and many states *have established* "little Hoover" commissions to survey their governments. [*27 words for 38*]

PASSIVE: The algal mats *are made up of* the interwoven filaments of several genera.

ACTIVE: The interwoven filaments of several genera *make up* the algal mats. [*11 words for 13*]

PASSIVE: Many of the remedies *would* probably *be shown to be* faith cures.

ACTIVE: Many of the remedies *were* probably faith cures. [*8 words for 12*]

PASSIVE: Anxiety and emotional conflict *are lessened* when latency sets in. The total personality *is oriented* in a repressive, inhibitory fashion so as to maintain the barriers, and what Freud has called "psychic dams," against psychosexual impulses.

ACTIVE: When latency sets in, anxiety and emotional conflict *lessen.* The personality *inhibits* itself, maintaining its barriers—Freud's "psychic dams"—against psychosexual impulses. [*22 words for 36*]

Check the Stretchers

To be, itself, frequently ought not to be:

> He seems [to be] upset about something.
> She considered him [to be] perfect.
> This appears [to be] difficult.

Above all, keep your sentences awake by not putting them into those favorite stretchers of the passivists, *There is . . . which, It is . . . that,* and the like:

> Moreover, [there is] one segment of the population [which] never seeks employment.
> [There are] many women [who] never marry.

[There] is nothing wrong with it. [Nothing is. . . .]
[It is] his last book [that] shows his genius best.
[It is] this [that] is important.

Cut every *it* not referring to something. Next to activating your passive verbs, and cutting the passive *there is*'s and *it is*'s, perhaps nothing so improves your prose as to go through it systematically also deleting every *to be,* every *which, that, who,* and *whom* not needed for utter clarity or for spacing out a thought. All your sentences will feel better.

Beware the Of-and-Which Disease

The passive sentence frequently breaks out in a rash of *of*'s and *which*'s, and even the active sentence may suffer. Diagnosis: something like sleeping sickness. *With*'s, *in*'s, *to*'s, and *by*'s also inflamed. Surgery imperative. Here is an actual case:

Many biological journals, especially those *which* regularly publish new scientific names, now state *in* each issue the exact date *of* publication *of* the preceding issue. *In* dealing *with* journals *which* do not follow this practice, or *with* volumes *which* are issued individually, the biologist often needs *to* resort *to* indexes... *in order to* determine the actual date *of* publication *of* a particular name.

Note *of publication of* twice over, and the three *which*'s. The passage is a sleeping beauty. The longer you look at it, the more useless little attendants you see. Note the inevitable passive voice *(which are issued)* in spite of the author's active efforts. The *of*'s accompany extra nouns, *publication* repeating *publish,* for instance. Remedy: (1) eliminate *of*'s and their nouns, (2) change *which* clauses into participles, (3) change nouns into verbs. You can cut more than a third of this passage without touching the sense (39 words for 63):

Many biological journals, especially those regularly *publishing* new scientific names, now give the date of each preceding issue. With journals not *following* this practice, and with some books, the biologist must turn to indexes . . . *to date* a particular name.

I repeat: you can cut most *which*'s, one way or another, with no loss of blood. Participles can modify their antecedents directly, since they are verbal adjectives, without an intervening *which:* "a car *which was* going south" is "a car going south"; "a train *which is* moving" is "a moving train." Similarly with the adjective itself: "a song *which was* popular last year" is "a song popular last year"; "a person *who is* attractive" is "an attractive person." Beware of this whole crowd: *who are, that was, which are.*

If you need a relative clause, remember *that.* *Which* has almost completely displaced it in laboured writing. *That* is still best for restrictive clauses, those necessary to definition: "A house that faces north is cool" (a participle would save a word: "A house facing north is cool"). *That* is tolerable; *which* is downright oppressive. *Which* should signal the nonrestrictive clause (the afterthought): "The house, which faces north, is a good buy." Here you need *which.* Even restrictive clauses must turn to *which* when complicated parallels arise. "He preaches the brotherhood of man *that* everyone affirms" elaborates like this: "He preaches the brotherhood of man *which* everyone affirms, *which* all the great philosophies support, but *for which* few can make any immediate concession." Nevertheless, if you need relatives, a *that* will often ease your sentence and save you from the *which*'s.

Verbs and their derivatives, especially present participles and gerunds, can also help to cure a string of *of*'s. Alfred North Whitehead, usually of clear mind, once produced this linked sausage: "Education is the acquisition *of* the art *of* the utilization *of* knowledge." Anything to get around the three *of*'s and the three heavy nouns would have been better: "Education instills the art of using knowledge"—"Education teaches us to use knowledge well." Find an active verb for *is the acquisition of,* and shift *the utilization of* into some verbal form: the gerund *using,* or the infinitive *to use.* Shun the *-tion*'s! Simply change your surplus *-tion*'s and *of*'s— along with your *which* phrases—into verbs, or verbals *(to use, learning).* You will save words, and activate your sentences.

Avoid "The Use Of"

In fact, both *use,* as a noun, and *use,* as a verb, are dangerously wordy words. Since *using* is one of our most basic concepts, other words in your sentence will already contain it.

He uses rationalization. [He rationalizes.]
He uses the device of foreshadowing. [He foreshadows.]
Through [the use of] logic, he persuades.
His [use of] dialogue is effective.

The utilization of and *utilize* are only horrendous extremes of the same pestilence, to be stamped out completely.

Break the Noun Habit

Passive writing adores the noun, modifying nouns with nouns in pairs, and even in denser clusters—which then become official jargon. Break up these logjams, let the language flow, make one noun of the pair an adjective:

> *Teacher militancy* **is not as marked in Pittsburgh.** [*Teachers* **are not so** *militant* **in Pittsburgh.** *7 words for 8*]

Or convert one noun to a verb:

> *Consumer demand* **is falling in the area of services.** [**Consumers** *are demanding* **fewer services.** *5 words for 9*]

Of course, nouns have long served English as adjectives: as in "*rail*road," "*railroad* station," "*court*house," and "*noun* habit." But modern prose has aggravated the tendency beyond belief; and we get such monstrosities as *child sex education course* and *child sex education curriculum publication deadline reminder*—whole strings of nothing but nouns. Education, sociology, and psychology produce the worst noun-stringers, the hardest for you not to copy if you take these courses. But we have all caught the habit. The nouns *level* and *quality,* used as adjectives, have produced a rash of redundancies. A meeting of "high officials" has now unfortunately become a meeting of "high-*level* officials." The "finest cloth" these days is always "finest *quality* cloth." Drop those two redundant nouns and you will make a good start, and will sound surprisingly original. In fact, using the noun *quality* as an adjective has become almost obsessive—*quality food, quality wine, quality service, quality entertainment, high-quality drilling equipment*—blurring all distinctions of *good, fine, excellent, superb, superior,* in one dull and

inaccurate cliché. A good rule: DON'T USE NOUNS AS ADJECTIVES.
You can drop many an excess noun:

WORDY	DIRECT
advance notice	notice
long in size	long

WORDY	DIRECT
puzzling in nature	puzzling
of an indefinite nature	indefinite
of a peculiar kind	peculiar
in order to	to
by means of	by
in relation to	with
in connection with	with
1986-model car	1986 car
at this point in time	at this time; now

Wherever possible, find the equivalent adjective:

of great importance	important
highest significance level	highest significant level
government spending	governmental spending
reaction fixation	reactional fixation
teaching excellence	excellent teaching
encourage teaching quality	encourage good teaching

Or change the noun to its related participle:

advance placement	advanced placement
uniform police	uniformed police
poison arrow	poisoned arrow

Or make the noun possessive:

reader interest	reader's interest
veterans insurance	veterans' insurance

Or try a cautious *of:*

colour lipstick	colour of lipstick
significance level	level of significance

Of all our misused nouns, *type* has become particularly pestilential and trite. Advertisers talk of *detergent-type cleansers* instead of *detergents;* educators, of *apprentice-type situations* instead of *apprenticeships;* newspapermen, of *fascist-type organizations* instead of *fascistic organizations.* We have forgotten that making the individual stand for the type is the simplest and oldest of metaphors: "Give us this day our daily bread." A twentieth-century supplicant might have written "bread-type food."

The active sentence transmits the message by putting each word unmistakably in its place, a noun as a noun, an adjective as an adjective, with the verb—no stationary *is*—really carrying the mail. Recently, after a flood, a newspaper produced this apparently succinct and dramatic sentence: **Dead animals cause water pollution.** (The word *cause,* incidentally, indicates wasted words.) That noun *water* as an adjective throws the meaning off and takes 25 percent more words than the essential active message: **Dead animals pollute water.** As you read your way into the sentence, it seems to say *dead animals cause water* (which is true enough), and then you must readjust your thoughts to accommodate *pollution.* The simplest change is from *water pollution* (noun-noun) to *polluted water* (adjective-noun), clarifying each word's function. But the supreme solution is to make *pollute* the verb it is, and the sentence a simple active message in which no word misspeaks itself. Here are the possibilities, in a scale from most active and clearest to most passive and wordiest, which may serve to chart your troubles if you get tangled in causes and nouns:

> **Dead animals pollute water.**
> **Dead animals cause polluted water.**
> **Dead animals cause water pollution.**
> **Dead animals are a factor in causing the pollution of water.**
> **Dead animals are a serious factor in causing the water pollution situation.**
> **Dead farm-type animals are a danger factor in causing the post-flood clearance and water pollution situation.**

So the message should now be clear. Write simple active sentences, outmanoeuvring all passive eddies, all shallow *is*'s, *of*'s, *which*'s, and *that*'s, all overlappings, all rocky clusters of nouns: they take you off your course, delay your delivery, and wreck many a straight and gallant thought.

Avoid Excessive Distinctions and Definitions

Too many distinctions, too many nouns, and too much Latin make pea soup:

> **Reading is a processing skill of symbolic reasoning sustained by the interfacilitation of an intricate hierarchy of substrata factors that have been mobilized as a psychological working system and pressed into service in accordance with the purpose of the reader.**

This comes from an educator, with the wrong kind of education. He is saying:

> **Reading is a process of symbolic reasoning aided by an intricate network of ideas and motives.** [*16 words for 40*]

Except with crucial assumptions and implications (see 77–81), try *not* to define your terms. If you do, you are probably either evading the toil of finding the right word, or defining the obvious:

> **Let us agree to use the word signal as an abbreviation for the phrase "the simplest kind of sign." (This agrees fairly well with the customary meaning of the word "signal.")**

That came from a renowned semanticist, an authority on the meanings of words. The customary meaning of a word *is* its meaning, and uncustomary meanings come only from careful punning. Don't underestimate your readers, as this semanticist did.

The definer of words is usually a bad writer. Our semanticist continues, trying to get his signals straight and grinding out about three parts sawdust to every one of meat. In the following excerpt, I have bracketed his sawdust. Read the sentence first as he wrote it: then read it again, omitting the bracketed words:

> **The moral of such examples is that all intelligent criticism [of any instance] of language [in use] must begin with understanding [of] the motives [and purposes] of the speaker [in that situation].**

Here, each of the bracketed phrases is already implied in the others. Attempting to be precise, the writer has beclouded himself. Naturally, the speaker would be "in that situation"; naturally, a sampling of language would be "an instance" of language "in use." *Motives* may not be *purposes*, but the difference here is insignificant. Our semanticist's next sentence deserves some kind of immortality. He means "Muddy language makes trouble":

> **Unfortunately, the type of case that causes trouble in practise is that in which the kind of use made of language is not transparently clear. . . .**

Clearly, transparency is hard. Writing is hard. It requires constant attention to meanings, and constant pruning. Count your words, and make your words count.

EXERCISES

1. *Clear up the blurred ideas, and grammar, in these sentences from students' papers and official prose, making each word say what it means, and counting your words to make sure your version has fewer.*

    1. Tree pruning may be done in any season of the year. [11 words]
    2. After reading a dozen books, the subject is still as puzzling as ever. [13]
    3. The secret teller vote used in the past was this time a recorded teller vote. [15]
    4. The courses listed herein are those which meet the university-level requirements which were stated above. [16]
    5. Records can be used in the Audio Room by individual students for their suggested listening assignments. [16]
    6. My counter was for refunds for which the customer had already paid for. [13]
    7. Entrance was gained by means of the skylight. [8]
    8. The reason we give this test is because we are anxious to know whether or not you have reflexes that are sufficiently fast to allow you to be a safe worker. [31]

2. *Find in your textbooks two or three passages suffering from the passive voice, the of-and-which disease, the the-use-of contagion, and the noun habit ("which shows the effect of age and intelligence level upon the use of the reflexes and the emergence of child behaviour difficulties") and rewrite them in clear English.*

3. *Recast these sentences in the active voice, clearing out all passive constructions, saving as many words as you can, and indicating the number saved:*

1. The particular topic chosen by the instructor for study in his section of English 2 must be approved by the Steering Committee. [Start with "The Steering Committee," and don't forget the economy of an apostrophe-*s*. I managed 14 words for 22.]
2. Avoidance of such blunders should not be considered a virtue for which the student is to be commended, any more than he would be praised for not wiping his hands on the tablecloth or polishing his shoes with the guest towels. [Begin "We should not"; try *avoiding* for *avoidance*. I dropped *virtue* as redundant and scored 27 for 41.]
3. The first respect in which too much variation seems to exist is in the care with which writing assignments are made. ["First, care in assigning"—8 for 21.]
4. The remaining variations that will be mentioned are concerned not with the assignment of papers but with the marking and grading of them. ["Finally, I shall mention"—14 for 23.]
5. The difference between restrictives and nonrestrictives can also be better approached through a study of the different contours that mark the utterance of the two kinds of elements than through confusing attempts to differentiate the two by meaning. ["One can differentiate restrictives"—I managed 13 for 38. The writer is dead wrong, incidentally: meaning is the true differentiator. See 219–21.]

4. *Eliminate the italicized words in the following passages, together with all their accompanying wordiness, indicating the number of words saved (my figures again are merely guides; other solutions that come close are quite good).*

1. *There is* a certain tendency to defend one's own position *which* will cause the opponent's argument to be ignored. [13 for 19]
2. *It is* the other requirements *that* present obstacles, some *of which* may prove insurmountable in the teaching of certain subjects. [11 for 20]
3. In the sort of literature-centred course being discussed here, *there is* usually a general understanding *that* essays will be based on the various literary works *that* are studied, the theory being *that* both the instruction in literature and *that* in writing will be made more effective by this interrelationship. [21 for 50]
4. The person *whom* he met was an expert *who was* able to teach the fundamentals quickly. [13 for 16]
5. They will take a pride *which is* wholly justifiable in being able to command a prose style *that is* lucid and supple. [13 for 22]

5. *To culminate this chapter, clear up the wordiness, especially the italicized patches, in these two official statements, one from an eminent
linguist, one from an eminent publisher.*

1. The work *which is* reported *in this* study *is* an investigation *of* language *within* the social context *of* the community *in which it is
spoken. It is* a study *of* a linguistic structure *which is* unusually complex, but no more than the social structure *of* the city *in which it*
functions. [I tried two versions, as I chased out the *which*'s; 29 for 52,
and 22 for 52.]

2. Methods *which are* unique to the historian *are illustrated* throughout
the volume *in order* to show how history *is written* and how historians
work. The historian's approach to his subject, *which* leads to the
asking of provocative questions and to a new understanding of complex events, situations, and personalities *is probed.* The manner *in
which* the historian reduces masses of chaotic fact—and occasional
fancy—to reliable meaning, and the way *in which* he formulates explanations and tests them *is examined and clarified* for the student. *It is
its* emphasis on historical method *which* distinguishes this book from
other source readings in western civilization. The problems *which are
examined* concern *themselves with* subjects *which are dealt with
by* most courses in western civilization. [66 for 123. The all-time
winner from a student is 45 words.]

9
Words

Here is the word. Sesquipedalian or short, magniloquent or low, Latin or Anglo-Saxon, Celtic, Danish, French, Spanish, Indian, Hindustani, Dutch, Italian, Portuguese, Choctaw, Swahili, Chinese, Hebrew, Turkish, Greek—English contains them all, a million words at our disposal, if we are disposed to use them. No language is richer than English. But our spoken vocabularies average only about 2800 words, our expository vocabularies probably fewer than 8000. We all have a way to go to possess our heritage.

VOCABULARY

Build Your Stock Systematically

If you can increase your hoard, you increase your chances of finding the right word when you need it. Read as widely as you can, and look words up the second or third time you meet them. I once knew a man who swore he learned three new words a day from his reading by using each at least once in conversation. I didn't ask him about *polyphiloprogenitive* or *antidisestablishmentarianism*. It depends a little on the crowd. But the idea is sound. The bigger the vocabulary, the more various the ideas one can get across with it—the more the shades and intensities of meaning.

132

The big vocabulary also needs the little word. The vocabularian often stands himself on a Latin cloud and forgets the Anglo-Saxon ground—the common ground between him and his audience. So do not forget the little things, the *stuff, lint, get, twig, snap, go, mud, coax.* Hundreds of small words not in immediate vogue can refresh your vocabulary. The Norse and Anglo-Saxon adjectives in -*y* (*muggy, scrawny, drowsy*) for instance, rarely appear in sober print. The minute the beginner tries to sound dignified, in comes a misty layer of words a few feet off the ground and nowhere near heaven, the same two dozen or so, most of them verbs. One or two will do no harm, but any accumulation is fatal—words like *depart* instead of *go:*

accompany—go with	place—put
appeared—looked *or* seemed	possess—have
arrive—come	prepare—get ready
become—get	questioned—asked
cause—make	receive—get
cease—stop	relate—tell
complete—finish	remain—stay
continue—keep on	remove—take off
delve—dig	retire—go to bed
discover—find	return—go back
indicate—say	secure—get
locate—find	transform—change
manner—way	verify—check

Through the centuries, English has added Latin derivatives alongside the Anglo-Saxon words already there, keeping the old with the new: after the Anglo-Saxon *deor* (now *deer*) came the *beast* and then the *brute,* both from Latin through French, and the *animal* straight from Rome. We have the Anglo-Saxon *cow, sheep,* and *pig* alongside Latin (through French) *beef, mutton,* and *pork.* Although we use more Anglo-Saxon in assembling our sentences (*to, by, with, though, is*), well over half our total vocabulary comes one way or another from Latin. The things of this world tend to be Anglo-Saxon (*man, house, stone, wind, rain*); the abstract qualities, Latin and French (*value, duty, contemplation*).

Most of our big words are Latin and Greek. Your reading acquaints you with them; your dictionary will show you their prefixes and roots. Learn the common prefixes and roots (see Exercise 3 at the end of this chapter), and you can handle all kinds of foreigners at first encounter; *con-cession* (going along with), *ex-clude* (lock out), *pre-fer* (carry before), *sub-version* (turning under), *trans-late* (carry across), *claustro-phobia* (dread of being locked in), *hydro-phobia* (dread of water), *ailuro-philia* (love of cats), *megalo-cephalic* (big-headed), *micro-meter* (little measurer). You can even, for fun, coin a word to suit the occasion: *megalopede* (big-footed). You can remember that *intramural* means "within the (university) walls," and that "intermural sports," which is the frequent mispronunciation and misspelling, would mean something like "wall battling wall," a physical absurdity.

Besides owning a good dictionary, you should refer, with caution, to a thesaurus, a treasury of synonyms ("together-names"), in which you can find the word you couldn't think of; the danger lies in raiding this treasury too enthusiastically. Checking for meaning in a dictionary will help assure that you have expanded, not distorted, your vocabulary.

ABSTRACT AND CONCRETE

Learn Their Powers, Separate and Combined

Every good stylist has perceived, in one way or another, the distinction between the abstract and the concrete. Tangible things—things we can touch—are "concrete"; their qualities, along with all our emotional, intellectual, and spiritual states, are "abstract." The rule for a good style is to be as concrete as you can, to illustrate tangibly your general propositions, to use *shoes* and *ships* and *sealing wax* instead of *commercial concomitants*.

But abstraction, a "drawing out from," is the very nature of thought. Thought moves from concrete to abstract. In fact, *all* words are abstractions. *Stick* is a generalization of all sticks, the crooked and the straight, the long and the short, the peeled and the shaggy. No word fits its object like a glove, because words are not things: words represent ideas of things. They are the means by which we class eggs and tents and trees so that we can handle them as ideas—not as actual things but as *kinds* or *classes* of things.

Abstract words can attain a power of their own, as the rhetorician heightens attention to their meanings. This ability, of course, does not come easily or soon. I repeat, you need to be as concrete as you can, to illustrate tangibly, to pin your abstractions down to specifics. But once you have learned this, you can move on to the rhetoric of abstraction, which is a kind of squeezing of abstract words for their specific juice.

Abraham Lincoln does exactly this when he concentrates on *dedication* six times within the ten sentences of his dedication at Gettysburg: "We have come to *dedicate.* . . . It is rather for us to be here *dedicated.* . . ." Similarly, T. S. Eliot refers to "faces/Distracted from distraction by distraction" *(Four Quartets).* Abstractions can, in fact, operate beautifully as specifics: "As a knight, Richard the Lion-Hearted was a *triumph;* as a king, he was a *disaster."* Many rhetorical patterns likewise concentrate on abstract essences:

> . . . tribulation works patience, and patience experience, and experience hope. (Rom. v.3–4)
> The humble are proud of their humility.
> Care in your youth so you may live without care.

An able writer like Samuel Johnson can make a virtual poetry of abstractions, as he alliterates and balances them against each other (I have capitalized the alliterations and italicized the balances):

> Dryden's performances were always hasty, either *Excited* by some *External occasion,* or *Extorted* by some *domestic necessity;* he *ComPosed without Consideration* and *Published without Correction.*

Notice especially how *excited* ("called forth") and *extorted* ("twisted out"), so alike in sound and form, so alike in making Dryden write, nevertheless contrast their opposite essential meanings.

So before we disparage abstraction, we should acknowledge its rhetorical power; and we should understand that it is an essential distillation, a primary and natural and continual mental process. Without it, we could not make four of two and two. So we make abstractions of abstractions to handle bigger and bigger groups of ideas. *Egg* becomes *food,* and *food* becomes *nourish-*

ment. We also classify all the psychic and physical qualities we can recognize: *candour, truth, anger, beauty, negligence, temperament.* But because our thoughts drift upward, we need always to look for the word that will bring them nearer earth, that will make our abstractions seem visible and tangible, that will make them graspable—mentioning a *handle,* or a *pin,* or an *egg,* alongside our abstraction, for instance.

But the writer's ultimate skill perhaps lies in making a single object represent its whole abstract class. I have paired each abstraction below with its concrete translation:

> *Friendliness* **is the salesman's best asset.**
> *A smile* **is the salesman's best asset.**
>
> *Administration of proper proteins* **might have saved John Keats.**
> *A good steak* **might have saved John Keats.**
>
> **To** *understand* **the world by** *observing all of its geological details.* . . .
> **To** *see* **the world in** *a grain of sand.* . . .

METAPHOR

Bring Your Words to Life

As you have probably noticed, I frequently use metaphors—the most useful way of making our abstractions concrete. The word is Greek for "transfer" (*meta* equals *trans* equals *across; phor* equals *fer* equals *ferry*). Metaphors illustrate our general ideas at a single stroke. Many of our common words are metaphors, *grasp* for "understanding," for instance, which compares the mind to something with hands, *transferring* the physical picture of the clutching hand to the invisible mental act.

Metaphor seems to work at about four levels, each with a different clarity and force. Suppose you wrote "he swelled and displayed his finery." You have transferred to a man the qualities of a peacock to make his appearance and personality vivid. You have chosen one of the four ways to make this transfer:

I. SIMILE: **He was like a peacock.**
                He displayed himself as a peacock does.
                He displayed himself as if he were a peacock.

II. PLAIN METAPHOR: **He was a peacock.**

III. IMPLIED METAPHOR: **He swelled and displayed his finery.**
                He swelled and ruffled his plumage.
                He swelled, ruffling his plumage.

IV. DEAD METAPHOR: **He strutted.**

I. Simile.   The simile is the most obvious form the metaphor can take, and hence would seem elementary. But it has powers of its own, particularly where the writer seems to be trying urgently to express the inexpressible, comparing his subject to several different possibilities, no one wholly adequate. In *The Sound and the Fury,* Faulkner thus describes two jaybirds (my italics):

> [they] **whirled up on the blast** *like gaudy scraps of cloth or paper* **and lodged in the mulberries, . . . screaming into the wind that** *ripped* **their harsh cries onward and away** *like scraps of paper or of cloth* **in turn.**

The simile has a high poetic energy. D. H. Lawrence uses it frequently, as here in *The Plumed Serpent* (my italics):

> **The lake was quite black,** *like a great pit.* **The wind suddenly blew with violence, with a strange ripping sound in the mango trees,** *as if some membrane in the air were being ripped.*

II. Plain Metaphor.   The plain metaphor makes its comparison in one imaginative leap. It is shorthand for "as if he were a peacock"; it pretends, by exaggeration *(hyperbole),* that he *is* a peacock. We move instinctively to this kind of exaggerated comparison as we try to convey our impressions with all their emotional impact. "He was a maniac at Frisbee," we might say, or "a dynamo." The metaphor is probably our most common figure of speech: *the pigs, the swine, a plum, a gem, a phantom of delight, a shot* *in the arm.* It may be humorous or bitter; it may be simply and aptly visual: "The road was a ribbon of silver." Thoreau extends a metaphor through several sentences in one of his most famous passages:

> **Time is but a stream I go a-fishing in. I drink at it; but while I drink I see the sandy bottom and detect how shallow it is. Its thin current slides away, but eternity remains. I would drink deeper; fish in the sky, whose bottom is pebbly with stars.**

III. Implied Metaphor. The implied metaphor is even more widely used. It operates most often among the verbs, as in *swelled, displayed,* and *ruffled,* the verbs suggesting "peacock." Most ideas can suggest analogues of physical processes or natural history. Give your television system *tentacles* reaching into every home, and you have compared TV to an octopus, with all its lethal and wiry suggestions. You can have your school spirit *fall below zero,* and you have implied that your school spirit is like temperature, registered on a thermometer in a sudden chill. Malcolm Cowley writes metaphorically about Nathaniel Hawthorne's style, first in a direct simile *(like a footprint)* and then in a metaphor implying that phrases are people walking at different speeds:

> **He dreamed in words, while walking along the seashore or under the pines, till the words fitted themselves to his stride. The result was that his eighteenth-century English developed into a natural, a *walked,* style, with a phrase for every step and a comma after every phrase like a footprint in the sand. Sometimes the phrases hurry, sometimes they loiter, sometimes they march to drums.***

IV. Dead Metaphor. The art of resuscitation is the metaphorist's finest skill. It comes from liking words and paying attention to what they say. Simply add onto the dead metaphor enough implied metaphors to get the circulation going again: *He strutted, swelling and ruffling his plumage. He strutted* means by itself "walked in a pompous manner." By bringing the metaphor back to life, we keep the general meaning but also restore the physical picture of a peacock puffing up and spreading his feathers. We recognize

---

The Portable Hawthorne (New York: Viking, 1948).

strut concretely and truly for the first time. We know the word, and we know the man. We have an image of him, a posture strongly suggestive of a peacock.

Perhaps the best dead metaphors to revive are those in proverbial clichés. See what Thoreau does (in his *Journal*) with *spur of the moment:*

> **I feel the spur of the moment thrust deep into my side. The present is an inexorable rider.**

Or again, when in *Walden* he speaks of wanting "to improve *the nick of time,* and notch it on my stick too," and of not being *thrown off the track* "by every nutshell and mosquito's wing that falls on the rails." In each case, he takes the proverbial phrase literally and physically, adding an attribute or two to bring the old metaphor back alive.

You can go too far, of course. Your metaphors can be too thick and vivid, and the obvious pun brings a howl of protest. I have myself advised scholars against metaphors because they are so often overworked and so often tangled in physical impossibilities, becoming "mixed" metaphors. "The violent population explosion has paved the way for new intellectual growth" looks pretty good—until you realize that explosions do not pave, and that new vegetation does not grow up through solid pavement. Changing *paved* to *cleared* would clear the confusion. The metaphor, then, is your most potent device. It makes your thought concrete and your writing vivid. It tells in an instant how your subject looks to you. But it is dangerous. It should be quiet, almost unnoticed, with all details agreeing, and all absolutely consistent with the natural universe.

ALLUSION

Illuminate the Dim with a Familiar Light

Allusions also illustrate your general idea by referring it to something else, making it take your reader as Wellington took Napoleon, making you the Mickey Mantle of the essay, or the Mickey

Mouse. Allusions depend on common knowledge. Like the metaphor, they illustrate the remote with the familiar—a familiar place, or event, or personage. "He looked . . . like a Japanese Humphrey Bogart," writes William Bittner of French author Albert Camus, and we instantly see a face like the one we know so well (a glance at Camus's picture confirms this allusion as surprisingly accurate). Perhaps the most effective allusions depend on a knowledge of literature. When Thoreau writes that "the winter of man's discontent was thawing as well as the earth," we get a secret pleasure from recognizing this as an allusive borrowing from the opening lines of Shakespeare's *Richard III:* "Now is the winter of our discontent / Made glorious summer by this sun of York." Thoreau flatters us by assuming we are as well read as he. We need not catch the allusion to enjoy his point, but if we catch it, we feel a sudden fellowship of knowledge with him. We now see the full metaphorical force, Thoreau's and Shakespeare's both, heightened as it is by our remembrance of Richard Crookback's twisted discontent, an allusive illustration of all our pitiful resentments now thawing with the spring.

Allusions can also be humorous. The hero of Peter De Vries's "The Vale of Laughter," alluding to Lot's wife looking back on Sodom (Gen. 19.26) as he contemplates adultery for a moment, decides on the path toward home and honour:

> **If you look back, you turn into a pillar of salt. If you look ahead, you turn into a pillar of society.**

DICTION

Reach for Both the High and the Low

"What we need is a mixed diction," said Aristotle, and his point remains true twenty-three centuries and several languages later. The aim of style, he says, is to be clear but distinguished. For clarity, we need common, current words; but, used alone, these are commonplace, and as ephemeral as everyday talk. For distinction, we need words not heard every minute, unusual words, large words, foreign words, metaphors; but, used alone, these become bogs, vapours, or at worst, gibberish. What we need is a diction that weds the popular with the dignified, the clear current with the sedgy margins of language and thought.

Not too low, not too high; not too simple, not too hard—an easy breadth of idea and vocabulary. English is peculiarly well endowed for this Aristotelian mixture. The long abstract Latin words and the short concrete Anglo-Saxon ones give you all the range you need. For most of your ideas, you can find Latin and Anglo-Saxon partners. In fact, for many ideas, you can find a whole spectrum of synonyms from Latin through French to Anglo-Saxon, from general to specific—from *intrepidity* to *fortitude* to *valour* to *courage* to *bravery* to *pluck* to *guts.* Each of these *denotes* or specifies the same thing: being brave. But each has a different *connotation,* or aura of meaning (see Glossary, 265). You can choose the high word for high effect, or you can get tough with Anglo-Saxon specifics. But you do not want all Anglo-Saxon, and you must especially guard against sobriety's luring you into all Latin. Tune your diction agreeably between the two extremes.

Indeed, the two extremes generate incomparable zip when tumbled side by side, as in *incomparable zip, inconsequential snip, megalomaniacal creep,* and the like. Rhythm and surprise conspire to set up the huge adjective first, then to add the small noun, like a monumental kick. Here is a passage from Edward Dahlberg's *Can These Bones Live,* which I opened completely at random to see how the large fell with the small (my italics):

> **Christ walks on a *visionary sea;* Myshkin . . . has his ecstatic premonition of infinity when he has an *epileptic fit.* We know the inward size of an artist by his *dimensional thirsts.* . . .**

This mixing of large Latin and small Anglo-Saxon, as John Crowe Ransom has noted, is what gives Shakespeare much of his power:

> **This my hand will rather
> The multitudinous seas incarnadine,
> Making the green one red.**

The short Anglo-Saxon *seas* works sharply between the two magnificent Latin words, as do the three short Anglo-Saxons that bring the big passage to rest, contrasting the Anglo-Saxon *red* with its big Latin kin, *incarnadine.* William Faulkner, who soaked himself in Shakespeare, gets much the same power from the same mixture. He is describing a very old Negro woman in *The Sound and the Fury* (the title itself comes from Shakespeare's *Macbeth,* the source of the *multitudinous seas* passage). She has been fat, but now she is wrinkled and completely shrunken except for her stomach:

> . . . a paunch almost dropsical, as though muscle and tissue had been courage or fortitude which the days or the years had consumed until only the indomitable skeleton was left rising like a ruin or a landmark above the somnolent and impervious guts. . . .

The impact of that short, ugly Anglo-Saxon word *guts,* with its slang metaphorical pun, is almost unbearably moving. And the impact would be nothing, the effect slurring, without the grand Latin preparation.

A good diction takes work. It exploits the natural, but does not come naturally. It demands a wary eye for the way meanings sprout, and it demands the courage to prune. It has the warmth of human concern. It is a cut above the commonplace, a cut above the inaccuracies and circumlocutions of speech, yet within easy reach. Clarity is the first aim; economy, the second; grace, the third; dignity, the fourth. Our writing should be a little strange, a little out of the ordinary, a little beautiful, with words and phrases not met every day but seeming as right and natural as grass. A good diction takes care and cultivation.

It can be overcultivated. It may seem to call attention to itself rather than to its subject. Suddenly we are aware of the writer at work, and a little too pleased with himself, reaching for the elegant cliché and the showy phrase. Some readers find this very fault with my own writing, though I do really try to saddle my maverick love of metaphor. If I strike you in this way, you can use me profitably as a bad example, along with the following passage. I have italicized elements that individually may have a certain effectiveness, but that cumulatively become mannerism, as if the writer were watching himself gesture in a mirror. Some of his phrases are redundant; some are trite. Everything is somehow cozy and grandiose, and a little too nautical:

> *There's* little excitement *ashore* when merchant ships
> from *faraway* India, Nationalist China, or Egypt *knife*
> *through* the *gentle swells* of Virginia's Hampton Roads. This
> *unconcern* may simply reflect the *nonchalance* of people who
> live by *one of the world's great seaports.* Or perhaps *it's*
> *just* that *folk* who *dwell* in the *home towns* of atomic subma-
> rines and Mercury astronauts are not likely to be impressed
> by a visiting freighter, *from however distant a realm.* . . . *Up-*
> *stream a bit* and also *to port,* the mouth of the Elizabeth River
> leads to Portsmouth and a major naval shipyard. *To star-*
> *board lies* Hampton, where at Langley Air Force Base the
> National Aeronautics and Space Administration prepares
> to send a man *into the heavens.*

EXERCISES

1. *As a warmup, clear the preceding example of its overdone phrases.*
2. *Revise the following sentences to make them more vivid and distinct by replacing as many of the abstract terms as possible with concrete terms.*

   1. For the better part of a year, he was without gainful employment.
   2. Of the students who go to university outside their own country, seventy percent do not go back after completing their studies.
   3. A sizable proportion of those people who use long-distance movers are large-corporation employees whose moving expenses are entirely underwritten by their companies.
   4. His great-grandfather once ran successfully for high public office, but he never served because his opponent mortally wounded him in a duel with pistols.
   5. There was a severe disturbance in Jackson prison one day in the spring —convicts, armed with makeshift weapons, took some of the prison personnel hostage.
   6. Her husband had one extramarital relationship after another and finally disappeared with a hotel dining room employee in one of our larger western cities.
   7. Rejected by the military because of an impairment of his vision, Ernest became a journalist with a Toronto newspaper.
   8. Disadvantaged people are often maltreated by the very social-service agencies ostensibly designed to help them.
   9. The newspaper reported that a small foreign car had overturned on the expressway just north of town.
   10. The new contract offers almost no change in the fringe-benefit package.

3. *Look up in your dictionary six of the Latin and Greek constituents listed below. Illustrate each with several English derivatives closely translated, as in these two examples:* con *(with)*—convince *(conquer with),* conclude *(shut with),* concur *(run with);* chron- *(time)*—chronic *(lasting a long time),* chronicle *(a record of the time),* chronometer *(timemeasurer).*

LATIN: *a- (ab-), ad-, ante-, bene-, bi-, circum-, con-, contra-, di- (dis-), e- (ex-), in- (two meanings), inter-, intra-, mal-, multi-, ob-, per-, post-, pre-, pro-, retro-, semi-, sub- (sur-), super-, trans-, ultra-.*

GREEK: *a- (an-), -agogue, allo-, anthropo-, anti-, apo-, arch-, auto-, batho-, bio-, cata-, cephalo-, chron-, -cracy, demo-, dia-, dyna-, dys-, ecto-, epi-, eu-, -gen, geo-, -gon, -gony, graph-, gyn-, hemi-, hepta-, hetero-, hexa-, homo-, hydr-, hyper-, hypo-, log-, mega-, -meter, micro-, mono-, morph-, -nomy, -nym, -pathy, penta-, -phagy, phil-, -phobe (ia), -phone, poly-, pseudo-, psyche-, -scope, soph-, stereo-, sym- (syn-), tele-, tetra-, theo-, thermo-, tri-, zoo-.*

4. *Revise the following sentences so as to clear up the illogical or unnatural connections in their metaphors and similes.*

   1. The violent population explosion has paved the way for new intellectual growth.
   2. The book causes a shock, like a bucket of icy water suddenly thrown on a fire.
   3. The whole social fabric will become unstuck.
   4. The tangled web of Jack's business crumbled under its own weight.
   5. His last week had mirrored his future, like a hand writing on the wall.
   6. The recent economic picture, which seemed to spell prosperity, has wilted beyond repair.
   7. They were tickled to death by the thunderous applause.
   8. Stream of consciousness fiction has gone out of phase with the new castles in the air of fantasy.
   9. The murmured protests drifted from the convention floor to the podium, cracking the façade of his imperturbability.
   10. Richard was ecstatic with his success. He had scaled the mountain of difficulties and from here on out he could sail with the breeze.

5. *Write a sentence for each of the following dead metaphors, bringing it to life by adding implied metaphorical detail, as in "She bridled, snorting and tossing her mane," or by adding a simile, as in "He was dead wrong, laid out like a corpse on a slab."*

   dead centre, pinned down, sharp as a tack, stick to, whined, purred, reflected, ran for office, yawned, take a course.

6. *Write a sentence for each of the following, in which you allude either humorously or seriously to:*

1. A famous—or infamous—person (Caesar, Napoleon, Barnum, Trudeau, Stalin, Picasso, Bogart)
2. A famous event (the Declaration of Independence, the Battle of Waterloo, Confederation, the Battle of the Bulge, the signing of the Magna Carta, Cartier's arrival in Canada, the 1984 Conservative landslide)
3. A notable place (Athens, Rome, Paris, London Bridge, Jerusalem, the Vatican)
4. This famous passage from Shakespeare, by quietly borrowing some of its phrases:

> To be, or not to be—that is the question:
> Whether 'tis nobler in the mind to suffer
> The slings and arrows of outrageous fortune,
> Or to take arms against a sea of troubles,
> And by opposing end them.

7. *Write a paragraph in which you mix your diction as effectively as you can, with the big Latin word and the little Anglo-Saxon, the formal word and just the right touch of slang, working in at least two combinations of the extremes, on the pattern of* multitudinous seas, diversionary thrust, incomparable zip, *underlining these for your instructor's convenience.*

8. *Write a* TERRIBLE ESSAY. *Have some fun with this perennial favorite, in which you reinforce your sense for clear, figurative, and meaningful words by writing the muddiest and wordiest essay you can invent, gloriously working out all your bad habits. Organize in the usual way, with a thesis, a good beginning, middle, and end, but parody the worst kind of sociological and bureaucratic prose. Here are the rules:*

1. Put EVERYTHING in the passive voice.
2. Modify nouns *only* with nouns, preferably in strings of three or four, never with adjectives: *governmental spending* becomes *government level spending;* an *excellent idea* becomes *quality program concept.*
3. Use only big abstract nouns—as many *-tion's* as possible.
4. Use no participles: not *dripping faucets* but *faucets which drip;* and use as many *which's* as possible.
5. Use as many words as possible to say the least.
6. Work in as many trite and wordy expressions as possible: *needless to say, all things being equal, due to the fact that, in terms of, as far as that is concerned.*
7. Sprinkle heavily with *-wise-*type and *type-*type expressions, and say *hopefully* every three or four sentences.

8. Compile and use a basic terrible vocabulary: *situation, aspect, function, factor, phase, process, procedure, utilize, the use of,* and so on. The class may well cooperate in this.

9. *Refine your sense of diction and meanings still further by writing an* IRONIC ESSAY, *saying the opposite of what you mean, as in "The party was a dazzling success," "The Rockheads are the solidest group in town," "Our team is the best in the West."*

10
Research

Now to consolidate and advance. Instead of eight or nine hundred words, you will write three thousand. Instead of a self-propelled debate or independent literary analysis, you will write a scholarly argument. You will also learn to use the library, and to take notes and give footnotes. You will learn the ways of scholarship. You will learn to acknowledge your predecessors as you distinguish yourself, to make not only a bibliography, but a contribution.

The research paper is very likely not what you think it is. *Research* is searching again. You are looking, usually, where others have looked before; but you hope to see something they have not. Research is not combining a paragraph from the *Encyclopaedia Britannica* and a paragraph from *Encyclopedia Canadiana* with a slick pinch from *Maclean's.* That's robbery. Nor is it research even if you carefully change each phrase and acknowledge the source. That's drudgery. Even in some high circles, I am afraid, such scavenging is called research. It is not. It is simply a cloudier condensation of what you have done in school as a "report"— sanctioned plagiarism to teach something about ants or Ankara, a tedious compiling of what is already known. That such material is new to you is not the issue: it is already in the public stock.

CHOOSING YOUR SUBJECT

Pick Something That Interests You

First get yourself a subject. You need not shake the world. Such subjects as "Subsidizing University Students," "College Versus

University," "Excluding the Press from Trials," or the changing valuation of a former best-seller well suit the research paper. Bigger subjects, of course, will try your mettle: nuclear power, abortion, federal powers, endangered species as against public need. The whole question of governmental versus private endeavour affords many lively issues for research and decision, perhaps in your own locality and your local newspaper.

You can stir your own interests and turn up a number of good ideas for research by reading the newspapers—*The Christian Science Monitor* is especially fruitful—and by browsing the current magazines such as *Maclean's, Saturday Night, Psychology Today, Scientific American, Atlantic Monthly, Saturday Review,* and many another. Other good sources are interviews on TV, film documentaries, and even arguments in the coffee shop or pub.

Work with a Thesis

Once you have spotted a subject that interests you, lean toward your inclination about it and write it into a tentative thesis sentence. Though tentative, any stand *for* or *against* will save you time in further searching, and help you establish manageable bounds.

Since you will be dealing mostly with facts in the public stock and with ideas with other people's names on them, what can you do to avoid copycatting? You move from facts and old ideas to new ideas. In other words, you begin by inquiring what is *already* known about a subject, then, as you collect inferences and judgments, you begin to perceive fallacies, to form conclusions of your own, to reinforce or to change your working thesis. Here the range is infinite. Every old idea needs new assertion. Every new assertion needs judgment. Here you are in the area of values, where everyone is in favour of virtue but in doubt about what is virtuous. Your best area of research is in some controversial issue, where you can add, and document, a new judgment of "right" or "wrong." I have put it bluntly to save you from drowning in slips of paper.

Unless you have a working hypothesis to keep your purpose alive as you collect, or at least a clear question to be answered, you may collect forever, forever hoping for a purpose. If you have a thesis, you will learn—and then overcome—the temptations of collecting only the supporting evidence and ignoring the obverse facts and whispers of conscience. If further facts and good arguments persuade you to the other side, so much the better. You will be the stronger for it.

Persuade Your Reader You Are Right

You do not search primarily for facts. You do not aim to summarize everything ever said on the subject. You aim to persuade your reader that the thesis you believe in is right. You persuade him by (1) letting him see that you have been thoroughly around the subject and that you know what is known of it and thought of it, (2) showing him where the wrongs are wrong, and (3) citing the rights as right. *Your* opinion, *your* thesis, is what you are showing; all your quotations from all the authorities in the world are subservient to *your* demonstration. You are the reigning authority. You have, for the moment, the longest perspective and the last word. So, pick a thesis, and move into the library.

USING THE LIBRARY

Start with the Encyclopedias

Find the *Encyclopaedia Britannica,* and you are well on your way. The *Britannica* will survey your subject and guide you to your sources. It is not, usually, a basic source in itself, but each article will refer you, at the end, to several authorities. If someone's initials appear at the end, look them up in the contributors' list. The author of the article is an authority himself; you should mention him in your paper, and also look him up to see what books he has written on the subject. Furthermore, the contributors' list will name several works, which will swell your bibliography and aid your research. The index will also refer you to data scattered through all the volumes. Under "Medicine," for instance, it directs you to such topics as "Academies," "Hypnotism," "Licensing," "Mythology," and so on. The *Encyclopedia Canadiana, Collier's Encyclopedia,* and *Chambers's Encyclopaedia,* though less celebrated, will here and there challenge *Britannica's* reign, and the one-volume *Columbia Encyclopedia* is a fine shorter reference.

The *World Almanac and Book of Facts,* a paperbacked lode of news and statistics (issued yearly since 1868), can provide a factual nugget for almost any subject. Other good ones are *Webster's Biographical Dictionary,* the *Dictionary of Canadian Biography,* and *Webster's New Geographical Dictionary;* their concise entries lead quickly to thousands of people and places. And don't overlook the atlases: *The Times Atlas of the World, The National Atlas of Canada.* Another treasure-trove is *The Oxford English Dictionary* (twelve volumes and supplement—abbreviated *OED* in footnotes), which gives the date a word, like *highwayman,* first appeared in print, and traces changing usages through the years.

Explore your library's reference works. You will find many encyclopedias, outlines, atlases, and dictionaries providing more intensive coverage than the general works on the arts, history, philosophy, literature, the social sciences, the natural sciences, business, and the technologies. Instructors in subjects you may be exploring can guide you to the best references. For a list of Canadian reference sources, see 289–90.

Next Find the Card Catalogue

The catalogue's 3 × 5 cards list all the library's holdings—books, magazines, newspapers, atlases—and alphabetize (1) authors, (2) publications, and (3) general subjects, from *A* to *Z*. You will find *John Adams* and *The Anatomy of Melancholy* and *Atomic Energy,* in that order, in the *A* drawers. Page 151 illustrates the three kinds of cards (filed alphabetically) on which the card catalogue will list the same book—by author, by subject, and by title.

You will notice that the bottom of the card shows the Library of Congress's cataloguing number (Q175.W6517) and the number from the older, but still widely used, Dewey Decimal System (501). Your library will use one or the other to make its own "call number," typed in the upper left hand corner of its cards—the number you will put on your slip when you sign out the book.

Author Card: the "Main Entry"

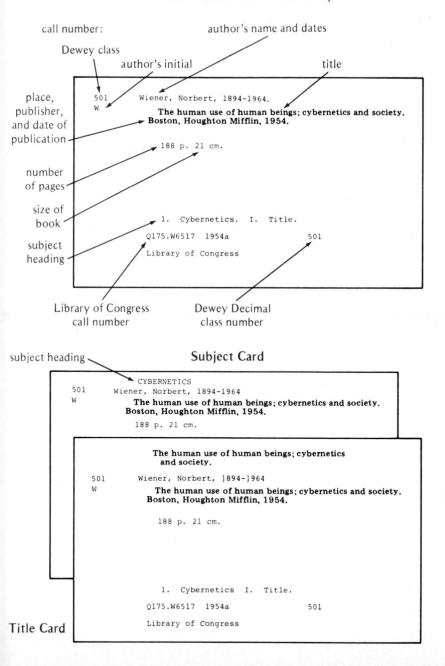

call number: author's name and dates

Dewey class

author's initial   title

place,
publisher,
and date of
publication

> 501
> W
>   Wiener, Norbert, 1894-1964.
>   The human use of human beings; cybernetics and society.
>   Boston, Houghton Mifflin, 1954.
>
>   188 p. 21 cm.

number
of pages

size of
book

subject
heading

>   1. Cybernetics.   I.   Title.
>
>   Q175.W6517 1954a   501
>
>   Library of Congress

Library of Congress
call number

Dewey Decimal
class number

subject heading

Subject Card

> CYBERNETICS
> 501   Wiener, Norbert, 1894-1964
> W   The human use of human beings; cybernetics and society.
>   Boston, Houghton Mifflin, 1954.
>
>   188 p. 21 cm.

>   The human use of human beings; cybernetics
>   and society.
> 501   Wiener, Norbert,]894-]964
> W   The human use of human beings; cybernetics and society.
>   Boston, Houghton Mifflin, 1954.
>
>   188 p. 21 cm.
>
>
>
>   1. Cybernetics I. Title.
>
>   Q175.W6517 1954a   501
>
>   Library of Congress

Title Card

Learn the Catalogue's Inner Arrangements

Since some alphabetical entries run on, drawer after drawer—
New York City, New York State, New York Times, for instance—knowing the arrangements *within* these entries will help you find your
book.

1. Not only men and women but organizations and institu-
   tions can be "authors" if they publish books or magazines.

   The Hudson's Bay Company
   The University of British Columbia
   The Department of External Affairs

2. Initial *A, An, The,* and their foreign equivalents (*Ein, El,
   Der, Une,* and so forth) are ignored in alphabetizing a title:
   A Long Day in a Short Life is alphabetized under *L*. But
   French surnames are treated as if they were one word: *De la
   Mare* as if *Delamare, La Rochefoucauld* as if *Larochefoucauld.*
3. Cards are usually alphabetized *word by word: Stock Market* comes before *Stockard* and *Stockbroker*. "Short before
   long" is another way of putting it, meaning that *Stock* and
   all its combinations with separate words precede the
   longer words beginning with *Stock-*. Whether a compound
   word is one or two makes the apparent disorder. Hy-
   phenations are treated as two words. The sequence would
   run thus:

   Stock
   Stock-Exchange Rulings
   Stock Market
   Stockard

4. Cards on one subject are arranged alphabetically by author. Under *Anatomy,* for instance, you will run from
   "Abernathy, John" to "Yutzy, Simon Menno," and then
   suddenly run into a title—*An Anatomy of Conformity*—which
   happens to be the next large alphabetical item after the
   subject *Anatomy.*

5. Identical names are arranged in the order (a) person, (b) titles and places, as they fall alphabetically.

MacDonald, J. E. H.   **Quebec (Province)**
Macdonald, Sir John A.   **Quebec, University of**
Macdonald College   **Quebec City**
Macdonald: His Life and World
   [by P. B. Waite]

"Quebec," the province, precedes the other "Quebecs" because "Province" (which appears on the card only in parentheses) is not treated as part of its name. "The University of Quebec" precedes "Quebec City" because no words or letters actually follow the "Quebec" of its title.

6. Since *Mc, M', and Mac* are all filed as if they were *Mac,* they go by the letter following them: *M'Coy, McDermott, Machinery, MacKenzie.*

7. Other abbreviations are also filed as if spelled out: *Dr. Zhivago* would be filed as if beginning with *Doctor; St. Joan* as if with *Saint; Mrs. Miniver* as if with *Mistress*— except that many libraries now alphabetize *Mr.* and *Mrs.* as spelled, and *Ms.* has found its place in the alphabetizing.

8. Saints, popes, kings, and people are filed, in that order, by name and not by appellation (do not look under *Saint* for St. Paul, nor under *King* for King Henry VIII). The order would be:

Paul, Saint
Paul VI, Pope
Paul I, Emperor of Russia
Paul, Jean

9. An author's books are filed first by collected works, then by individual titles. Different editions of the same title follow chronologically. Books *about* an author follow the books *by* him.

That is the system. Now you can thumb through the cards filed under your subject—"Cancer," or "Television," or

"Mowat"—to see what books your library has on it, and you can look up any authorities your encyclopedia has mentioned. Two or three of the most recent books will probably give you all you want, because each of these will refer you, by footnote and bibliography, to important previous works.

Find the Indexes to Periodicals and Newspapers

Indexes to periodicals do for articles what the card catalogue does for books. Some index by subjects only, others by subjects and authors. Begin with the *Reader's Guide to Periodical Literature*—an index of articles (and portraits and poems) in more than one hundred magazines. Again, take the most recent issue, look up your subject, and make yourself a bibliographical card for each title—spelling out the abbreviations of titles and dates according to the key just inside the cover. If you don't spell them out fully, your cards may be mysteries to you when you sit down to write. You can drop back a few issues and years to collect more articles; and if your subject belongs to the recent past (after 1907), you can drop back to the right year and track your subject forward. (*Poole's Index to Periodical Literature* provides similar guidance to American and English periodicals from 1802 to 1906). The *Canadian Periodical Index* and *Canadian News Index* are useful guides to Canadian materials.

You can do the same with the *New York Times Index,* beginning with 1913. It will probably lead you to news that appeared in any paper. The *Social Sciences Index* and the *Humanities Index* do for scholarly journals what the *Reader's Guide* does for the popular ones. (These two *Indexes* were the *International Index* [until 1965] and the *Social Sciences and Humanities Index* [until 1974].) If you are searching for an essay that may be in a book rather than a magazine, your guide is the *Essay and General Literature Index.* Add to these the *Book Review Digest* (since 1905), the *Biography Index* (which nicely collects scattered references), and the *Current Biography Index,* and you will probably need no more. But if you should need more, consult Constance M. Winchell's *Guide to Reference Books,* which is also a valuable guide to encyclopedias and dictionaries, and Dorothy Ryder's *Canadian Reference Sources.*

MAKING YOUR CARDS

Before you start toward the library, get some 3 × 5 cards for your bibliography. Plan on some ten or fifteen sources for your three thousand words of text. As you pick up an author or two, and some titles, start a bibliographical card for each: *one card for each title.* Leave space to the left to put in the call number later, and space at the top for a label of your own, if needed. Put the author (last name first) on one line, and the title of his work on the next, leaving space to fill in the details of publication when you get to the work itself—for books, place of publication, publisher, and date; for magazine articles, volume number, date, and pages. Italicize (that is, underscore) titles of books and magazines; put titles of articles *within* books and magazines in quotation marks. The card catalogue will supply the call numbers, and much of the other publishing data you need; but check and complete all your publishing data when you finally get the book or magazine in your hands, putting a light √ in pencil to assure yourself that your card is authoritative, that quotations are word for word and all your publishing data accurate, safe to check your finished paper against. Get the author's name as it appears on the title page, adding details in brackets, if helpful: Smith, D[elmar] P[rince]. Get all the information, to save repeated trips to the library. You will simplify some of the publishing data for your "Works Cited" (see 191–93), but get it all down now to be sure.

Take Brief Notes

Some people abhor putting notes on bibliographical cards. A separate card for bibliography and other cards for notes—written only on one side for ease of manipulation and viewing—are certainly more orderly and thorough. But the economy of taking notes directly on bibliographical cards is, I have found, well worth the slight clutter. Limiting yourself to what you can put on the front and back of one bibliographical card will restrain your notes to the sharp and manageable. You can always add another note card if you must. If you find one source offering a number of irresistible quotations, put each one separately on a 3 × 5 card (with author's name on each), so you can rearrange them later for writing.

However you do it, keep your notes brief. Read quickly, with an eye for the general idea and the telling point. Holding a clear thesis in mind will guide and limit your note taking. Some of your sources will need no more than the briefest summary: "Violently opposed, recommends complete abolition." This violent and undistinguished author will appear in your paper only among several others in a single footnote to one of your sentences: "Opposition, of course, has been tenacious and emphatic."[2]

Suppose you are writing a paper denying an interpretation of Louis Riel as a Saviour of minority rights. John Coulter, you find, says he is (Anthony 61). Here is a perfect piece of opposition, a *con,* to set your thesis against, to explain and qualify. But don't copy too much. Summarize the author's point, jot down some facts you might use, and copy down directly, within distinct quotation marks, only the most quotable phrases, such as his calling Riel a "dark and haunting symbol" (see Geraldine Anthony's quotation of Coulter, 184).

Take care with page numbers. When your passage runs from one page to the next—from 29 over onto 30, for instance—put "(29–30)" after it, *but also mark the exact point where the page changed.* You might want to use only part of the passage and then be uncertain as to which of the pages contained it. An inverted L-bracket and the number "30" after the last word of page 29, will do nicely: "All had ⌐30 occurred earlier." Do the same even when the page changes in midword with a hyphen: "having con-⌐21 vinced no one."

When preparing a research paper on a piece of literature, you would also make a bibliographical card for the edition you are using, and would probably need a number of note cards for summaries and quotations from the work itself—one card for each item, for convenience in sorting.

Take Care Against Plagiarism

If you borrow an idea, cite your source. If you have an idea of your own and then discover that someone has beaten you to it, swallow your disappointment and cite your predecessor. Or you can get back some of your own by saying, in a footnote, "I discover that Smith agrees with me on this point," explaining, if possible, what Smith has overlooked, or his differing emphasis. Your "Works Cited" will list Smith's article for all future reference. A danger lies in copying out phrases from your source as you summarize what it says, and then incorporating them in your essay, without remembering that those phrases are not yours. The solution is, again, to take down and mark quotations accurately in your notes, to summarize succinctly *in your own words,* as far away from the original as possible, and always to credit your sources.

YOUR FIRST DRAFT

Plot Your Course

Formal outlines, especially those made too early in the game, can take more time than they are worth, but a long paper with notes demands some planning. First, draft a beginning paragraph, incorporating your thesis. Then read through your notes, arranging them roughly in the order you think you will use them, getting the opposition off the street first. If your thesis is strongly argumentative, you can sort into three piles: *pro*'s, *con*'s, and *in-between*'s (often simple facts). Now, by way of outline, you can simply make three or four general headings on a sheet of paper, with ample space between, in which you can jot down your sources in the order, *pro* and *con,* that is best for your argument. Our paper on Louis Riel would block out something like this:

I. **Riel, the historical figure**

        PRO   **CON**

                                     Revising Riel's image (Morton)

      But other commentators (Pannekeok)

II. **Riel in Manitoba Riel's contribution (Thomas)**

                                   But Flanagan—Riel "inflexible." Execution of Scott (Morton)

III. Riel's mental state

Riel: self and cause
identified (Flanagan)
Streak of stubbornness
(Flanagan)
Unbalanced mind (Wallace)

Name "David"
(Flanagan)

IV. Riel in Saskatchewan
Métis situation and
the Battle of Batoche
—surveys and land
claims (Laurence
and Stanley)

The trial (Morton,
Flanagan)

The trial and
execution (Coulter,
Anthony, Stanley)

V. Confusion of views—
newspapers
Riel as mythical hero
(Montreal Gazette,
Winnipeg Free Press)

Riel as mythical rebel
(Toronto Star)

VI. The real Riel—a
mystery

Outline More Fully for the Finished Product

You can easily refine this rough blocking into a full topic outline,
one that displays your points logically, not necessarily in the
actual sequence of your writing. You can make this outline best
after your first draft has stretched and squeezed your material

into handsomer shape. The principle of outlining is to rank equivalent headings—keeping your headings all as nouns, or noun phrases, to make the ranks apparent as in the full outline of our sample paper (171).

But *begin to write soon.* You have already begun to write, of course, in getting your thesis down on paper, and then drafting a first paragraph to hold it. Now that you have blocked out your argument or your course, however roughly, plunge into your first draft.

Put in Your References as You Go

The Modern Language Association of America, in conformity with many journals in the social sciences and sciences, recommends a system of citations that simplifies your job considerably. A list of "Works Cited" at the end of your paper—the usual bibliography—now replaces all footnotes merely identifying a work. Previously, on first mention, you would have made the following footnote:

> [1]**Thomas Flanagan,** *Louis "David" Riel* **(Toronto: University of Toronto Press, 1979), p. 29.**

Now you save all that for your "Works Cited," where you would have had to repeat it anyway. You skip the footnote altogether, putting in your paper no more than the author's name and the page number, omitting the old and unnecessary *p.:*

> **The handling of the Scott execution, for Flanagan, shows Riel to have been "inflexible"** (*Louis* **29).**

If you have two Flanagan entries, as in the above example, simply include a short title in addition to the usual page number. More details on the new system will follow in a moment. But the old problem of handling footnotes and numbering them in your first draft has vanished. All you do is mention your author's name— last name alone suffices—and then add the page number in parenthesis where you usually would have put a footnote number. Now you limit your footnotes to your own commentary or explanation, which of course may include other authors and even quotations handled in the same way. These few footnotes you may type directly into your draft, surrounding them with triple parentheses: (((. . .)))—the easiest distinction you can make.

YOUR FINAL DRAFT

Reset Your Long Quotations

Your final draft will change in many ways, as the rewriting polishes up your phrases and turns up new and better ideas. But some changes are merely presentational. The triple parentheses of your first draft will disappear, along with the quotation marks around the *long* quotations, since you will single-space and indent, *without quotation marks,* all quotations of more than fifty words, to simulate the appearance of a printed page. You will do the same with shorter quotations, if you want to give them special emphasis, and also with passages of poetry. Some instructors prefer, and some handbooks recommend, that you double-space your long inset quotations, setting them off by triple spacing, above and below, as you would in an essay submitted for publication.

Differentiate Those Page Numbers

Notice that you cite, or quote, in three different ways: (1) indirect quotation or reference, (2) direct quotation in your running text, (3) direct quotation set apart from your running text and single-spaced. Accordingly, you punctuate the page-parenthesis in three slightly different ways.

1. With an indirect quotation or reference, you simply include the parenthesis, like any parenthesis, *within* the sentence, or within the phrase—that is, *before* any and all punctuation marks:

  . . . as Anderson (291) and others believe, but not. . . .

  . . . as others, including Anderson (291), believe.

  Anderson believes the evidence inconclusive (291).

2. With a direct quotation in your running text, put the page-parenthesis *after* the closing quotation mark but *before* the punctuation, thus including the parenthesis within *your* sentence.

  He thinks them "quite daffy" (213), but concedes. . . .

  As Belweather says, "Many of these proposals for investigation are quite daffy" (213).

3. But when you inset and single-space a quotation, you *omit* quotation marks, and put the page-parenthesis *after* the final period and a few spaces farther along—with no period following it:

  . . . a culture, a commonly shared, learned, and remembered history as a group, which it transmits through the generations. (218)

What if an author has more than one work? I repeat for clarity. Simply devise a short label for each. Suppose Samuelson has both a book and an article you want to cite—I'm making these up: *Physiological Differences in Simian Primates* and "The Oral and Nasal Physiology of *Pongo Pygmaeus.*" Your reference then might read: Samuelson finds the neocortex inadequate for language (*Physiological* 291), and ". . . the larynx is too high" ("Oral" 13).

THE DETAILS OF "WORKS CITED"

Handle with care so that your readers can find what you found, and you too can find it again. Note that the new system condenses most publishers' names: "Holt, Rinehart and Winston" becomes "Holt"; "Dunne Press, Inc." becomes "Dunne"; "Alfred A. Knopf" became "Knopf." Spacing is like this:

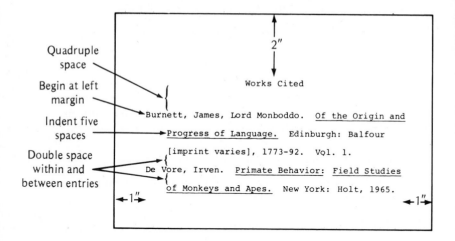

Books

You indicate books that give no place or date of publication as follows:

Segal, Annette. *The Question of Rights.* **N.p.: Bell, n.d.**

When listing other works by the same author, use three hyphens and a period instead of repeating the name:

Two Authors; More Than One Entry for Same Author(s)

Jones, Bingham, and Samuel Maher. *The Kinescopic Arts and Sciences.* **Princeton: Little House, 1970.**

---. **"Television and Vision: The Case for Governmental Control."** *Independent Review* **7 (1969): 18–31.**

Jones and Maher also wrote the second entry, which alphabetizes second with its *T* following the *K* of *Kinescopic.* If Jones alone had written "Television and Vision," it would come first, with his name in full, and the "Kinescopic" entry would follow as it stands.

Books that are monographs in a series look like this:

Thornbury, Ethel Margaret. *Henry Fielding's Theory of the Comic Prose Epic.* **Univ. of Wisconsin Studies in Language and Literature, no. 37. Madison, Wis.: U. of Wisconsin P., 1931.**

Magazines

With scholarly journals that number their pages consecutively throughout the year, you give volume number, the year, and the pages an article covers, with no comma following title and all in Arabic numbers, but with spaces between numbers and punctuations:

> **Solovyov, Vladimir. "The Paradox of Russian Vodka."**
> *Michigan Quarterly Review* **21 (1982): 406–19.**

With weekly and monthly magazines that begin numbering their pages anew with each issue, give the full date:

> **Hahn, Emily. "Getting Through to Others." Part 1.** *The New*
> *Yorker* **17 Apr. 1978: 38–103.**

Newspapers

Newspaper articles sometimes need more detail. Alphabetize by title—by *Trouble* in the following item:

> **"The Trouble with Fiction" (editorial).** *New York Times* **10**
> **Apr. 1984: 4.8.**

You have added "editorial" in parenthesis after the quotation marks but before the period. Here again the full date is necessary. The "4.8" indicates "Section 4, page 8." With newspapers that letter their sections—*A, B, C, D*—give the letter and page-number, just as it appears in the newspaper—*8B* or *D*-4.

If the article has a byline, you include the author. If the article is mostly an interview with one authority, bracket that authority as your key, since you will be quoting him in your essay:

> **[Mills, Jay.] "Chipmunks Are Funny People." Associated**
> **Press News Release.** *Back Creek Evening Star* **15 Oct.**
> **1983: D4, D8.**

Source Within Source

When you find a useful quotation, or a complete essay, within another source or collection, include both in your "Works Cited."

> **Caldwell, Abraham B. "The Case for a Streaming Con-
> sciousness."** *American Questioner* **62 (1979): 37–49. Qtd.
> Mendenhall.**

You then also cite Mendenhall fully in your "Works Cited."

> **Small, David R. "The Telephone and Urbanization." In** *An-
> nals of American Communication:* **401–18.**

Again, cite the *Annals* fully in your "Works Cited." You may
simplify citations of articles in encyclopedias.

> **Peters, Arnold. "Medicine."** *Encyclopaedia Britannica.* **11th
> ed. 1911.**

> **"Jackal."** *Encyclopaedia Britannica: Micropaedia.* **1980 ed.**

You need neither volume nor page numbers in alphabetized
encyclopedias, only the edition you are citing. The entry on
"Medicine" was initialed "A.P.," and you have looked up the
author's name in the contributors' list. The article on the
"Jackal" was anonymous, to be alphabetized in your "Works
Cited" under *J.*

Editions

Alphabetize editions by the author's name, but cite the editor:

> **Shakespeare, William.** *Romeo and Juliet.* **In** *An Essential
> Shakespeare.* **Ed. Russell Fraser. New York: Prentice-
> Hall, 1972.**

But alphabetize by the editor, when you have referred to his
introduction and notes:

> **Cowley, Malcolm, ed.** *The Portable Hawthorne.* **With intro-
> duction and notes. New York: Viking, 1948.**

> **Quackenbush, Colby. Afterword** *The Scarlet Letter.* **By Na-
> thaniel Hawthorne. New York: Dunne, 1983.**

In the second entry, Quackenbush has contributed only an "Afterword" with no editor specified, and you have referred only to
his remarks. If, on the other hand, you quote from both the novel
and Quackenbush, you would list by *Hawthorne:*

Hawthorne, Nathaniel. *The Scarlet Letter.* With afterword by
Colby Quackenbush. New York: Dunne, 1983.

Other Details

Gillies, George L. "Henry Smith's 'Electra.' " *Speculation* 2
(1881): 490–98.

This example shows where to put the period when the title of an
article ends in a quotation. The original title would have had
double quotation marks around the poem.

Schwartz, P[aul] F[riedrich]. *A Quartet of Thoughts.* New
York: Appleton, 1943.

[Lewes, George H.] "Percy Bysshe Shelley." *Westminster
Review* 35 (1841): 303–44.

These entries bracket useful details not appearing in the published work. Keep famous initials as initials: T. S. Eliot, H. G.
Wells, D. H. Lawrence.

Pamphlets and other oddities require common sense:

"The Reading Problem." Mimeographed pamphlet. Center
City, Arkansas: Concerned Parents Committee, 25 Dec.
1979.

Racial Integration. House Committee on Health, Education,
and Welfare, U. S. Congress, 101st Cong., 2nd sess.,
1969, H. Rep. 391 to accompany H. R. 6128.*

Briefly include the details to help others hunt them down.

Recordings, films, and tapes also require some ingenuity.
Do not cite microfilms and other reproductions of things in
print. Simply cite the book, article, or newspaper as if you had
it in hand. But other media are forms of publication in themselves, to be cited as clearly as possible if you use them. The
American Library Association recommends the following ways
of citation.†

---

*For recalcitrant cases, the current edition of *Style Manual,* U. S. Government
Printing Office, is helpful.

†Eugene B. Fleischer, *Style Manual for Citing Microform and Nonprint Media* (Chicago: American Library Association, 1978).

DISC

O'Neill, Eugene. *Long Day's Journey into Night.* **Sound Recording. Caedmon, 1972. 3 discs TRS350. Disc 3, Side 2.**

CASSETTE

Bogard, Charles. *"Ree-deep, ribbid": Herpetologist Charles Bogard Studies the Frog and Its Call.* **Sound Recording. Center for Cassette Studies, 1971. Cassette 010 13460.**

Other non-print items follow the same pattern, with the square brackets containing "[Motion Picture]" or "[Filmstrip]" to indicate the kind.

Omit Unnecessary Abbreviations

DO NOT USE these old favorites:

ibid.—*ibidem* ("in the same place"), meaning the title and page recently cited. Instead, *use the author's last name and page,* preferably phrased as part of your text: ". . . as Claeburn also makes clear (28)."

op. cit.—*opere citato* ("in the work cited"), meaning a work referred to again after several others have intervened. Again, *use the author's last name and page:* ". . . too small for vocalization (Adams 911)."

loc. cit.—*loco citato* ("in the place cited"). Simply repeat the page number: ". . . as Smith says (31). He cites, however, some notable exceptions (31)."

p., pp.—"page, pages." These old standbys are now redundant: *Omit them completely.* As we have seen, the number alone within parentheses suffices in the text, as it does in "Works Cited" as well.

l., ll.—"line, lines." These you would probably not need anyway, since they concern certain kinds of literary and textual scholarship, but, as you see, they are confusing, since they look like the numerals 1 and 11. If you ever need them, just write "line" and "lines."

Use Only the Convenient Abbreviations

The following conventional abbreviations remain useful (do *not* italicize them):

cf.—*confer* ("bring together," or "compare"); do not use for "see."

et al.—*et alii* ("and others"); does not mean "and all"; use after the first author in multiple authorships: "Ronald Elkins et al."

Two more Latin terms, also not italicized, are equally handy:

passim—Not an abbreviation, but a Latin word meaning "throughout the work; here and there." Use when a writer makes the same point in many places within a single work; use also for statistics you have compiled from observations and tables scattered throughout his work.

sic—a Latin word meaning "so"; "this is so"; always in brackets—[sic]—because used only within quotations following some misspelling or other surprising detail to show that it really was there, was "so" in the original and that the mistake is not yours.

Other useful abbreviations are:

c. or **ca.**	*circa,* "about" (c. 1709)
ch., chs.	chapter, chapters, with Arabic numerals, "ch. 12."
ed.	edited by, edition, editor
ms., mss.	manuscript, manuscripts
n.d.	no date given
n.p.	no place of publication given
rev.	revised
tr., trans.	translated by
vol., vols.	volume, volumes (use only with books: *Forsythe Saga,* vol. 3.)

A footnote using some of these might go like this:

[3]See Donald Allenberg et al., *Population* 308–12; cf. Weiss 60. Dillon, passim, takes a position even more conservative than Weiss's. See also A. H. Hawkins 71–83 and ch. 10. Records sufficient for broad comparisons begin only ca. 1850.

Abbreviate Books of the Bible, Even the First Time

The Bible and its books, though capitalized as ordinary titles, are never italicized. Spell them out in your running text: "The Bible begins with Genesis." You refer to them also directly in your text, within parentheses—abbreviated, with no commas, and with Arabic numerals: Mark 16.6; Jer. 4.24; 1 Sam. 18.33. No comma—only a space—separates name from numbers; periods separate the numbers, *with no spacing.* The dictionary gives the accepted abbreviations: Gen., Exod., Lev., Deut. Make biblical references like this:

> **There is still nothing new under the sun (Eccl. 1.9); man still does not live by bread alone (Matt. 4.4).**
>
> **As Ecclesiastes tells us, "there is no new thing under the sun" (1.9).**

Abbreviate Plays and Long Poems After First Mention

After first mention, handle plays and long poems like biblical citations. Your "Works Cited" will contain the edition you are using. Italicize the title (underscore on typewriter or in handwriting): Merch. 2.4.72–75 (this is *The Merchant of Venice,* Act II, scene iv, lines 72–75), Caesar 5.3.6, Ham. 1.1.23; Iliad 9.93 (=Book IX, line 93), PL 4.918 (=*Paradise Lost,* Book IV, line 918). Notice: no comma between short-title and numbers; periods and no spaces between numbers. Use the numbers alone if you have already mentioned the title, or have clearly implied it, as in repeated quotations from the same work.

For the most part, I have based these instructions on the *MLA Handbook for Writers of Research Papers,* second edition (1984), compiled by the Modern Language Association of America following the customs for work in literature and the humanities. The social and natural sciences use slightly different conventions; for papers in the social and natural sciences, consult your instructor about the correct style, or style manual, to follow.

A good general manual is the current edition of Kate L. Turabian, *A Manual for Writers of Term Papers, Theses, and Dissertations* (Chicago and London: The University of Chicago Press). A larger reference popular with scholars is *A Manual of Style* (the "Chicago Style Manual"), also published by the University of Chicago Press. Both the *MLA Handbook* and the Chicago *Manual* list other manuals for the various disciplines—engineering, geology, linguistics, psychology, and medicine, for example.

SAMPLE RESEARCH PAPER

Here is a complete research paper, with everything laid out in typescript and properly spaced, as if you had done it. The writer has followed out his own interest in Canadian history, as anyone might explore an interest in automobiles, kites, piccolos, or whatever. The writer has found a lively argumentative area, right down the alley of his personal interest in Louis Riel's role in the development of Canada. The back of the first page shows note-cards for his first three citations, each one different: (1) a summarized reference, (2) a full quotation, single-spaced and inset, (3) a brief quotation followed by summarized information.

Our paper combines title-page with outline. Perhaps more common is the separate title-page. Notice especially how the three footnotes contain only authorial amplification (173, 183), and how the writer easily refers to his sources, both in his footnotes and in his text. To set up a separate title-page, centre the title four inches down from the top, with capitals and small letters—NOT all in capitals:

Was Riel a Madman or a Hero?

[quadruple space]

Michel Laflamme

[12 to 15 lines of space]

English 0312

Prof. Gamache

April 1985

Notice also the spacing of "Works Cited," with the hanging indentation five spaces in for clear distinction, but otherwise everything double-spaced (191–93). Anonymous titles fall into alphabetical place among the alphabetized authors, with no "Anon."
crowding them all in at first.

Michel Laflamme
English 0312
Professor Gamache
April 1, 1985

Was Riel a Madman or a Hero?

Thesis: Although both his defenders and detractors may remain
        unconvinced, the evidence suggests that Louis Riel
        was neither an unblemished hero and martyr nor an
        insane revolutionary, and that the myth has, in fact,
        far outdistanced the reality of his character and
        deeds.

  I. Riel, the historical figure: the conflicting views of
      him and his actions
 II. His role in Manitoba
      A. The establishment of the province, 1869-70
          1. The Métis vs. the new settlers
          2. The Manitoba Act
      B. The execution of Scott
      C. The loss of power and exile
III. Riel's mental problems
 IV. Riel in Saskatchewan
      A. His mental state
      B. The Battle of Batoche
      C. Trial and execution
  V. The real Riel vs. the myth

Riel's Trial, Con.

Riel's trial was not a travesty but was well
run and honestly conducted.

Morton, "Reflections" F2

Riel revised.   Con

"Each generation rewrites history to suit its own
purposes and Riel, as a man with a powerful
sense of his own importance, might well
be satisfied that he is getting his due. But
other ancestors also have their rights."

Morton, "Reflections" F2

Riel's Trial. Pro

He was convicted by the jury "after one hour and
twenty minutes deliberation." A juror, fifty
years later, said "We tried Riel for treason
and he was hanged for the murder of
Scott."

Stanley, _Patriot_ 22

Was Riel a Madman or a Hero?

Louis Riel, leader of the Métis uprisings
in later nineteenth-century Manitoba and Saskat-
hewan, has been characterized as both hero and
madman, seditionist and political idealist. In
recent years, with the growth of the human
rights movement in North America and the concom-
mitant growth of consciousness of minorities and
their often oppressed situations, Riel's character and career have undergone reassessment,
some claim revision, in order to rectify what
has been called, by Riel's current defenders, a
grave misrepresentation of history. The treatment of Riel, and of the Métis generally, is
singled out as a clear instance of Canadian
racism and a chronicle of injustice.[1] Perhaps
these claims are true, but their truth or
falsity do not necessarily clarify the truth

Opening
Invitation

(Funneling to)

---

[1] This conflict of views has been discussed
often, in particular by Hartwell Bowsfield in
the selection of essays he edited, Louis Riel:
The Rebel and the Hero and in Louis Riel: Rebel
of the Western Frontier or Victim of Politics
and Prejudice; George F. G. Stanley in his
pamphlet Louis Riel: Patriot or Rebel is also
useful.

2
M. Laflamme
Eng. 0312

Thesis   about the enigmatic Riel. Although both his

defenders and his detractors may remain uncon-

vinced, the evidence suggests that he was really

neither an unblemished hero nor an insane revo-

lutionary; his myth has, in fact, far outdis-

tanced the reality of his character and deeds.

Opposition: The case against Riel has been developed
Con

from a number of sources; among the more impor-

tant are the historical record, as interpreted

by writers convinced of the efficacy of a Cana-

dian national destiny and of the dangers of Riel's

vision for the Métis people, and the evidence

of Riel's personal life, including his psycho-

logical breakdown, which reflects the image of a

Pro   very complex and troubled personality. But the

same sources have also been used to argue Riel's

heroism and to prove he was driven by the highest

of ideals. His detractors consider such readings

of the record, however, as attempts to revise

history. Desmond Morton, for example, considers

Con   the reassessment of the Riel case revisionist:

Newspaper   Each generation rewrites history to suit its
Source Cited   own purposes and Riel, as a man with a
with Short   powerful sense of his own importance, might
Title and   well be satisfied that he is getting his
Page in   due. But other ancestors also have their
Parenthesis   rights. If Canadians in 1985 want to pardon

3
M. Laflamme
Eng. 0312

> Riel to please voters in Quebec or the West,
> they should not harbor the illusion that
> they are righting some savage injustice of
> the past. ("Reflections" F 2)

For Morton, evidently the actions of Riel, as a

leader of the Métis people during the events in

Manitoba preceding its establishment, in 1870,

as a Canadian province and in Saskatchewan in

1885, leading to his trial and execution for

"levying war upon Her Majesty"—high treason—

justified the treatment accorded him by the

Government of Canada and its leader, Sir John A.

Macdonald.

But other commentators vigorously disagree

with Morton's kind of assessment, urging the

view that Riel's goals in both Manitoba and

Saskatchewan were reasonable and properly

motivated by a perception of what was best for

the Métis and for westerners generally. The

historian Fritz Pannekeok discusses the genuine

fear of the Métis that "union with Canada would

mean a Protestant supremacy" (67). He points out

that "bigots . . . sought to discredit the

Catholic Church, their morals and their

lifestyles, and the Canadians who invaded the

*Topic
Sentence
(Pro)*

*Quotation
Marks, Page
in
Parenthesis,
Period After*

[Métis] settlement in the later 1860s confirmed

Same Page
Repeated
the fears of the Métis" (67). The unrest of the

people of Assiniboia (the earlier name of the

territory) was also fueled by the realization of

the long-established residents "that although

their settlement was still isolated, it was the

object of expansionist aspirations on the part

Further
Evidence
of both the United States and Canada" (Thomas

737). New settlers were endangering the way of

life of the older inhabitants; little heed was

being paid to their needs and fears, or to the

conflicts among racially, linguistically, and

religiously different groups, each seeking to

establish itself while antagonizing the others.

Topic
Sentence
    In 1870, Riel was a major contributor to the

negotiations that produced the Manitoba Act of

the Canadian Parliament establishing the new

province, but because of his decision to sen-

tence to death Thomas Scott, a man "determined

to foment civil war to eliminate Métis power"

(Thomas 740), he destroyed any future he might

have had in the new province. He was driven into

Pro
exile. According to Lewis Thomas, the fears of

the Métis, those noted by Pannekeok, were

5
M. Laflamme
Eng. 0312

justified: the Ontario militia volunteers, in
Manitoba as part of a Canadian force sent to
establish order, "seemed bent on nothing short
of assassinating all the Métis" (742). They gave
vent to their anger over Scott's execution and
the hatred English Canadians harboured against
the French-speaking Métis. Riel, elected twice
to the Canadian Parliament as member for the
district of Provencher, was expelled from the
House of Commons, and, in 1875, he was banished
from the country for five years. This happened
despite the fact that, in 1871, he had offered
to help repel an attempted Fenian invasion with
the purpose to annex Manitoba to the United
States. He had supported Canada despite its
apparent rejection of him and the Métis people.
Thus, argue those who support Riel, he was a
victim of injustice and racism. However, other
evidence and interpretations of Riel's action in
Manitoba offered by Thomas Flanagan, a noted
Riel scholar, suggest a less positive view. The
handling of the Scott execution, for Flanagan,
shows Riel to have been "inflexible" (Louis 29).
He comments:

Further
Opposition
(Con)

6
M. Laflamme
Eng. 0312

> The execution was a ghastly mistake. For one
> thing it was morally repugnant because of
> the procedures followed. Scott was hastily
> tried for an unclear offense; he had no
> legal assistance nor did he enjoy any other
> benefits of fair play. He could not even
> understand the proceedings, which were
> conducted in French. The alleged legal
> deficiencies of Riel's own trial fifteen
> years later pale by comparison. (<u>Louis</u> 30)

In analyzing Riel's character, Flanagan also

suggests that idealism was not the only driving

motive behind Riel's actions: "Riel was an ambi-

tious man, but his ambition was fused with his

dedication to the cause of his people" (<u>Louis</u>

30). This fusion amounted to the identification

of Riel's self with his cause. Flanagan says,

"If the two [self and cause] become identified in

the mind of the individual, it becomes difficult,

even impossible, for him to remain objective

about himself. Any action, no matter how repre-

hensible it may seem to outsiders, can be justi-

fied for the sake of the cause" (<u>Louis</u> 30). So

it was that Riel ordered, unjustly and for evi-

dently political reasons (according to Flanagan)

to show that his "government possessed the sover-

eignty of a state" and to " 'make Canada respect

us' " [<u>Louis</u> 29]), that a man be put to death.

7
M. Laflamme
Eng. 0312

<u>This episode in Riel's life demonstrated his</u>   Topic
                                                            Sentence
<u>character.</u> In Flanagan's opinion, he had shown   (Con)

"considerable political acumen, as well as [an]

unfortunate streak of stubbornness. . . .

Unquestionably he enjoyed the role he played.

Politics was his natural métier, for it allowed

him to exercise his very great oratorical and

persuasive gifts. He also relished the exercise

of power and the prestige that went with it"

(<u>Louis</u> 31). It also suggests that there is some

truth in W. Stewart Wallace's assertion that

"Riel was a man of some ability, but of an

unbalanced mind" (631). By the time Manitoba

became Canada's fifth province, he was but

twenty-six years of age; his later activities as

leader of the 1885 uprising were the unfortunate

fulfillment of the promise of his youth.

The story of the Métis unrest in Saskatche-

wan in some ways repeats the Manitoba episode,

but with greater extremes of behaviour both by

Riel and by his opponents. <u>Again the evidence</u>   Thesis
                                                            Restated
<u>suggests that his actions cannot be interpreted</u>

<u>simply as those of a heroic leader or of an</u>

<u>egocentric madman.</u> According to Morton, "No one

else [other than Riel] had the capacity, the
influence or the imagination to orchestrate so
massive and dangerous an act of resistance to
Canada's transcontinental drive" ("Some" A 12).
This view seems to imply that, by resisting
Canada's expansion, Riel was behaving unreason-
ably. To the Métis of today "the battle Riel
waged against the federal government of 1885 is
still being fought" ("Métis" A 20). What he
fought, they say, was "against Ottawa's indifference to western grievances" ("Métis" A 20).
Each of these views has some supporting
evidence, but neither, alone, accurately or
justly explains Riel.

    After Riel left Manitoba for Montana in
1875, where he became an American citizen in
1883, he experienced a series of mental crises.
He had previous difficulties of this kind in his
early years, and in December 1874, during a
visit to Washington, D.C., he "had experienced a
mystical vision and an uncontrollable emotional

Evidence:
Specific
Illustration

seizure'' (Thomas 745). He was committed to
mental asylums of Longue Pointe and Beauport, in
Quebec, between 1876 and 1878, during which time

M. Laflamme
Eng. 0312

he adopted the name of "David," which he signed
with inverted commas—suggesting that this use
was metaphorical and that Riel was not suffering
a delusion.

In his essay on Riel's use of the name,
Flanagan suggests, with evidence to support the
possibility, that Louis may have chosen to use
"David" as an alias while a fugitive; or, perhaps, he chose that name because he saw similarities between himself and the biblical David and
between the Métis and the Jews (see "Louis
Riel's Name" 50-51). Whatever the reason, it is
clear he saw himself as a man with a mission—to
secure a land for his people and to establish a
peaceful relationship with non-francophones in
the West and in Eastern Canada. The course of
action he began early in 1885 was not intended
to start an armed conflict; according to Joseph
Kinsey Howard, Riel did not realize the
differences that existed between the situations
on the Saskatchewan and on the Red River:

> Actually, though none but a few of his
> intimates knew it, Riel had now decided upon
> a dangerous gamble—establishment of a
> Provisional Government under the protection
> of Métis cavalry, as he had done in Rupert's

Additional
Evidence:
Expert
Opinion
(Con)

Land. He looked upon this as a demonstration
rather than as an act of war, and it had
worked on Red River; he was convinced it was
the only way to bring Ottawa to terms. But
he was not thinking as clearly as he had
fifteen years before; his judgment had been
impaired by mental lapses, by years of
brooding exile, and perhaps most of all by
his emotional response to the enthusiasm
with which his people had received him in
Saskatchewan. (320)

If Howard is accurate, then Riel can hardly be

thought of as a conscious rebel leading his

people in fanatical dedication to an insane,

religious delusion. It was this interpretation

that, each for their own reasons, his defenders

and his enemies suggested at the time (see

Thomas 745). That Riel suffered from bouts of

intense emotional stress is clear; that he was

insane is not. He had been encouraged in the

religious conviction of his role as saviour of

his people by Bishop Bourget, and the need for

him to play this role was also confirmed by the

conviction of the Métis that "they had been

abandoned by everyone who had temporal power"

(Osler 186-187).

The loss of the Battle of Batoche had dire

consequences for Riel and for the Métis. Such

fears as the loss of their land resulting from

11
M. Laflamme
Eng. 0312

the surveys of 1869 in Manitoba and of the

surveys and the ignoring of their land claims in

Saskatchewan were only a pale foreshadowing of

what they had to fear after Batoche.[2] The

representation of the Métis heritage in the

twentieth century in such literary works as

Margaret Laurence's "The Loons," if they are

even only partly valid reflections of the

current situation, certainly argue the truth of

the Métis's fears in the nineteenth century.[3]

For Riel, the consequence was his execution.

Contem-
porary
Evidence

The trial of Riel has been discussed inces-

santly, beginning with a flurry of pamphlets

that began appearing soon after his execution,

highly emotional in their defence of the man and

also highly vigorous in attacking the Macdonald

government. Some sought to arouse American

sympathy, since Riel had become an American. The

Topic
Sentence

[2]A fuller discussion of these surveys and
land claims and the relevance to the Métis in
Manitoba and in Saskatchewan, and therefore to
Riel, is contained in George F. G. Stanley's
biography of Riel (see Louis Riel 57-59, 295-99).

Footnote
Citing Further
Evidence

[3]A list of twenty-nine literary works in
Lussier's collection of essays (see 198-200)
dealing with the Riel story is by no means
complete. It does not, in fact, include
Laurence's.

Amplifying
Footnote

government, predictably, published its own just-

ification, for example, the Interior Depart-

ment's "Facts," published in 1887. From the

extensive list included with the Dictionary of

Canadian Biography Riel entry, it would appear

that the controversy caused the Riel story very

early to lose its reality as an historical

event, to become part of the mythology of Canada—

with almost as many permutations as can be found

in Canadian society itself (see Thomas 751).

Contem-   Of all the things written about the Riel
porary
Evidence trial, however, none has had the range of

influence that John Coulter, the Irish-born

dramatist, created through his plays on the

subject, first performed in 1950, revived in

1975 and later broadcast on the CBC. According

to Geraldine Anthony, "Coulter's Canadian plays

emphasize that spirit of rebellion against

injustice so familiar to the heart of an Irish-

man" (61). He identified Riel's fight with that

of the Irish against the British. In the 1975

program notes, as quoted by Anthony, Coulter

called Riel a "dark and haunting symbol nagging

our political conscience. . . . I see in his

13
M. Laflamme
Eng. 0312

uprisings . . . the early beginnings of movements all over the world in which an emerging
people . . . insist on being left alone to
mature" (61). This assessment seems to ignore,
at the least, Riel's own expressed political
affinity for conservative rather than liberal
movements (see Flanagan, "Political Thought"
154-157). It is clear that these plays did much
to intensify the image of Riel as hero. After
they reawakened interest in an apparent protector
of an oppressed minority, particularly during
the era of activism against the oppression of
minorities of the sixties and seventies, the
Riel of history was further obscured. They led
to ceremonial honouring of Riel's burial place,
by today's Métis and today's politicians, as the
resting place of a "hero and martyr" deserving
of a posthumous pardon from today's Canadian
Parliament ("The Métis" B 4). It is this image
that is being defended by such moves as M. P.
Bill Yurko's private member's bill introduced in
1983 to grant Riel a pardon. According to Yurko,
the hanging of the Métis's Chief on Monday,
November 15, 1885, is "a blot on Canadian
justice" ("Independent" A 8).

But the research of such scholars as
Flanagan and Morton seem to lead to another
conclusion—that Riel's trial was not, as Coulter
represents it, a travesty, but was well run and
honestly conducted (see, e.g., Morton,
"Reflections" F 2). Thomas calls the treason
charge "a legal rationalization" (750), but even
his account suggests that Riel had a good chance
of avoiding a death sentence by following his
lawyer's advice—to build an insanity plea. Not
only did he not do as advised, he spoke in such
clear and impassioned terms on his own behalf

Pro   that he confounded all attempts to prove that he
was "not an accountable being, that he was
unable to distinguish between right and wrong on
political and religious subjects"—the judgment
of Francois Xavier Valade, one of the three
doctors appointed to examine him (Thomas 751).
He was convicted by the jury "after one hour and
twenty minutes [sic] deliberation" (Stanley,
Patriot 22). One of the jurors, fifty years
later, said, according to Stanley, "We tried
Riel for treason, and he was hanged for the
murder of Scott" (Patriot 23).

15
M. Laflamme
Eng. 0312

That the comment of the juror, if what he   Argument
(Con)
said was true, suggests Riel was unjustly hanged

is clear, but that juror was only one man

recalling distant events; he may well have been

falsely interpreting the jury's feelings. Even

if the jurors did feel he should die for killing

Scott, they may have been convinced at the trial

that he was also guilty of treason. According to

Morton, Riel's trial "was conducted . . . with

painful propriety and respect for law and

procedure as they existed in 1885. . . . The

verdict was inevitable" ("Reflections" F 2).

It is hard to deny, according to Stanley,   Further
Evidence
that the execution of Riel was "determined by   (Pro)

political expediency, that, in the final analy-

sis, it represented the careful assessment by

the Canadian government of the relative voting

strengths and political loyalties of the two

racial groups in Canada" (Patriot 23). It was

also reported that Macdonald had said, "He shall

hang . . . though every dog in Quebec bark in

his favour" (Stanley, Louis Riel 367). No doubt,

from the evidence given by Stanley (Louis Riel

421) of the Ontario pressure on Macdonald to

uphold the death sentence, the hatred of Protestant for Catholic and of Englishman for French-
man motivated many who influenced the Prime
Minister after the trial in Regina. No clear
picture, either of justice done for proper
reasons or of persecution and martyrdom, emerges
from a review of the evidence.

Thesis
Restated
    The confusion of views of Riel makes any
assessment of his proper place difficult. He has
become the hero of a number of camps: to the
Métis he is still a beloved leader; to many
French of Canada, he is the symbol of their
fight to preserve their language and culture; to
a number, he is the martyred victim of Ontario
Orangemen's hatred of Catholics and "Popery";
and to others, like John Coulter, he is the
symbol of the minorities' struggle to throw off
the oppression of a ruling class. A brief look
at recent newspaper accounts of reactions to
Riel's story, increasingly prominent because of
the 1985 centenary year of his death, reveals
the liveliness of each of the facets of the Riel
myth: in the Montreal Gazette it is noted that a
"school package [for Manitoba's French-language
schools] . . . concentrates on the role played by

17
M. Laflamme
Eng. 0312

Riel in the struggle for survival of franco-
phones in the West" ("Riel's Death" A 9); in
another issue of the same paper, the statements
of Métis leaders at his graveside call Riel "a
hero and a martyr" whose fight was for the Métis
("Homage" B 4). In a major Manitoba paper a
story was printed, during the separation refer-
endum campaign, giving an account of a group of
Oui supporters (attending a Canadian Labor Congress convention) who went to Riel's gravesite
and "honoured his gravestone with a few Oui
stickers and a couple of wreaths. . . . Louis
Leberge . . . [said], '. . . . To them, it was a
gesture that symbolized something. . . . Riel
asked for then what Quebecers are asking for
now' " ("Oui" WFP 2). And in the Toronto Star,
Michael Best reported the words of the
great-nephew of Riel: "He [Riel] was an honorable
man, who believed that what he was doing was for
the ultimate good of Canada as well as his
people. He shouldn't have been hung for that"
("Time" A 8). The remarks of the historian
Morton in the same paper (cited above) certainly
contrast with those of the young Riel and also
with the general tone of Best's article.

18
M. Laflamme
Eng. 0312

Expert
Opinions:
Summation

What does become apparent from all these

diverging views is that the real Louis Riel is

not their subject—it is the mythical Riel. An

historian referred to by Morton, Douglas Omran,

"noted a few years ago, Louis Riel has slowly

become the Canadian myth for all seasons"

("Reflections" F 2), and Stanley, Riel's bio-

grapher, said, "By historical accident rather

than by design he became the symbol of divisions

as old as the Franco-British struggle for the

control of North America" (Patriot 24). He also

seems to have come to symbolize divisions of our

times as well, as Coulter's view and dramatized

rendering of the Riel trial suggest.

Riel's own declared motives, in particular

those that sprang from his religious and basic-

ally conservative beliefs, have tended to fade

in the popular image of him. Realizations of

these facets of his life and deeds seem only to

be given importance by historical scholars.

Closing
Statements:
Conclusion
from
Evidence

Which Riel is more important seems to depend on

whether historical truth or dedication to a

cause he can be identified with is more impor-

tant. But even to the historian, the real Riel

remains something of a mystery.

19
M. Laflamme
Eng. 0312

Works Cited

Anthony, Geraldine. John Coulter. Boston: Twayne
     Publishers, 1976.

Best, "Time Changes Riel's Image from Villain to
     Hero." Toronto Star 24 July 1982: A 8.

Bowsfield, Hartwell, ed. Louis Riel: Rebel of
     the Western Frontier or Victim of Politics
     and Prejudice. Toronto: Copp Clark, 1969.

Campbell, Ron. "Oui Backers Visit Riel Grave."
     Winnipeg Free Press 8 May 1980:1.

Coulter, John. The Crime of Louis Riel. Toronto:
     Playwright's Co-op, 1976.

———. The Trial of Louis Riel. Ottawa: Oberon
     Press, 1968.

Flanagan, Thomas G. Louis "David" Riel:
     Prophet of the New World. Toronto:
     University of Toronto Press, 1979.

———. "Louis Riel's Name 'David,' " in A. S.
     Lussier: 48-65.

———. "The Political Thought of Louis Riel," in
     A. S. Lussier: 131-160.

Howard, Joseph. Strange Empire: The Story of
     Louis Riel. Toronto: Swan Publishing Co.,
     1952.

20
M. Laflamme
Eng. 0312

"Independent MP to Introduce Bill That Would
    Grant Riel a Pardon." Montreal Gazette 20
    September 1983: F 18.

Laurence, Margaret. "The Loons," A Bird in the
    House. Toronto: McClelland and Stewart,
    1974: 114-127.

Lussier, A. S., ed. Riel and the Métis: Riel
    Mini-Conference Papers. Winnipeg: Manitoba
    Metis Federation Press, 1979.

"The Métis Pay Homage to Riel at Annual
    Graveside Ceremony." Montreal Gazette 17
    November 1983: B 4.

"Métis Vow to Fight." Vancouver Sun 17 November
    1983: A 20.

Morton, Desmond. "Reflections on the Centenary
    of Louis Riel's Execution." The Sunday Star
    13 January 1985: F 2.

———. "Some Reflections on Louis Riel." Toronto
    Star 2 August 1982: A 12.

Osler, E. B. The Man Who Had to Hang: Louis
    Riel. Toronto: Longman's Green and Co., 1961.

Pannekeok, Fritz. "Some Comments on the Social
    Origins of the Riel Protest of 1869," in
    A. S. Lussier: 66-83.

"Riel Death to Be Remembered." Montreal

    Gazette 12 October 1984: A 9.

Stanley, George E. G. "Riel, Louis (David)"

    Encyclopedia Canadiana. 1966 ed.

———. "Riel, Louis." The Oxford Companion to

    Canadian History and Literature. Toronto:

    Oxford University Press, 1967: 712-713.

———. Louis Riel. Toronto: McGraw-Hill Ryerson

    Ltd., 1963.

———. Louis Riel, Patriot or Rebel? Ottawa:

    Canadian Historical Association Booklets,

    1970.

Thomas, Lewis H. "Riel." Dictionary of

    Canadian Biography, 1881-1890.

Wallace, W. Stewart. "Riel, Louis." The

    Macmillan Dictionary of Canadian Biography.

    London: Macmillan, 1963.

EXERCISES

1. *Consult the current* World Almanac and Book of Facts *for the date of some memorable event: the sinking of the* Titanic *or the* Lusitania, Lindbergh's *flight over the Atlantic, Canada's entry into war, the founding of the United Nations, the great stock-market crash, or the like. Now go to another collection, like* Facts on File, *and some of the other almanacs and yearbooks for the year of your event; write an essay entitled, let us say, "1929"—a synopsis of the monumental and the quaint for that year, as lively and interesting as you can make it.*

2. *Look up some event of the recent past (after 1913) in the* New York Times Index. *Write a paper on how the event is reported in the* Times *and in the other newspapers available in your library.*

3. *Choose a subject like the origin of man, the PLO, apartheid—anything that interests you—and compile a bibliographical list of the articles given in the* Reader's Guide, *beginning with the most recent issue and going backward in time until you have eight or ten titles. You may have to look under several headings, such as "archeology," "anthropology," and "evolution," for the origin of man; under "Israel," "Lebanon," and others in addition to "PLO" itself; and under "South Africa," "racism," and "apartheid" itself for apartheid. Then look in the scholarly* Indexes *(see 154), and make another bibliographical listing of your subject for the same period. Which articles appear in the* Humanities *or* Social Sciences Index *(or both) only? Which articles appear in the* Reader's Guide *only? Which appear in both the* Indexes *and the* Guide? *Write a brief commentary about the differences in coverage in these two (or three) indexes. What does comparing them tell you about research?*

4. *In the* Essay and General Literature Index, *look up three essays published in anthologies between 1965 and 1969 on Gerard Manley Hopkins, recording each entry and then following it by full data on the book, with call number, from the card catalogue.*

5. *Select some well-known literary work:* Barometer Rising, David Copperfield, Huckleberry Finn, Alice in Wonderland, The Wind in the Willows, A Farewell to Arms. *Describe how thoroughly it is catalogued by your library. Check cards for author, title, and subject. How many editions does the library have? Is the work contained within any* Works? *How many cards treat it as a subject? Does your library own a first edition? This last may require that you find the date of the first edition by looking up your author in an encyclopedia, checking available books about him, and perhaps checking in the British Library's* General Catalogue of Printed Books, *or, for a twentieth-century book,* United States Catalog of Printed Books, *or* Cumulative Book Index *to discover the earliest cataloguing.*

11
A Writer's Grammar

Theories of grammar have proliferated in the twentieth century, but the familiar nouns, verbs, adjectives, and other entities persist simply because they are the most handy. In spite of certain leaks in the system, traditional grammar can give writers the most help when they need it. Grammar tells us how sentences fit together meaningfully. On paper, we can see where the meanings slide. Here are some typical sliding sentences, each with slippage noted, each slippage discussed on the text pages given at the right.

They study hard, but *you* do not have to work all the time. [*You* does not agree with *They*.]	209–10
Hagar *goes* **east and** *learned* **about life.** [*Learned* does not agree in tense with *goes*.]	204
A *citizen* should support the government, but *they* should also be free to criticize it. [*They* does not agree with *citizen*.]	209–10
The *professor*, as well as the students, *were* glad the course was over. [*Were* does not agree with *professor*.]	200–02
As *he looked up*, a *light could be seen* in the window. [The subject has shifted awkwardly from *he* to *light*, and the verbal construction from active to passive.]	205

Now we knew: it was *him.* [*Him* does not agree   206
in case with the subject, *it.*]

Let's keep this between you and *I.* [*I* cannot be   207
the object of *between.*]

Can you and Shirley play doubles next Sunday   207
with *Bob and I?* [*I* cannot be the object of
with—with I?]

They accuse William Singleton Stone and *I* of   207
mismanaging their accounts. [*I* cannot be
the object of a verb—*accuse I?*]

The students always elect *whomever* is popular.   206
[*Whomever* cannot be the subject of the verb
is.]

She hated *me* leaving so early. [She hated not   208
me but the *leaving.*]

Bill told *Fred* that *he* failed the exam. [*He* can   212
mean either *Bill* or *Fred.*]

Each of the labourers performed *their* task.   209
[*Each* and *their* disagree in number.]

Father felt *badly.* [*Badly* describes Father's com-   210
petence, not his condition.]

He *spoke friendly.* [The verb requires an adverb,   210
like *warmly,* and *friendly,* though ending in
-ly, is an adjective, not an adverb.]

She said *on Tuesday* she *would call.* [The position   211–12
of *on Tuesday* confuses the times of *saying*
and *calling.*]

Walking to class, her *book* slipped from her   212
grasp. [*Walking* refers illogically to *book.*]

While *playing* the piano, the *dog* sat by me and   212
howled. [Dogs don't usually play pianos.]

With each of these, you sense that something is wrong. With a
little thought you can usually find the trouble. But what to do may
not be so readily apparent. We first need to understand something of the basic structure of grammar.

Know the Basic Parts of Speech

The parts of speech are the elements of the sentence. A grasp of the basic eight—nouns, pronouns, verbs, adjectives, adverbs, prepositions, conjunctions, and interjections—will give you a sense of the whole.

Nouns.   Nouns name something. A *proper noun* names a particular person, place, or thing. A *common noun* names a general class of things; a common noun naming a group as a single unit is a *collective noun*. A phrase or clause functioning as a noun is a *noun phrase* or a *noun clause*. Here are some examples:

> PROPER: **George, Halifax, Alberta, Europe, the British North America Act**
> COMMON: **stone, tree, house, girl, artist, nation, democracy**
> COLLECTIVE: **committee, family, quartet, herd, navy, clergy, kind**
> NOUN PHRASE: *Riding the surf* **takes stamina.**
> NOUN CLAUSE: *What you say* **may depend on** *how you say it.*

Pronouns.   As their name indicates, pronouns stand "for nouns." The noun a pronoun represents is called its *antecedent.* Pronouns may be classified as follows:

> PERSONAL *(standing for persons):* **I, you, he, she, we, they; me, him, her, us, them; his, our, and so on**
> POSSESSIVE *(indicating ownership):* **my, mine, yours, his, hers, ours, theirs, whose, its**—notice that none of them takes the usual possessive apostrophe-s: *ours* **not our's,** *its* **not it's.**
> REFLEXIVE *(turning the action back on the doer):* **I hurt** *myself.* **They enjoy** *themselves.*
> INTENSIVE *(emphasizing the doer):* **He** *himself* **said so.**
> RELATIVE *(linking subordinate clauses):* **who, which, that, whose, whomever, whichever, and so on**
> INTERROGATIVE *(beginning a question):* **who, which, what**
> DEMONSTRATIVE *(pointing to things):* **this, that, these, those, such**
> INDEFINITE *(standing for indefinite numbers of persons or things):* **any, each, few, some, anyone, no one, everyone, somebody, and so on**
> RECIPROCAL *(plural reflexives):* **each other, one another**

Note that pronouns describing nouns function as adjectives:

> PRONOUNS: *Few* would recognize *this.*
> PRONOUNS AS ADJECTIVES: *Few* readers would recognize *this* allusion.

Verbs.   Verbs express actions or states of being, present, past, or future. A verb may be *transitive,* requiring an object to complete the thought, or *intransitive,* requiring no object for completeness. Some verbs can function either transitively or intransitively. *Linking verbs* link the subject to a state of being.

> TRANSITIVE: He *put* his feet on the chair. She *sold* her old car. They *sang* a sad old song. She *lays* carpets.
> INTRANSITIVE: He *smiled.* She *cried.* They *sang* like birds. They *are coming.* He *lies* down.
> LINKING: He *is* happy. She *feels* angry. This *looks* bad. It *is* she.

Adjectives.   Adjectives narrow and specify nouns or pronouns. An *adjectival phrase* or *adjectival clause* functions in a sentence as a single adjective would.

> ADJECTIVES: The *red* house faces west. He was a *handsome* devil. The *old haunted* house was *empty.* We saw a *dancing* bear. We walked at a *leisurely* pace. *These* books belong to *that* student. [In the last example, demonstrative pronouns serve as adjectives.]
> ADJECTIVAL PHRASE: He had reached the end *of the book.*
> ADJECTIVAL CLAUSE: Here is the key *that unlocks the barn.*

Articles, which point out nouns, are classified with adjectives. *The,* the "definite" article, points to specific persons or things; *A* and *an,* the "indefinite" articles, point out persons or things as members of groups.

> ARTICLES: *The* hunter selected *a* rifle from *an* assortment.

Adverbs.   Adverbs describe verbs, adjectives, or other adverbs, completing the ideas of *how, how much, when,* and *where.* An *adverbial phrase* or *adverbial clause* functions as a single adverb would.

ADVERBS: **Though** *slightly* **fat, he runs** *quickly* **and plays** *extremely well.* **She runs** *fast.*
ADVERBIAL PHRASE: **He left** *after the others.* **He spoke** *with vigor.*
ADVERBIAL CLAUSE: **She lost the gloves** *after she left the store.*

Certain forms of verbs, alone or in phrases, serve as nouns, adjectives, and adverbs. *Participles* act as adjectives. *Present participles* are verbs plus *-ing,* and *past participles* are regular verbs plus *-ed* (see 273 for *Irregular verbs*). *Gerunds,* like present participles, are verbs plus *-ing* but work as nouns; past participles occasionally function as nouns, also. *Infinitives—to* plus a verb—serve as nouns, adjectives, or adverbs. Unlike participles and gerunds, infinitives can have subjects, which are always in the objective case.

PRESENT PARTICIPLES: *Feeling* **miserable and** *running* **a fever, she took to her bed.** [adjectives]
PAST PARTICIPLES: **The nurses treated the** *wounded* **soldier.** [adjective] **The nurses treated the** *wounded.* [noun]
GERUND PHRASE: *His going* **ended the friendship.** [noun, subject of sentence]
INFINITIVES: *To err* **is human;** *to forgive,* **divine.** [nouns, subjects of sentence]
I saw *him* [to] **go.** [phrase serving as noun, object of *saw; him* subject of *to go*]
Ford is the man *to watch.* [adjective]
Coiled, the snake waited *to strike.* [adverb]

Prepositions.   A preposition links a noun or pronoun to another word in the sentence. A preposition and its object form a *prepositional phrase,* which acts as an adjective or adverb:

By *late afternoon,* **Williams was exhausted.** [as adverb, modifying *was exhausted*]
He walked TO *his car* **and drove** FROM *the field.* [as adverbs, modifying *walked* and *drove*]
The repairman opened the base OF *the telephone.* [as adjective, modifying *base*]

Conjunctions.   Conjunctions join words, phrases, and clauses. *Coordinating* conjunctions—*and, but, or, nor, yet, so, still, for*—join equals:

> Mary *and* I won easily.
> Near the shore *but* far from home, the bottle floated.
> He was talented, *yet* he failed.
> Could you take Karl *and* me water-skiing.

Subordinating conjunctions attach clauses to the basic subject-and-verb:

> *Since* it was late, they left.
> He worked hard *because* he needed an *A.*
> They stopped *after* they reached the spring.

Interjections. Interjections interrupt the usual flow of the sentence to emphasize feelings:

> But, *oh,* the difference to me.
> Mr. Dowd, *alas,* has ignored the evidence.
> The consumer will suddenly discover that, *ouch,* his dollar
>   is cut in half.

AGREEMENT: NOUNS AND VERBS

Make Your Verb and Its Subject Agree

Match singulars with singulars, plurals with plurals. First, find the verb, since that names the action—*sways* in the following sentence: "The poplar tree *sways* in the wind, dropping yellow leaves on the lawn." Then ask *who* or *what* sways, and you have your simple subject: *tree,* a singular noun. Then make sure that your singular subject matches its singular verb. (A reminder: contrary to nouns, the majority of singular verbs end in *s*—the actor performs; actors perform.) You will have little trouble except when subject and verb are far apart, or when the number of the subject itself is doubtful. (Is *family* singular or plural? What about *none?* What about *neither he nor she?*)

Subject and Verb Widely Separated

FAULTY: *Revision* of their views about markets and averages *are* mandatory.

REVISED: *Revision* of their views about markets and averages *is* mandatory.

Sidestep the plural constructions that fall between your singular subject and its verb:

> FAULTY: The *attention* of the students *wander* out the window.   Mistaken
>
> REVISED: The *attention* of the students *wanders* out the window.   Plurals
>
> FAULTY: The *plaster*, as well as the floors, *need* repair.
>
> REVISED: The *plaster*, as well as the floors, *needs* repair.

Collective nouns *(committee, jury, herd, group, family, kind, quartet)* are usually considered single units in Canada (although often plural in British usage); give them singular verbs, or plural members:

> FAULTY: Her *family were* ready.   Collective
>
> REVISED: Her *family was* ready.   Nouns
>
> FAULTY: The *jury have disagreed* among themselves.
>
> REVISED: The *jurors have disagreed* among themselves.
>
> FAULTY: These *kind* of muffins *are* delicious.
>
> REVISED: *These muffins are* delicious.
>
> REVISED: *This kind* of muffin *is* delicious.

Watch out for the indefinite pronouns—*each, neither, anyone, everyone, no one, none, everybody, nobody.* Each of these is (not *are*) singular in idea, yet each one flirts with the crowd from which it singles out its idea: each of *these,* either of *them,* none of *them.* Give all of them singular verbs.

> *None* of these men *is* a failure.   Indefinite
>
> *None* of the class, even the best prepared, *wants* the test.   Pronouns
>
> *Everybody,* including the high-school kids, *goes* to Andy's Drive-In.
>
> *Neither* the right nor the left *supports* the issue.

None of them are is very common. From Shakespeare's time to ours, it has persisted alongside the more precise *none of them is,* which seems to have the edge in careful prose.

When one side of the *either-or* contrast is plural, you have a problem, conventionally solved by matching the verb to the nearer noun:

> **Either the players or the coach** *is* **bad.**   "Either-Or"

Since *players is* disturbs some feelings for plurality, the best solution is probably to switch your nouns:

> **Either the coach or the players *are* bad.**

When both sides of the contrast are plural, the verb is naturally also plural:

> **Neither the rights of man nor the needs of the commonwealth *are* relevant to the question.**

Don't let a plural noun in the predicate lure you into a plural verb:

> FAULTY: **His most faithful rooting *section are* his family and his girl.**
> REVISED: **His most faithful rooting *section is* his family and his girl.**
> REVISED: **His family and his girl *are* his best rooting section.**

ALIGNING THE VERBS

Verbs have *tense* (past, present, future), *mood* (indicative, imperative, subjunctive), and *voice* (active, passive). These can sometimes slip out of line, as your thought slips, so a review should be useful here:

Use the Tense That Best Expresses Your Idea

Each tense (from Latin *tempus,* meaning time) has its own virtues for expressing what you want your sentences to say. Use the *present tense,* of course, to express present action: "Now she *knows.* She *is leaving.*" Use the present also for habitual action: "He *sees* her every day," and for describing literary events: "Hamlet *finds* the king praying, but he *is* unable to act; he *lets* the opportunity slip." And use the present tense to express timeless facts: "The Greeks knew the world *is* round." The present can also serve for the future: "Classes begin next Monday." Apply the *past tense* to all action before the present:

> **One day I *was watching* television when the phone *rang;* it *was* the police.**
> **In the center of the cracked façade, the door *sagged;* rubble *lay* all around the foundations.**

Use the *future tense* for action expected after the present:

> **He *will finish* it next year.**
> **When he *finishes* next year, . . . [The present functioning as future]**
> **He *is going to finish* it next year. [The "present progressive" *is going* plus an infinitive, like to *finish,* commonly expresses the future.]**

Use the *present perfect tense* for action completed ("perfected") but relevant to the present moment:

> **I *have gone* there before.**
> **He *has sung* forty concerts.**
> **She *has driven* there every day.**

Use the *past perfect tense* to express "the past of the past":

> **"When we *arrived* [past], they *had finished* [past perfect]."**

Similarly, use the *future perfect tense* to express "the past of the future":

> **When we *arrive* [future], they *will have finished* [future perfect].**
> **You *will have worked* thirty hours by Christmas. [future perfect].**
> **The flare *will signal* [future] that he *has started* [perfect].**

Set your tense, then move your reader clearly forward or back from it as your thought requires:

> **Hamlet *finds* the king praying. He *had sworn* instant revenge the night before, but he *will achieve* it only by accident and about a week later. Here he *is* unable to act; he *loses* his best opportunity.**

Shifting tenses

But avoid mixtures like this: "Hamlet *finds* the king praying, but he *was* unable to act; he *let* the opportunity slip." Here, all the verbs should be in the present, corresponding to *finds*.

Confusing the past tense of *lie* with the verb *lay* is a frequent error. *Lie* is intransitive, taking no object: *Lie* down; I *lie* down; I *lay* down yesterday; I have *lain* down often. *Lay* is transitive, taking an object: I *lay* carpets; I *laid* one yesterday; I have *laid* them often. When someone says incorrectly "He is *laying* down," ask yourself the impudent questions "Who is Down?" or "Is he laying goosefeathers?"—and you might remember to say, and write: "He is *lying* down."

Keep Your Moods in Mind

The *indicative mood,* which indicates matters of fact (our usual verb and way of writing), and the *imperative mood,* which commands ("Do this," "Keep your moods in mind"), will give you no trouble. The *subjunctive mood,* which expresses an action or condition not asserted as actual fact, occasionally will. The conditional, provisional, wishful, suppositional ideas expressed by the subjunctive are usually subjoined (*subjunctus,* "yoked under") in subordinate clauses. The form of the verb is often plural, and often in past tense, even though the subject is singular, and the condition present or future.

> **He looked as if he *were* confident.**
> **If I *were* you, Miles, I would ask her myself.**
> **If this *be* error, and upon me [*be*] proved. . . .**
> ***Had* he *been* sure, he would have said so.**
> **I demand that he *make* restitution.**
> **I move that the nominations *be closed,* and that the secretary**
> **   *cast* a unanimous ballot.**

Don't let *would have* (colloquial *would've*) seep into your conditional clause from your main clause:

> FAULTY: **If he *would have known,* he never would have said**
> **   that.**
> REVISED: **If he *had known,* he never would have said that.**
> REVISED: **Had he *known,* he never would have said that.**

Be careful not to write *would of* or *should of* for *would have*
(would've) or *should have (should've)*.   "Would've"

Don't Mix Active and Passive Voice

One parting shot at our friend the passive. Avoid misaligning
active with passive in the same sentence:

> **As he *entered* the room, muttering *was heard* [he *heard*].**   Mixed voices
> **After they *laid out* the pattern, electric shears *were used* [they
> *used* electric shears].**

You can also think of this as an awkward shift of subject, from
he to *muttering,* from *they* to *shears.* Here is a slippery sample,
where the subject stays the same:

> FAULTY: **This plan *reduces* taxes and *has been used* success-
> fully in three other cities.**
> REVISED: **This plan *reduces* taxes and *has been* successful in**   Past tense;
> **three other cities.**   not passive
> REVISED: **This plan *reduces* taxes and *has proved* workable in**   voice
> **three other cities.**

REFERENCE OF PRONOUNS

Match Your Pronouns to What They Stand For

Pronouns stand for *(pro)* nouns. They *refer* to nouns already
expressed *(antecedents),* or they stand for conceptions (people,
things, ideas) already established or implied, as in *"None of
them* is perfect." Pronouns must agree with the singular and plural ideas they represent, and stand clearly as subjects or objects.

When a relative pronoun *(who, which, that)* is the subject of
a clause, it takes a singular verb if its antecedent is singular, a
plural verb if its antecedent is plural:

> Phil is the only *one* of our swimmers WHO *has* won three gold
> medals. [The antecedent is *one*, not *swimmers*.]
> Phil is one of the best *swimmers* WHO *have* ever been on the
> team. [The antecedent is *swimmers*, not *one*.]

Pronouns may stand either as subjects or objects of the action,
and their form changes accordingly.

Use Nominative Pronouns for Nominative Functions

Those pronouns in the predicate that refer to, or complement,
the subject are troublesome; keep them nominative:

Subjective   **He discovered that it was *I*.**
Complement   **It was *they* who signed the treaty.**

Another example is that of the pronoun in *apposition* with the
subject (that is, *positioned near, applied to,* and meaning the same
thing as, the subject):

Apposition   ***We* students would rather talk than sleep.**
with Subject

After *than* and *as,* the pronoun is usually the subject of an
implied verb:

Implied Verb   **She is taller than *I* [am].**
You are as bright as *he* [is].
She loves you as much as *I* [do].

But note: "She loves you as much as [she loves] *me.*" Match your
pronouns to what they stand for, subjects for subjects, objects for
objects. (But a caution: use an objective pronoun as the subject
of an infinitive. See 199, 208).

Use a nominative pronoun as subject of a noun clause. This
is the trickiest of pronominal problems, because the subject of
the clause also looks like the object of the main verb:

> FAULTY: The sergeant asked *whomever* did it to step for-
> ward.
> REVISED: The sergeant asked *whoever* did it to step forward.

Similarly, parenthetical remarks like *I think, he says,* and *we believe* often make pronouns seem objects when they are actually subjects:

FAULTY: **Ellen is the girl** *whom* **I think** *will succeed.*
REVISED: **Ellen is the girl** *who* **I think** *will succeed.*

Use Objective Pronouns for Objective Functions

Compound objects give most of the trouble. Try the pronoun by itself: "invited *me,*" "sent *him,*" and so forth. These are all correct:

The mayor invited my wife and *me* **to dinner.** [*not* **my wife and** *I*]   Compound Objects
Between *her* **and** *me,* **an understanding grew.**
They sent it to Stuart and *him.*
. . . for you and *me.*

Again, *see if the pronoun would stand by itself* ("for I"? No, *for me*):

FAULTY: **The credit goes to** *he* **who tries.** ["to he"?]
REVISED: **The credit goes to** *him* **who tries.**

Pronouns in apposition with objects must themselves be objective:

FAULTY: **The mayor complimented us both—Bill and** *I.*   Apposition with Object
REVISED: **The mayor complimented us both—Bill and** *me.*

FAULTY: **She gave the advice specifically to us—Helen and** *I.*
REVISED: **She gave the advice specifically to us—Helen and** *me.*

FAULTY: **Between us—Elaine and** *I*—**an understanding grew.**
REVISED: **Between us—Elaine and** *me*—**an understanding grew.**

FAULTY: **He would not think of letting** *we* **girls help him.**
REVISED: **He would not think of letting** *us* **girls help him.**

Notice this one:

> FAULTY: **Will you please help Leonard and *I* find the man-ager?**
> REVISED: **Will you please help Leonard and *me* find the man-ager?**

Leonard and me are objective both as objects of the verb *help* and
as subjects of the shortened infinitive *to find.* Subjects of infinitives are always in the objective case, as in "She saw *him* go";
"She helped *him* find his keys."

Use a Possessive Pronoun Before a Gerund

Since gerunds are *-ing* words used as nouns, the pronouns attached to them must say what they mean:

> FAULTY: **She disliked *him* hunting.**
> REVISED: **She disliked *his* hunting.**

The object of her dislike is not *him* but *hunting.*

Keep Your Antecedents Clear

If an antecedent is missing, ambiguous, vague, or remote, the
pronoun will suffer from "faulty reference."

> MISSING: **In Alberta *they* produce a lot of oil.**
> REVISED: **Alberta produces a lot of oil.**

> AMBIGUOUS: **Paul smashed into a girl's car *who* was visiting his sister.**
> REVISED: **Paul smashed into the car of a *girl* visiting his sister.**

> VAGUE: **Because Ann had never spoken before an audi-ence, she was afraid of *it.***
> REVISED: **Because Ann had never spoken before an audi-ence, she was afraid.**

REMOTE: The castle was built in 1537. The rooms and
furnishings are carefully kept up, but the entrance is now guarded by a coin-fed turnstile.
It still belongs to the Earl.

REVISED: The castle, which still belongs to the Earl, was
built in 1537. The rooms and furnishings are
carefully kept up, but the entrance is now
guarded by a coin-fed turnstile.

This poses a special problem, especially when heading a sentence
("This is a special problem"). Many good stylists insist that every
this refer back to a specific noun—*report* in the following example:

The commission submitted its *report. This* proved windy,   *"This"*
evasive, and ineffectual.

Others occasionally allow (as I do) a more colloquial *this,* referring back more broadly:

The commission submitted its report. This ended the matter.

Give an Indefinite or General Antecedent
a Singular Pronoun

FAULTY: *Each* of the students hoped to follow in *their*
teacher's footsteps.

REVISED: *Each* of the students hoped to follow in *his* [or *his*
or *her*] teacher's footsteps.

REVISED: *All* of the students hoped to follow in *their*
teacher's footsteps. [Here, we have a single class.]

FAULTY: If the *government* dares to face the new philosophy,
they should declare *themselves.*

REVISED: If the *government* dares to face the new philosophy,
it should declare *itself.*

Keep Person and Number Consistent

Don't slip from person to person *(I* to *they);* don't fall among
singulars and plurals—or you will get bad references:

FAULTY: *They* have reached an age when *you* should know better.

REVISED: *They* have reached an age when *they* should know better.

FAULTY: A motion *picture* can improve upon a book, but *they* usually do not.

REVISED: A motion *picture* can improve upon a book, but *it* usually does not.

MODIFIERS MISUSED AND MISPLACED

Keep Your Adjectives and Adverbs Straight

The adjective sometimes wrongly crowds out the adverb: "He played a *real* conservative game." And the adverb sometimes steals the adjective's place, especially when the linking verb looks transitive but isn't *(feels, looks, tastes, smells),* making the sense wrong: "He feels *badly*" (adverb) means incompetence, not misery. The cure is to modify your nouns with adjectives, and everything else with adverbs:

He played a *really* conservative game. [adverb]
He feels *bad*. [adjective]
This tastes *good*. [adjective]
I feel *good*. [adjective—spirit]
I feel *well*. [adjective—health]
This works *well*. [adverb]

Some words serve both as adjectives and adverbs: *early, late, near, far, hard, only, little, right, wrong, straight, well, better, best, fast,* for example, to be squeezed for their juice.

Think *little* of *little* things.

Near is a hard case, serving as an adjective *(the near future)* and as an adverb of place *(near the barn),* and then also trying to serve for *nearly,* the adverb of degree:

FAULTY: We are nowhere *near* knowledgeable enough.
REVISED: We are not *nearly* knowledgeable enough.

FAULTY: It was a *near* treasonous statement.
REVISED: It was a *nearly* treasonous statement.

FAULTY: With Dodge, he has a tie of *near-*filial rapport.
REVISED: With Dodge, he has an *almost* filial rapport.

Slow has a long history as an adverb, but *slowly* keeps the upper hand in print. Notice that adverbs usually go after, and adjectives before:

The *slow* freight went *slowly.*

Make Your Comparisons Complete

Ask yourself "Than what?"—when you find your sentences ending with a *greener* (adjective) or a *more smoothly* (adverb):

FAULTY: The western prairie is *flatter.*
REVISED: The western prairie is *flatter than* the northern tundra.

FAULTY: He plays more *skillfully.*
REVISED: He plays more *skillfully than* most boys his age.

FAULTY: Jane told her more than Ellen.
REVISED: Jane told her more than she told Ellen.

FAULTY: His income is lower than a *busboy.*
REVISED: His income is lower than a *busboy's.*

Don't Let Your Modifiers Squint

Some modifiers squint in two directions at once. Place them to modify one thing only.

FAULTY: They agreed *when both sides ceased fire* to open negotiations.
REVISED: They agreed to open negotiations *when both sides ceased fire.*

FAULTY: Several delegations *we know* have failed.
REVISED: *We know* that several delegations have failed.

FAULTY: They hoped to try *thoroughly* to understand.
REVISED: They hoped to try to understand *thoroughly*.

FAULTY: He resolved to *dependably* develop plans.
REVISED: He resolved to develop *dependable* plans.

Don't Let Your Modifiers or References Dangle

The *-ing* words (the gerunds and participles) tend to slip loose from the sentence and dangle, referring to nothing or the wrong thing.

FAULTY: Going home, the walk was slippery. [participle]
REVISED: Going home, I found the walk slippery.

FAULTY: When getting out of bed, his toe hit the dresser. [gerund]
REVISED: When getting out of bed, he hit his toe on the dresser.

Infinitive phrases also can dangle badly:

FAULTY: To think clearly, some logic is important.
REVISED: To think clearly, you should learn some logic.

Any phrase or clause may dangle:

FAULTY: When only a freshman [phrase], Jim's history teacher inspired him.
REVISED: When Jim was only a freshman, his history teacher inspired him.

FAULTY: After he had taught thirty years [clause], the average student still seemed average.
REVISED: After he had taught thirty years, he found the average student still average.

EXERCISES

1. *Straighten out these disagreements and misalignments:*

1. These kinds of questions are sheer absurdities.
2. Conservatism, as well as liberalism, are summonses for change in Canadian life, as we know it.
3. Neither the make of his car nor the price of his stereo impress us.
4. Her family were bitter about it.
5. The grazing ground of both the antelope and the wild horses are west of this range.
6. The campus, as well as the town, need to wake up.
7. The extinction of several species of whales are threatened.
8. None of the group, even Smith and Jones, want to play.
9. If I would have studied harder, I would have passed.
10. First he investigated the practical implications, and then the moral implications that were involved were examined.

2. *Revise these faulty pronouns, and their sentences where necessary:*

1. None of us are perfect.
2. Doug is the only one of the boys who always stand straight.
3. He took my wife and I to dinner.
4. She disliked him whistling the same old tune.
5. He will give the ticket to whomever wants it: he did it for you and I.
6. My mother insists on me buying my own clothes: the average girl likes their independence.

3. *Straighten out these adjectives and adverbs:*

1. The demonstration reached near riot proportions.
2. It smells awfully.
3. The dress fitted her perfect.
4. He has a reasonable good chance.
5. His car had a special built engine.

4. *Complete and adjust these partial thoughts.*

1. He swims more smoothly.
2. The pack of a paratrooper is lighter than a soldier.
3. The work of a student is more intense than his parents.

5. *Unsquint these modifiers:*

   1. She planned on the next day to call him.
   2. They asked after ten days to be notified.
   3. The party promised to completely attempt reform.
   4. Several expeditions we know have failed.

6. *Mend these danglers:*

   1. What we need is a file of engineers broken down by their specialties.
   2. Following the games on television, the batting average of every player was at his fingertips.
   3. When entering the room, the lamp fell over.
   4. After he arrived at the dorm, his father phoned.

7. *Correct the following:*

   1. No one likes dancing backward all their lives.
   2. His pass hit the wide receiver real good.
   3. The ball was laying under the bench.
   4. If they would of come earlier, they would of seen everything.
   5. I feel badly about it.

8. *Cure the following:*

   1. The professor as well as the students were glad the course was over.
   2. We study hard at university, but you do not have to work all the time.
   3. As he looked up, a light could be seen in the window.
   4. A citizen should support the government, but they should also be free to criticize it.
   5. She hated me leaving so early.
   6. This is one of the best essays that has been submitted.

12
Punctuation, Spelling, Capitalization

Punctuation gives the silent page some of the breath of life. It marks the pauses and emphases with which a speaker points his meaning. Loose punctuators forget what every good writer knows: that even silent reading produces an articulate murmur in our heads, that language springs from the breathing human voice, that the beauty and meaning of language depend on what the written word makes us *hear,* on the sentence's tuning of emphasis and pause. Commas, semicolons, colons, periods, and other punctuation transcribe our meaningful pauses to the printed page.

THE PERIOD: MARKING THE SENTENCE

A period marks a sentence, a subject completed in its verb:

She walked.

A phrase—which lacks a verb, though it may contain a verb *form* (see 199)—subordinates this idea, making it *depend* on some other main clause:

While walking, **she thought.**

A subordinate clause does the same, making the whole original sentence subordinate:

While she walked, **she thought.**

Like a period, and a question mark, an exclamation mark marks a sentence, but much more emphatically: *Plan to revise!* Use it sparingly if you want it to count rhetorically.

Take special care not to break off a phrase or clause with a period, making a fragment that looks like a sentence but isn't (unless you intend a rhetorical fragment—see 113–14, and don't use the comma as a period (see 225).

> FAULTY: **She dropped the cup. Which had cost twenty dollars.**
> REVISED: **She dropped the cup, which had cost twenty dollars.**

> FAULTY: **He swung furiously, the ball sailed into the lake.**
> REVISED: **He swung furiously. The ball sailed into the lake.**

THE COMMA

Here are the four basic commas:

> I. THE INTRODUCER—after introductory phrases and clauses.
> II. THE COORDINATOR—between "sentences" joined by *and, but, or, nor, yet, so, still, for.*
> III. THE INSERTER—a PAIR around any inserted word or remark.
> IV. THE LINKER—when adding words, phrases, or clauses.

I. The Introducer.   A comma after every introductory word or phrase makes your writing clearer, more alive with the breath and pause of meaning:

> **Indeed, the idea failed.**
> **After the first letter, she wrote again.**
> **In the autumn of the same year, he went to Paris.**

Without the introductory comma, your reader frequently expects something else:

> **After the first letter she wrote, she. . . .**
> **In the autumn of the same year he went to Paris, he. . . .**

But beware! What looks like an introductory phrase or clause may actually be the subject of the sentence *and should take no comma.* A comma can break up a good marriage of subject and verb. The comma in each of these is an interloper, and should be removed:

> **That handsome man in the ascot tie, is the groom.**
> **The idea that you should report every observation, is wrong.**
> **The realization that we must be slightly dishonest to be truly kind, comes to all of us sooner or later.**

If your clause-as-subject is unusually long, or confusing, you may relieve the pressure by inserting some qualifying remark after it, between two commas:

> **The idea that you should report every observation, *however insignificant,* is wrong.**
> **The realization that we must be slightly dishonest to be truly kind, *obviously the higher motive,* comes to all of us sooner or later.**

II. The Coordinator.   Between "sentences" joined by coordinate conjunctions. You will often see the comma omitted when your two clauses are short: "He hunted and she fished." But nothing is wrong with "He hunted, and she fished." The comma, in fact, shows the slight pause you make when you say it.

Think of the "comma-and" **(, and)** as a unit equivalent to the period. The period, the semicolon, and the "comma-and" **(, and)** all designate independent clauses—independent "sentences"— but give different emphases:

.   **He was tired. He went home.**
;   **He was tired; he went home.**
, and   **He was tired, and he went home.**

A comma tells your reader that another subject and predicate are coming:

> **He hunted the hills and dales.**
> **He hunted the hills, and she fished in the streams.**
> **She was naughty but nice.**
> **She was naughty, but that is not our business.**
> **Wear your jacket or coat.**
> **Wear your jacket, or you will catch cold.**
> **It was strong yet sweet.**
> **It was strong, yet it was not unpleasant.**

Of course, you may use a comma in *all* the examples above if your sense demands it. The contrasts set by *but, or,* and *yet* often urge a comma, and the even stronger contrasts with *not* and *either-or* demand a comma, whether or not full predication follows:

> **It was strong, yet sweet.**
> **It was a battle, not a game.**
> **. . . either a bird in the hand, or two in the bush.**

Commas signal where you would pause in speaking.

The meaningful pause also urges an occasional comma in compound predicates, usually not separated by commas:

> **He granted the usual permission and walked away.**
> **He granted the usual permission, and walked away.**

Both are correct. In the first sentence, however, the granting and walking are perfectly routine, and the temper unruffled. In the second, some kind of emotion has forced a pause, and a comma, after *permission.* Similarly, meaning itself may demand a comma between the two verbs:

> **He turned and dropped the vase.**
> **He turned, and dropped the vase.**

In the first sentence, he turned the vase; in the second, himself. Your , **and** in compound predicates suggests some touch of drama, some meaningful distinction, or afterthought.

You need a comma before *for* and *still* even more urgently. Without the comma, their conjunctive meaning changes; they assume their ordinary roles, *for* as a preposition, *still* as an adjective or adverb:

> **She liked him still. . . . [That is, either *yet* or *quiet!*]**
> **She liked him, still she could not marry him.**
> **She liked him for his money.**
> **She liked him, for a good man is hard to find.**

An observation: *for* is the weakest of all the coordinators. Almost a subordinator, it is perilously close to *because*. *For* can seem moronic if cause and effect are fairly obvious: "She liked him, for he was kind." Either make a point of the cause by full subordination—"She liked him *because* he was kind"—or flatter the reader with a semicolon: "She liked him; he was kind." *For* is effective only when the cause is somewhat hard to find: "Blessed are the meek, for they shall inherit the earth."

To summarize the basic point about the comma as coordinator: put a comma before the coordinator *(, and , but , or , nor , yet , so , still , for)* when joining independent clauses, and add others necessary for emphasis or clarity.

III. The Inserter.   Put a PAIR of commas around every inserted word, phrase, or clause—those expressions that seem parenthetical and are called "nonrestrictive." When you cut a sentence in two to insert something necessary, you need to tie off *both* ends, or your sentence will die on the table:

> **St. John's, Newfoundland looks promising. [, Newfoundland,]**
> **When he packs his bag, however he goes. [, however,]**
> **The car, an ancient Packard is still running. [, an ancient Packard,]**
> **April 10, 1985 is agreeable as a date for final payment. [, 1985,]**
> **John Jones, Jr. is wrong. [, Jr.,]**
> **I wish, Sandra you would do it. [, Sandra,]**

You do not mean that 1985 is agreeable, nor are you telling John Jones that Junior is wrong. Such parenthetical insertions need a PAIR of commas:

> **The case, *nevertheless*, was closed.**
> **She will see, *if she has any sense at all*, that he is right.**
> **Sam, *on the other hand*, may be wrong.**
> **Note, *for example*, the excellent brushwork.**
> **John Jones, *M.D.*, and Bill Jones, *Ph.D.*, doctored the punch to perfection.**
> **He stopped in Timmins, *Ontario*, for two hours.**

The same rule applies to all *nonrestrictive* remarks, phrases, and clauses—all elements simply additive, explanatory, and hence parenthetical:

> **John, *my friend*, will do what he can.**
> **Andy, *his project sunk, his hopes shattered*, was speechless.**
> **The taxes, *which are reasonable*, will be paid.**
> **That man, *who knows*, is not talking.**

Think of *nonrestrictive* as "nonessential" to your meaning, hence set off by commas. Think of *restrictive* as essential and "restricting" your meaning, hence not set off at all (use *which* for nonrestrictives, *that* for restrictives; see 124).

> **RESTRICTIVES:**
> **The taxes that are reasonable will be paid.**
> **Southpaws who are superstitious will not pitch on Friday nights.**
> **The man who knows is not talking.**
>
> **NONRESTRICTIVES:**
> **The taxes, which are reasonable, will be paid.**
> **Southpaws, who are superstitious, will not pitch on Friday nights.**
> **The man, who knows, is not talking.**

The difference between restrictives and nonrestrictives is one of meaning, and the comma-pair signals that meaning. How many grandmothers do I have in the first sentence below (restrictive)? How many in the second (nonrestrictive)?

My grandmother who smokes pot is ninety.
My grandmother, who smokes pot, is ninety.

In the first sentence, I still have two grandmothers, since I am distinguishing one from the other by my restrictive phrase (no commas) as the one with the unconventional habit. In the second sentence, I have but one grandmother, about whom I am adding an interesting though nonessential, nonrestrictive detail within a pair of commas. Read the two aloud, and you will hear the difference in meaning, and how the pauses at the commas signal that difference. Commas are often optional, of course. The difference between a restictive and a nonrestrictive meaning may sometimes be very slight. For example, you may take our recent bridegroom either way (but not halfway):

That handsome man, in the ascot tie, is the groom. [nonre-
strictive]
That handsome man in the ascot tie is the groom. [restric-
tive]

Your meaning will dictate your choice. But use **PAIRS** of commas or none at all. Never separate subject and verb, or verb and object, with just one comma.

Some finer points. One comma of a pair enclosing an inserted remark may coincide with, and, in a sense, overlay, a comma "already there":

In each box, a bottle was broken.
In each box, however, a bottle was broken.

The team lost, and the school was sick.
The team lost, in spite of all, and the school was sick.

The program will work, but the cost is high.
The program will work, of course, but the cost is high.

Between the coordinate clauses, however, a semicolon might have been clearer:

The team lost, in spite of all; and the school was sick.
The program will work, of course; but the cost is high.

Beware: *however,* between commas, cannot substitute for *but,* as in the perfectly good sentence: "He wore a hat, *but* it looked terrible." You would be using a comma where a full stop (period or semicolon) should be:

WRONG:
He wore a hat, however, it looked terrible.

RIGHT *(notice the two meanings):*
He wore a hat; however, it looked terrible.
He wore a hat, however; it looked terrible.

But a simple , **but** avoids both the ambiguity of the floating *however* and the ponderosity of anchoring it with a semicolon, fore or aft: "He wore a hat, but it looked terrible."

Another point. *But* may absorb the first comma of a pair enclosing an introductory remark (although it need not do so):

At any rate, he went.
But, at any rate, he went.
But at any rate, he went.
But [,] if we want another party, we had better clean up.
The party was a success, but [,] if we want another one, we
**   had better clean up.**

But avoid a comma *after* "but" in sentences like this:

I understand your argument, but [,] I feel your opponent
**   has a stronger case.**

Treat the "he said" and "she said" of dialogue as a regular parenthetical insertion, within commas, and without capitalizing, unless a new sentence begins:

"I'm going," he said, "whenever I get up enough nerve."
"I'm going," he said. "Whenever I get up enough nerve, I'm
**   really going."**

And Canadian usage puts the comma *inside* ALL quotation marks:

"He is a nut," she said.
She called him a "nut," and walked away.

Finally, the comma goes after a parenthesis, never before:

> **On the day of her graduation (June 4, 1985), the weather
> turned broiling hot.**

IV. The Linker. This is the usual one, linking on additional
phrases and afterthoughts:

> **They went home, having overstayed their welcome.**
> **The book is too long, overloaded with examples.**

It also links items in series. Again, the meaningful pause demands
a comma:

> **words, phrases, or clauses in a series**
> **to hunt, to fish, and to hike**
> **He went home, he went upstairs, and he could remember
> nothing.**
> **He liked oysters, soup, roast beef, and song.**

Put a linker before the concluding *and.* By carefully separating all
elements in a series, you keep alive a final distinction long ago
lost in the daily press, the distinction Virginia Woolf makes (see
114): "urbane, polished, brilliant, imploring and commanding
him. . . ." *Imploring and commanding* is syntactically equal to each
one of the other modifiers in the series. If Woolf customarily
omitted the last comma, as she does not, she could not have
reached for that double apposition. The muscle would have been
dead. These other examples of double apposition will give you
an idea of its effectiveness:

> **They cut out his idea, root and branch.**
> **He lost all his holdings, houses and lands.**
> **He loved to tramp the woods, to fish and hunt.**

A comma makes a great deal of difference, of sense and distinction.

But adjectives in series, as distinct from nouns in series,
change the game a bit. Notice the difference between the following two strings of adjectives:

a good, unexpected, natural rhyme
a good old battered hat

With adjectives in series, only your sense can guide you. If each seems to modify the noun directly, as in the first example above, use commas. If each seems to modify the total accumulation of adjectives and noun, as with *good* and *old* in the second phrase, do not use commas. Say your phrases aloud, and put your commas in the pauses that distinguish your meaning.

Finally, a special case. Dramatic intensity sometimes allows you to join clauses with commas instead of conjunctions:

She sighed, she cried, she almost died.
I couldn't do it, I tried, I let them all get away.
It passed, it triumphed, it was a good bill.
I came, I saw, I conquered.

The rhetorical intensity of this construction—the Greeks called it *asyndeton*—is obvious. The language is breathless, or grandly emphatic. As Aristotle once said, it is a person trying to say many things at once. The subjects repeat themselves, the verbs overlap, the idea accumulates a climax. By some psychological magic, the clauses of this construction usually come in three's. The comma is its sign. But unless you have a stylistic reason for such a flurry of clauses, go back to the normal comma and conjunction, the semicolon, or the period.

FRAGMENTS, COMMA SPLICES, AND RUN-ONS

These are the most persistent problems in using the comma—either missing it or misusing it. The rhetorical fragment, as we have seen (114), may have great force: "So what." But the grammatical one needs repairing with a comma:

FAULTY: **She dropped the cup. Which had cost twenty dollars.**
REVISED: **She dropped the cup, which had cost twenty dollars.**

FAULTY: He does not spell everything out. But rather hints that something is wrong, and leaves the rest up to the reader.

REVISED: He does not spell everything out, but rather hints . . . , and leaves. . . .

FAULTY: . . . and finally, the book is obscure. Going into lengthy discussions and failing to remind the reader of the point.

REVISED: . . . and finally, the book is obscure, going into lengthy discussion. . . .

FAULTY: Yet here is her husband treating their son to all that she considers evil. Plus the fact that the boy is offered beer.

REVISED: Yet here is her husband treating their son to all that she considers evil, especially beer.

FAULTY: He points out that one never knows what the future will bring. Because it is actually a matter of luck.

REVISED: He points out that one never knows what the future will bring, because it is actually a matter of luck.

FAULTY: They are off. Not out of their minds exactly but driven, obsessed.

REVISED: They are off, not out of their minds exactly, but driven, obsessed.

Beware the Comma Splice, and the Run-On

The comma splice is the beginner's most common error, the opposite of the fragment—putting a comma where we need a period rather than putting a period where we need a comma—splicing two sentences together with a comma:

> The comma splice is a common error, it is the opposite of a fragment.   Comma Splice

Of course, you will frequently see comma splices, particularly in fiction and dialogue, where writers are conveying colloquial speed and the thoughts come tumbling fast. Some nonfiction writers borrow this same speed here and there in their prose. But

you should learn to recognize these as comma splices and generally avoid them because they may strike your reader as the errors
of innocence. Like the rhetorical fragment, a comma splice between short clauses can be most effective (see *asyndeton,* 224): "If
speech and cinema are akin to music, writing is like architecture;
it endures, it has weight."*

The run-on sentence (fortunately less common) omits even
the splicing comma, running one sentence right on to another
without noticing:

Run-On   **The comma splice is a common error it is the opposite of
a fragment.**

Here the writer is in deeper trouble, having somehow never
gotten the feel of a sentence as based on subject and verb, and
thus needing special help. But most of us can see both the comma
splice and run-on as really being two sentences, to be restored
as such:

   **The comma splice is a common error. It is the opposite of
a fragment.**

Or to be coordinated by adding a conjunction after the comma:

   The comma splice is a common error, and it is. . . .

Or to be subordinated by making the second sentence a phrase:

   The comma splice is a common error, the opposite. . . .

Here are some typical comma splices:

   She cut class, it was boring.
   The class was not merely dull, it was useless.
   Figures do not lie, they mislead.
   He was more than satisfied, he was delighted.

Each of these pulls together a pair of closely sequential sentences. But a comma without its *and* or *but* will not hold the
coordination. Either make them the sentences they are:

---

*Italics added. Richard Lloyd-Jones, "What We May Become," *College Composition
and Communication* 33 (1952): 205.

> She cut class. It was boring.
> Figures do not lie. They mislead.

Or coordinate them with a colon or dash (with a semicolon *only* if they contrast sharply):

> The class was not merely dull: it was useless.
> He was more than satisfied—he was delighted.

Or subordinate in some way:

> She cut class because it was boring.
> The class was not merely dull but useless.
> More than satisfied, he was delighted.

Here are some more typical splices, all from one set of papers dealing with Shakespeare's *The Tempest.* I have circled the comma where the period should be:

> She knows nothing of the evil man is capable of, to her every
>   man is beautiful.
> The question of his sensibility hovers, we wonder if he is
>   just.
> Without a doubt, men discourage oppression, they strive to
>   be free.
> Ariel is civilized society, besides being articulate, he has
>   direction and order.
> Stephano and Trinculo are the comics of the play, never
>   presented as complete characters, they are not taken
>   seriously.

You will accidentally splice with a comma most frequently when adding a thought (a complete short sentence) to a longer sentence:

> The book describes human evolution in wholly believable
> terms, comparing the social habits of gorillas and chimpan-
> zees to human behaviour, it is very convincing. [Either
> "... believable terms. Comparing ... ," or "human behavi-
> our. It. . . ."]

Conjunctive adverbs (*however, therefore, nevertheless, moreover, furthermore,* and others) may also cause comma splices and trouble:

> She continued teaching, however her heart was not in it.

Here are three mendings:

> **She continued teaching, but her heart was not in it.**
> **She continued teaching; however, her heart was not in it.**
> **She continued teaching; her heart, however, was not in it.**

Similarly, transitional phrases *(in fact, that is, for example)* may splice your sentences together:

> **He disliked discipline, that is, he really was lazy.**

You can strengthen the weak joints like this:

> **He disliked discipline; that is, he really was lazy.**
> **He disliked discipline, that is, anything demanding.**

SEMICOLON AND COLON

Use the semicolon only where you could also use a period, unless desperate. This dogmatic formula, which I shall loosen up in a moment, has saved many a punctuator from both despair and a reckless fling of semicolons. Confusion comes from the belief that the semicolon is either a weak colon or a strong comma. It is most effective as neither. It is best, as we have seen (102), in pulling together and contrasting two independent clauses that could stand alone as sentences:

> **The dress accents the feminine. The pants suit speaks for freedom.**
> Semicolon **The dress accents the feminine; the pants suit speaks for freedom.**

This compression and contrast by semicolon can go even farther, allowing us to drop a repeated verb in the second element (note also how the comma marks the omission):

> **Golf demands the best of time and space; tennis demands the best of personal energy.**

> **Golf demands the best of time and space; tennis, the best of personal energy.**
> **Tragedy begins with the apple; comedy, with the banana peel.***

Use a semicolon with a transitional word *(moreover, therefore, then, however, nevertheless)* to signal close contrast and connection:

> **He was lonely, blue, and solitary; moreover, his jaw ached.**

Used sparingly, the semicolon emphasizes your crucial contrasts; used recklessly, it merely clutters your page. *Never* use it as a colon: its effect is exactly opposite. A colon, as in the preceding sentence, signals the meaning to go ahead; a semicolon, as in this sentence, stops it. The colon is a green light; the semicolon is a stop sign.

Consequently, a wrong semicolon frequently makes a fragment. *Use a semicolon only where you could also use a period*—forget the exceptions—or you will make semicolon-fragments like the italicized phrases following the erroneous semicolons circled below:

> **The play opens on a dark street in Montreal;***one streetlight giving the only illumination.*
> **The geese begin their migration in late August or early September;***some groups having started, in small stages, a week or so earlier.*

Each of those semicolons should have been a comma.

Of course, you may occasionally need a semicolon to unscramble a long line of phrases and clauses, especially those in series and containing internal commas:

> **Writing is hard because we often must discover our ideas by writing them out, clarifying them on paper; because we must also find a clear and reasonable order for ideas the mind presents simultaneously; and because we must find, by trial and error, exactly the right words to convey our ideas and our feelings about them.**

The colon waves the traffic on through the intersection: "Go right ahead," it says, "and you will find what you are looking for."

---

*Adapted from Guy Davenport, *Life,* 27 Mar. 1970: 12.

The colon emphatically and precisely introduces a series, the clarifying detail, the illustrative example, and the formal quotation:

Colon   **The following players will start: Corelli, Smith, Jones, Baughman, and Stein.**
Pierpont lived for only one thing: money.
In the end, it was useless: Adams really was too green.
We remember Sherman's words: "War is hell."

PARENTHESIS AND DASH

The dash says aloud what the parenthesis whispers. Both enclose interruptions too extravagant for a pair of commas to hold. The dash is the more useful—since whispering tends to annoy—and will remain useful only if not overused. It can serve as a conversational colon. It can set off a concluding phrase—for emphasis. It can bring long introductory matters to focus, concluding a series of parallel phrases: "—all these are crucial." It can insert a full sentence—a clause is really an incorporated sentence—directly next to a key word. The dash allows you to insert—with a kind of shout!—an occasional exclamation. You may even insert—and who would blame you?—an occasional question. The dash affords a structural complexity with all the tone and alacrity of talk.

With care, you can get much the same power from a parenthesis:

Many philosophers have despaired (somewhat unphilosophically) of discovering any certainties whatsoever.
Thus did Innocent III (we shall return to him shortly) inaugurate an age of horrors.
But in such circumstances (see page 34), be cautious.
Delay had doubled the costs (a stitch in time!), so the plans were shelved.

But dashes seem more generally useful, and here are some special points. When one of a pair of dashes falls where a comma would be, it absorbs the comma:

If one wanted to go, he certainly could.
If one wanted to go—whether invited or not—he certainly
**   could.**

Not so with the semicolon:

He wanted to go—whether he was invited or not; she had
**   more sense.**

To indicate the dash, type two hyphens (--) flush against the
words they separate—not one hyphen between two spaces, nor
a hyphen spaced to look exactly like a hyphen.

Put commas and periods *outside* a parenthetical group of
words (like this one), even if the parenthetical group could stand
alone as a sentence (see the preceding "Innocent III" example).
(But if you make an actual full sentence parenthetical, put the
period inside.)

Change has had its way with the parenthesis around numbers. Formal print and most guides to writing, including this one,
still hold to the full parenthesis:

The sentence really has only two general varieties: (1) the   Numbered
**   "loose" or strung-along, in Aristotle's phrase, and (2)**   Items
**   the periodic.**
He decided (1) that he did not like it, (2) that she would not
**   like it, and (3) that they would be better off without it.**

Popular print now omits the first half of the parenthesis:

. . . decided 1) that he did not like it, 2) that she. . . .

But for your papers—keep the full parenthesis.

BRACKETS

Brackets indicate your own words inserted or substituted within
a quotation from someone else: "Byron had already suggested
that [they] had killed John Keats." You have substituted "they"
for "the gentlemen of the *Quarterly Review*" to suit your own
context; you do the same when you interpolate a word of expla-

nation: "Byron had already suggested that the gentlemen of the *Quarterly Review* [especially Croker] had killed John Keats." *Do not use parentheses:* they mark the enclosed words as part of the original quotation. Don't claim innocence because your typewriter lacks brackets. Just leave spaces and draw them in later, or type slant lines and tip them with pencil or with the underscore key: *[. . .]*

In the example below, you are pointing out with a *sic* (Latin for "so" or "thus"), which you should not italicize, that you are reproducing an error exactly as it appears in the text you are quoting:

> **"On no occassion [sic] could we trust them."**

Similarly you may give a correction after reproducing the error:

> **"On the twenty-fourth [twenty-third], we broke camp."**
> **"In not one instance [actually, Baldwin reports several instances] did our men run under fire."**

Use brackets when you need a parenthesis within a parenthesis:

> **(see Donald Allenberg, *The Future of Television* [New York, 1973]: 15–16)**

Your instructor will probably put brackets around the wordy parts of your sentences, indicating what you should cut:

> **In fact, [the reason] he liked it [was] because it was different.**

QUOTATION MARKS AND ITALICS

Put quotation marks around quotations that "run directly into your text" (like this), but *not* around quotations set off from the text and indented. You normally inset poetry, as it stands, without quotation marks:

> **An aged man is but a paltry thing,**
> **A tattered coat upon a stick, unless**
> **Soul clap its hands and sing. . . .**

But if you run it into your text, use quotation marks, with virgules (slants) showing the line-ends: "An aged man is but a paltry thing,/A tattered coat. . . ." Put periods and commas *inside* quotation marks; put semicolons and colons *outside:*

> **Now we understand the full meaning of "give me liberty, or**   Periods
> **give me death."**
> **"This strange disease of modern life," in Arnold's words,**   Commas
> **remains uncured.**
> **In Greece, it was "know thyself"; in Canada, it is "know thy**   Semicolons
> **neighbour."**
> **He left after "God Save the Queen": he could do nothing**   Colons
> **more.**

Although logic often seems to demand the period or comma outside the quotation marks, convention has put them inside for the sake of appearance, even when the sentence ends in a single quoted word or letter:

> **Clara Bow was said to have "It."**
> **Mark it with "T."**

If you have seen the periods and commas outside, you were reading a British book or some of Canada's little magazines.

When you have dialogue, signal each change of speaker with a paragraph's indentation:

> **"What magazines in the natural sciences should I read**
> **regularly?" inquired the student.**
> **"Though moderately difficult, *Scientific American* and**
> ***Science* are always worth your time, but you'll want to ex-**
> **plore afield from these," responded his advisor.**

If in a dialogue a single speaker carries on for several paragraphs, place quotation marks before *each* paragraph, but after only the *last* paragraph.

Omit quotation marks entirely in *indirect* quotations:

> **She asked me if I would help her.**
> **The insurance agent told Mr. Jones that his company would**
> **pay all valid claims within thirty days.**
> **In his review of the play, J. K. Beaumont praised the plot as**
> **strong and incisive, but faulted the dialogue as listless**
> **and contrived in a few scenes. [Here, you are summariz-**
> **ing the reviewer's comments.]**

If you are quoting a phrase that already contains quotation marks, reduce the original double marks (") to single ones ('):

	ORIGINAL	YOUR QUOTATION
Single Quotation Marks (on the Right)	Hamlet's "are you honest?" is easily explained.	He writes that "Hamlet's 'are you honest?' is easily explained."

Notice what happens when the quotation within your quotation falls at the end:

ORIGINAL	YOUR QUOTATION
A majority of the informants thought *infer* meant "imply."	Kirk reports that "a majority of the informants thought *infer* meant 'imply.' "

And notice that a question mark or exclamation point falls between the single and the double quotation marks at the end of a quotation containing a quotation:

"Why do they call it 'the Hippocratic oath'?" she asked.
"Everything can't be 'cool'!" he said.

But heed the following exception:

"I heard someone say, 'Is anyone home?' " she declared.

Do not use *single* quotation marks for your own stylistic flourishes; use *double* quotation marks or, preferably, none:

It was indeed an "affair," but the passion was hardly "grand."
It was indeed an affair, but the passion was hardly grand.
Some "cool" pianists use the twelve-tone scale.

Once you have thus established this slang meaning of *cool,* you may repeat the word without quotation marks. In general, of course, you should favour that slang your style can absorb without quotation marks.
Do not use quotation marks for calling attention to words as

words. Use italics (an underscore when typing) for the words, quotation marks for their meanings.

> **This is taking *tergiversation* too literally.**   Italics
> **The word *struthious* means "like an ostrich."**

Similarly, use italics for numbers as numbers and letters as letters:

> **He writes a *5* like an *s*.**
> **Dot your *i*'s and cross your *t*'s.**

But common sayings like "Watch your p's and q's" and "from A to Z" require no italics.

Use quotation marks for titles *within* books and magazines: titles of chapters, articles, short stories, songs, and poems, and for unpublished works, lectures, courses, TV episodes within a series. But use italics for titles or names of books, newspapers, magazines, plays, films, TV series, long poems, sculptures, paintings, ships, trains, and airplanes.

> **Poe's description of how he wrote "The Raven" was at-**   Titles and
> **tacked in the *Atlantic Monthly* [or: the *Atlantic*.]**   Names
> **We saw Michelangelo's *Pietà*, a remarkable statue in white**
> **marble.**
> **We took the *Maid of the Mist* across the Niagara River.**
> **He read all of Frazer's *The Golden Bough*.**
> **His great-grandfather went down with the *Titanic*.**
> **She read it in the *Globe and Mail*.**
> **They loved *Saturday Night Fever* [film].**

Handle titles within titles as follows:

> **"*Tintern Alley*" and *Nature in Wordsworth* [book]**
> **" 'Tintern Abbey' and Natural Imagery" [article]**
> **"The Art of *Tom Jones*" [article]**
> ***The Art of* Tom Jones [book]**

In the last example, notice that what is ordinarily italicized, like the title of a book *(Tom Jones),* is set in roman when the larger setting is in italics.

Italicize foreign words and phrases, unless they have been

assimilated into English through usage (your dictionary should have a method for noting the distinction; if not, consult one that has):

> **The statement contained two clichés and one *non sequitur.***
> **The author of this naive exposé suffers from an *idée fixe.***

Other foreign expressions *not* italicized are: etc., e.g., et al., genre, hubris, laissez faire, leitmotif, roman à clef, raison d'être, tête-à-tête.

Use neither quotation marks nor italics for the Bible, for its books or parts (Genesis, Old Testament), for other sacred books (Koran, Talmud, Upanishad), nor for famous documents like the Magna Carta, the Charter of Rights, the Communist Manifesto, and the Gettysburg Address, nor for instrumental music known by its form, number, and key:

> **Beethoven's C-minor Quartet**
> **Brahms's Symphony No. 4, Opus 98**

When a reference in parentheses falls at the end of a quotation, the quotation marks *precede* the parentheses:

> **As Ecclesiastes tells us, "there is no new thing under the sun" (1.9).**

ELLIPSIS

1. Use three spaced periods . . . (the ellipsis mark) when you omit something from a quotation. Do *not* use them in your own text in place of a dash, or in mere insouciance.
2. If you omit the end of a sentence, put in a period (no space) and add the three spaced dots. . . .
3. If your omission falls after a completed sentence, just add the three spaced dots to the period already there. . . . The spacing is the same as for case 2.

Here is an uncut passage, followed by a shortened version illustrating the three kinds of ellipsis:

> To learn a language, learn as thoroughly as possible a few
> everyday sentences. This will educate your ear for all future
> pronunciations. It will give you a fundamental grasp of
> structure. And start soon.

> **(1)**
> To learn a language, learn . . . a few everyday sentences.
> **(2)**
> This will educate your ear. . . . It will give you a
> **(3)**
> fundamental grasp of structure. . . .

You can omit beginning and ending ellipses when you use a
quotation within a sentence:

> Lincoln was determined that the Union, "cemented with the
> blood of . . . the purest patriots," would not fail.

APOSTROPHE

It's may be overwhelmingly our most frequent misspelling as in
"The dog scratched *it's* ear." No, no! *It's* means *it is. Who's* means
who is. They're means *they are.* NO pronoun spells *its* possessive
with an apostrophe: *hers, its, ours, theirs, yours, whose, oneself.*

For nouns, add apostrophe *-s* to form the singular possessive: *dog's life, hour's work, Marx's ideas.* Add apostrophe *-s* even to
singular words already ending in *s: Yeats's poems, Charles's crown.*
Sis' plans and *the boss' daughter* are not what we say. We say *Sis-
suz* and *bossuz* and *Keatsuz,* and should say the same in our writing:
sis's, boss's, Keats's. Plurals *not* ending in *s* also form the possessive
by adding *'s: children's hour, women's rights.* But most plurals take
the apostrophe after the *s* already there: *witches' sabbath, ten cents'
worth, three days' time, the Joneses' possessions.*

I repeat, the rule for making singulars possessive is to add
's regardless of length and previous ending. French names ending in silent *s*-sounds also add *'s: Camus's works, Marivaux's life,
Berlioz's Requiem.* If your page grows too thick with double *s*'s,
substitute a few pronouns for the proper names, or rephrase: *the
death of Themistocles, the Dickens character Pip.*

The apostrophe can help to clarify clusters of nouns. These

I have actually seen: *Alistair Jones Renown Combo, the church barbecue chicken sale, the uniform policeman training program, the members charter plane.* And of course, *teachers meeting* and *veterans insurance* are so common as to seem almost normal. But an apostrophe chips one more noun out of the block. It makes your meaning one word clearer, marking *teachers'* as a modifier, and distinguishing *teacher* from *teachers.* Inflections are helpful, and the written word needs all the help it can get: *Jones's Renowned, church's barbecued, uniformed policeman's, members' chartered.* Distinguish your modifiers, and keep your possessions.

Compound words take the *'s* on the last word only: *mother-in-law's hat, the brothers-in-law's attitude* (all the brothers-in-law have the same attitude), *somebody else's problem.* Joint ownerships may similarly take the *'s* only on the last word *(Bill and Mary's house),* but *Bill's and Mary's* house is more precise, and preferable.

Again, possessive pronouns have no apostrophe: *hers, its, theirs, yours, whose, oneself.* Remember that *it's* means *it is,* and that *who's* means *who is;* for possession, use *its* and *whose.*

The double possessive uses both an *of* and an *'s: a friend of my mother's, a book of the teacher's, a son of the Joneses', an old hat of Mary's.* Note that the double possessive indicates one possession among several of the same kind: mother has several friends; the teacher, several books.

Use the apostrophe to indicate omissions: *the Spirit of '76, the Class of '02, can't, won't, don't.* Finally, use the apostrophe when adding a grammatical ending to a number, letter, sign, or abbreviation: *1920's;* his *3's* look like *8's; p's* and *q's;* he got four *A's;* too many *of's* and *and's;* she *X'd* each box; *K.O.'d* in the first round. (Some of these are also italics, or underlined when typed. See 235.) Contemporary usage omits the apostrophe in some of these: 1920s, *8*s, two *t*s.

HYPHEN

For clarity, hyphenate groups of words acting as one adjective or one adverb: *eighteenth-century attitude, early-blooming southern crocus, of-and-which disease.* Distinguish between a *high school,* and a *high-school teacher.* Similarly, hyphenate compound nouns when you need to distinguish, for example, *five sentence-exercises* from *five-sentence exercises.*

Hyphenate prefixes to proper names: *ex-Catholic, pro-Napoleon,* and all relatively new combinations like *anti-marriage.* Consult your dictionary.

Hyphenate after prefixes that demand emphasis or clarity: *ex-husband, re-collect* ("to collect again," as against *recollect,* "to remember"), *re-create, re-emphasize, pre-existent.* If you must break a word at the end of a line, hyphenate where your dictionary marks the syllables with a dot; *syl·lables, syl-lables.* If you must break a hyphenated word, break it after the hyphen: *self-/sufficient.* Don't hyphenate an already hyphenated word: *self-suf-/ficient.* It's hard on the eyes and the printer. When you write for print, underline those line-end hyphens you mean to keep as hyphens, making a little equals sign: self=/sufficient.

Hyphenate suffixes to single capital letters (*T-shirt, I-beam, X-ray*). Hyphenate *ex-champions* and *self-reliances.* Hyphenate to avoid double *i*'s and triple consonants: *anti-intellectual, bell-like.* Hyphenate two-word numbers: *twenty-one, three-fourths.* Use the "suspensive" hyphen for hyphenated words in series: "We have ten-, twenty-five-, and fifty-pound sizes."

VIRGULE (SLANT, SLASH)

Spare this "little rod" (/), and don't spoil your work with the legalistic *and/or.* Don't write "bacon and/or eggs"; write "bacon or eggs, or both." Likewise, don't use it for a hyphen: not "male/female conflict" but "male-female conflict." Use the virgule when quoting poetry in your running text: "That time of year thou mayst in me behold / When yellow leaves, . . ."

SPELLING

The dictionary is your best friend as you face the inevitable anxieties of spelling, but three underlying principles and some tricks of the trade can help immeasurably:

Principle I. Letters represent sounds: proNUNciation can help you spell. No one proNOUNcing his words correctly would make the familiar errors of "similiar" and "enviorment." Simply sound out the letters: *envIRONment* and *goverNment* and *FebRUary* and *intRAmural.* Of course, you will need to be wary of some words *not* pronounced as spelled: *Wednesday* pronounced "Wenzday," for instance. But sounding the letters can help your spellings. You can even say "convert*i*ble" and "indel*i*ble" and "plaus*i*ble" without sounding like a fool, and you can silently stress the *able* in words like "prob*able*" and "immov*able*" to remember the difficult distinction between words ending in *-ible,* and *-able.*

Consonants reliably represent their sounds. Remember that *c* and often *g* go soft before *i* and *e.* Consequently, you must add a *k* when extending words like *picnic* and *mimic—picnicKing, mimicKing—*to keep them from rhyming with *slicing* or *dicing.* Conversely, you just keep the *e* (where you would normally drop it) when making *peace* into *peacEable* and *change* into *changEable,* to keep the *c* and *g* soft.

Single *s* is pronounced *zh* in words like *vision, occasion, pleasure.* Knowing that *ss* hushes ("sh-h-h") will keep you from errors like *occassion,* which would sound like *passion.*

Vowels sound short and light before single consonants: *hat, pet, kit, hop, cup.* When you add any vowel (including *y*), the first vowel will say its name: *hate, Pete, kite, hoping, cupid.* Notice how the *a* in *-able* keeps the main vowel saying its name in words like *unmistakable, likable,* and *notable.* Therefore, to keep a vowel short protect it with double consonant: *petting, hopping.* This explains the troublesome *rr* in *occuRRence:* a single *r* would make it say *cure* in the middle. *Putting* a golf ball and *putting* something on paper must both use *tt* to keep from being pronounced *pewting.* Compare *stony* with *sonny* and *bony* with *bonny.* The *y* is replacing the *e* in *stone* and *bone,* and the rule is working perfectly. It works in any syllable that is accented: compare *forgeTTable* as against *markeTing, begiNNing* as against *buttoNing,* and *compeLLing* as against *traveLing.*

Likewise, when *full* combines and loses its stress, it also loses an *l.* Note the single and double *l* in *fulFILLment.* Similarly, *SOULful, GRATEful, AWful—*even *SPOONful.*

Principle II. This is the old rule of *i* before *e,* and its famous exceptions:

I before *e*
Except after *c,*
Or when sounded like *a*
As in *neighbour* and *weigh.*

It works like a charm: *achieve, believe, receive, conceive.* Note that *c* needs an *e* to make it sound like *s.* Remember also that *leisure* was once pronounced "lay-sure," and *foreign,* "forayn," and *heifer,* "hayfer." Memorize these important exceptions: *seize, weird, either, sheik, forfeit, counterfeit, protein.* Note that all are pronounced "ee" (with a little crowding) and that the *e* comes first. Then note that another small group goes the opposite way, having a long *i* sound as in German "Heil": *height, sleight, seismograph, kaleidoscope. Science* is a notable exception. *Financier,* another exception, follows its French origin and its original sound. *Deity* sounds both vowels as spelled.

Principle III. Most big words, following the Latin or French from which they came, spell their sounds letter for letter. Look up the derivations of the words you misspell (note that double *s,* and explain it). You will never again have trouble with *desperate* and *separate* once you discover that the first comes from *de-spero,* "without hope," and that SePARate divides equals, the PAR values in stocks or golf. Nor with *definite* or *definitive,* once you see the kinship of both with *finite* and *finish.* Derivations can also help you a little with the devilment of *-able* and *-ible,* since, except for a few ringers, the *i* remains from Latin, and the *-ables* are either French *(ami-able)* or Anglo-Saxon copies *(workable).* Knowing origins can help at crucial points: *resemblAnce* comes from Latin *simulAre,"* "to copy"; *existEnce* comes from Latin *existEre,* "to stand forth."

The biggest help comes from learning the common Latin prefixes, which, by a process of assimilation *(ad-similis,* "like to like"), account for the double consonants at the first syLLabic joint of so many of our words:

AD- **(toward, to):** *abbreviate* **(shorten down),** *accept* **(grasp to).**
CON- **(with):** *collapse* **(fall with),** *commit* **(send with).**
DIS- **(apart):** *dissect* **(cut apart),** *dissolve* **(loosen apart).**
IN- **(into):** *illuminate* **(shine into),** *illusion* **(playing into).**
IN- **(not):** *illegal* **(not lawful),** *immature* **(not ripe).**

INTER- (between): *interrupt* (break between), *interrogate* (ask between).

OB- (toward, to): *occupy* (take in), *oppose* (put to), *offer* (carry to).

SUB- (under): *suffer* (bear under), *suppose* (put down).

SYN- ("together"—this one is Greek): *symmetry* (measuring together), *syllogism* (logic together).

Spelling takes a will, an eye, and an ear. And a dictionary. Keep a list of your favourite enemies. Memorize one or two a day. Write them in the air in longhand. Visualize them. Imagine a blinking neon sign, with the wicked letters red and tall—defin**I**te —defin**I**te. Then print them once, write them twice, and blink them a few times more as you go to sleep. But best of all, make up whatever devices you can—the crazier the better—to remember their tricky parts:

DANCE attenDANCE.

EXISTENCE is TENSE.

There's IRON in this enviRONment.

The resisTANCE took its STANCE.

There's an ANT on the defendANT.

LOOSE as a goose.

LOSE loses an O.

ALLOT isn't A LOT.

Already isn't ALL RIGHT.

I for gaIety.

The LL in paraLLel gives me *el.*

PURr in PURsuit.

When an unaccented syllable leads to misspelling, you can also get some help by trying to remember a version of the word that accents the troublesome syllable: acad*e*my—acaDEMic; defin*i*tely—defiNItion; irrit*a*ble—irriTATE; prep*a*ration—prePARE.

Many foreign words, though established in English, retain their native diacritical marks, which aid in pronunciation; *naïveté, résumé, séance, tête-à-tête, façade, Fräulein, mañana, vicuña.* Many names are similarly treated: *Müller, Gödel, Göttingen, Poincaré, Brontë, Noël Coward, García Lorca, Havlíček.* As always, your dictionary is your best guide, as it is, indeed, to all words transliterated to English from different alphabets and systems of writing (Russian, Arabic, Chinese, Japanese, and so on).

Here are more of the perpetual headaches:

accept—except
accommodate
acknowledgment—
  judgment
advice—advise
affect—effect*
all right*—a lot*
allusion—illusion—
  disillusion*
analysis—analyzing
argue—argument
arrangement
businessman
capital (city)—capitol
  (building)*
censor—censure*
committee
complement—
  compliment*
continual—continuous*
controversy
council—counsel—
  consul*
criticize—criticism
curriculum*—career—
  occurrence
decide—divide—devices
desert—dessert
dilemma—condemn
disastrous
discreet—discrete*
embarrassment—
  harassment

eminent—imminent—
  immanent*
exaggerate
explain—explanation
familiar—similar
forward—foreword
genius—ingenious*—
  ingenous*
height—eighth
hypocrisy—democracy
irritable
its—it's*
lonely—loneliness
marriage—marital—martial
misspell—misspelling
Negroes—heroes—tomatoes
obstacle
possession
primitive
principal—principle*
proceed—precede—procedure
rhythm
questionnaire
stationary—stationery
succeed—successful
suppressed
their—they're
truly
until—till
unnoticed
weather—whether
who's—whose*

CAPITALIZATION

You know about sentences and names, certainly; but the following points are troublesome. Capitalize:

---

*In the Glossary of Usage.

1. Names of races, languages, and religions—Black, Caucasian, Mongolian, Protestant, Jewish, Christian, Roman Catholic, Indian, French, English.
2. North, South, East, and West *only when they are regions*—the mysterious East, the new Southwest—or parts of proper nouns: the West Side, North York.
3. The *complete* names of churches, rivers, hotels, and the like —the Knox Presbyterian Church, the Royal York Hotel, the Ottawa River (not Knox Presbyterian church, Royal York hotel, Ottawa river).
4. All words in titles, except prepositions, articles, conjunctions, and the "to" of infinitives. But capitalize even these if they come first or last, or if they are longer than four letters—"I'm Through with Love," *Gone with the Wind,* "I'll Stand By," *In Darkest Africa, How to Gain Friends and Influence People, To Catch a Thief.* Capitalize nouns, adjectives, and prefixes in hyphenated compounds—*The Eighteenth-Century Background, The Anti-Idealist* (but *The Antislavery Movement*). But hyphenated single words, the names of numbered streets, and the written-out numbers on your cheques are *not* capitalized after the hyphen: *Self-fulfillment, Re-examination. Forty-second Street, Fifty-four . . . Dollars.*

   When referring to magazines, newspapers, and reference works in sentences, footnotes, and bibliographies, you may drop the *The* as part of the title; the *Malahat Review,* the *Globe and Mail,* the *Encyclopaedia Britannica.* (Euphony and sense preserve *The* for a few: *The New Yorker, The Spectator.*)
5. References to a specific section of a work—the Index, his Preface, Chapter 1, Volume IV, Act II, but "scene iii" is usually not capitalized because its numerals are also in lower case.
6. Abstract nouns, when you want emphasis, serious or humorous—". . . the truths contradict, so what is Truth?"; Very Important Person; the Ideal.

Do not capitalize the seasons—spring, winter, midsummer.
Do not capitalize after a colon, unless what follows is normally capitalized:

> **Again we may say with Churchill: "Never have so many
> owed so much to so few."**
> *Culture, People, Nature: An Introduction to General Anthro-
> pology* **[title of book]**
> **Many lost everything in the earthquake: their homes had
> vanished along with their supplies, their crops, their
> livestock.**

Do not capitalize proper nouns serving as common nouns: *china,
cognac, napoleon* (a pastry), *chauvinist, watt* (electricity). Usage divides on some proper adjectives: *French* [*french*] *pastry, Cheddar* [*cheddar*] *cheese, German* [*german*] *measles, Venetian* [*venetian*] *blinds.* Also somewhat uncertain are names with lower-case
articles or prepositions like [Charles] de Gaulle, [John] von Neumann; in such cases, follow the lower-case form within sentences—*de Gaulle, von Neumann*—but always capitalize in full at
the beginning of a sentence: *De Gaulle, Von Neumann.* (Many
names, however, drop the article or preposition when the sur-
name appears alone: [Ludwig van] *Beethoven,* [Guy de] *Maupas-
sant.*) Breeds of animals, as in *Welsh terrier,* and products of a
definite origin, as in *Scotch whisky,* are less uncertain. When in
doubt, your best guides are your dictionary and, for proper
names, a biographical dictionary or an encyclopedia.

EXERCISES

1. *Correct these omissions of the comma, and, in your margin, label the
ones you insert as* INTRODUCER, COORDINATOR, INSERTER, *or* LINKER:

1. We find however that the greatest expense in renovation will be for
   labour not for materials.
2. They took chemistry fine arts history and English.
3. We met June 1 1982 to discuss the problem which continued to plague
   us.
4. A faithful sincere friend he remained loyal to his roommate even after
   the unexpected turn of events.
5. Though she was a part-time instructor teaching advanced calculus
   given at night during the winter did not intimidate her.

6. C. Wright Mills's *The Power Elite* which even after two decades is still one of the finest examples of sociological analysis available ought to be required reading in any elementary sociology course.
7. My father, who is a good gardener keeps things well trimmed.

2. *Correct these fragments, comma splices, and run-ons, adding commas and other marks as necessary:*

1. His lectures are not only hard to follow they are boring.
2. Stephano and Trinculo are the comics of the play never presented as complete characters they are not taken seriously.
3. The book deals with the folly of war its stupidity, its cruelty however in doing this the author brings in too many characters repeats episodes over and over and spoils his comedy by pressing too hard.
4. He left his second novel unfinished. Perhaps because of his basic uncertainty, which he never overcame.
5. She seems to play a careless game. But actually knows exactly what she is doing, and intends to put her opponent off guard.
6. His idea of democracy was incomplete, he himself had slaves.
7. She knows her cards that is she never overbids.
8. The problem facing modern architects is tremendous, it involves saving energy on a grand scale with untested devices and still achieving beautiful buildings.
9. The solution was elegant, besides being inexpensive, it was a wholly new approach.
10. Don't underestimate the future, it is always there.

3. *Add or subtract commas and semicolons as necessary in these sentences:*

1. Their travels are tireless, their budget however needs a rest.
2. They abhor economizing, that is, they are really spendthrifts.
3. Muller wants efficiency, Smithers beauty.
4. Abramson won the first set with a consistent backhand; some beautiful forehand volleys also helping at crucial moments.
5. The downtown parking problem remains unsolved; the new structures, the new meters, and the new traffic patterns having come into play about three years too late.

4. *Adjust the following sentences concerning the colon:*

1. Many things seem unimportant, even distasteful, money, clothes, popularity, even security and friends.
2. People faced with inflation, of which we have growing reminders daily, seem to take one of two courses; either economizing severely in hopes

of receding prices, or buying far beyond their immediate needs in fear of still higher prices.
   3. Depressed, refusing to face the reality of his situation, he killed himself, it was as simple as that.
   4. To let him go was unthinkable: to punish him was unbearable.

5. *Add quotation marks and italics to these:*

   1. Like the farmer in Frost's Mending Wall, some people believe that Good fences make good neighbours.
   2. Here see means understand, and audience stands for all current readers.
   3. For him, the most important letter between A and Z is I.
   4. Why does she keep crying Mother? he asked.
   5. In Canada, said the Chinese lecturer, people sing Home, Sweet Home; in China, they stay there.
   6. The boys' favourite books were Oliver Twist, the Bible, especially Ecclesiastes, and Beautiful Losers.
   7. Germaine Greer's The Female Eunuch is memorable for phrases like I'm sick of peering at the world through false eyelashes and I'm a woman, not a castrate.

6. *Make a list of your ten most frequent misspellings. Then keep it handy and active, removing your conquests and adding your new troubles.*
7. *Capitalize the following, where necessary:*

go west, young man.
the west left the confederation.
the east side of town
the introduction to *re-establishing liberalism in ontario*
east side, west side
the driver spoke only french.
she loved the spring.
health within seconds [book]
clear through life in time [book]
a doberman pinscher
the united church
the niagara river
my christian name begins with c.
the edmonton public library
the neo-positivistic approach [book]
the montreal gazette [add italics]
twenty-five dollars [on a cheque]
33 thirty-third street
the tundra occupies a large portion of northern canada.

13
The Written Examination

GRASPING THE ANSWER

We began with the thesis, that seminal organizer of knowledge and thought. We end with the same Big Idea now applied to written examinations. Here is my parting gift, guaranteed from experience. It will improve your results on any question, in any subject, asking for a discursive answer.

This is the secret: MAKE YOURSELF ANSWER THE QUESTION IN ONE SENTENCE. However well or poorly you are prepared, this forces all you know on the subject to its widest dimension. If you start your answer with this sentence, even desperately throwing in any old detail as it comes (as I used to do until I hit on the one-sentence idea), every detail will seem to illustrate your opening declaration, and your instructor will say, "Now *this* one is organized—a real grasp of the subject." So, start your answer with your seminal sentence, and your answer will sound like an essay. It will sound even more so if you have jotted down the points you want to cover, quickly saving best for last—the one you know best and can cover most fully. It will indeed *be* an essential essay. Your instructor, after all, needs no introduction.

Next point: incorporate the language of the question in your one-sentence opener. This works even with the broadest kind of question—those barn doors opened so wide you can drive in any kind of load:

1. **Discuss the fall of the Roman Empire.**
2. **What is the most valuable thing you have learned in this course?**
3. **Demonstrate your knowledge of the materials of this course.**

Your one-sentence openers might go like this:

1. The Roman Empire fell because of decay from within and attack from without.
2. The most valuable thing I have learned this term is that people usually conceal their true motivations from themselves.
3. The materials of this course illustrate biological evolution, particularly the role of mutation in the survival of the fittest.

Jot down your points, quickly arranging for ascending order, and you are off and running. Finally, try to paragraph, with a topic sentence if you can, about once a page.

AN HISTORICAL QUESTION

1. Summarize Gibbon's reasons for the fall of the Roman Empire.

One-Sentence Answer

The Roman Empire fell because of decay from within and attack from without.

Jotted Outline

1. Augustus
2. Tiberius-Caligula-Nero
3. Nerva, Trajan, Hadrian, the Antonines
4. Commodus
5. Mercenaries
6. Overextension
7. Rome and Byzantium
8. Goths

Answer

The Roman Empire fell because of decay from within and attack from without. After the five good emperors who extended the Pax Romana to the end of the second century A.D.—Nerva, Trajan, Hadrian, and the two Antonines—Gib-   Thesis

First Half:
Inner Decay
bon unfolds a long account of folly, luxuriance, insanity, and bloodshed. But he sees the seeds of decay already sown by the wily Augustus, as he calls him, who dissolved the remaining republican powers of the Senate under a fiction of senatorial authority that disguised a military dictatorship. This dictatorship of the emperor, now the "Caesar," expanded the borders but weakened the old Roman spirit of freedom and patriotic commitment.

Topic
Sentence
    Moral decay was also evident from the first years of the empire. Augustus had tried to reform the profligacy of the upper classes, banishing both his wife and daughter for flagrant lewdness, as well as the poet Ovid, who was somehow implicated in the daughter's scandalous behaviour, as the lecturer pointed out. That Rome could survive the inner decay displayed in the murderous orgies of Tiberius (A.D. 14–37), or in the insane Caligula (37–41), who made his horse a senator, or in the almost equally mad and more bloody Nero (54–68), is a wonder.

Topic
Sentence
    But Commodus (180–192), the adolescent wastrel who thought he was Hercules and fought men and beasts in the arena in Herculean costume—the son of good Marcus Aurelius Antoninus—begins Rome's long decline, in Gibbon's eyes. The few good emperors along the line could not sustain the overextended empire, defended by mercenaries rather than patriots, the leading citizens who were now luxuriating at home and keeping the populace happy with bread and circuses. The empire broke in two, with two loosely cooperating caesars, one in Rome, one in Byzantium. The tail began to wag the dog, as Byzantium gained ascendancy, and at one time as many as six caesars divided the power and luxuriated on the taxes.

Topic
Sentence:
Second Half,
Outer Attack
    The pressure of attack from without was sustained from the first on all the empire's borders—Scotland, Gaul, the Danube, the East. But how outer attack conspired with inner decay is nowhere better illustrated than in the account of the Goths, whose future king Alaric conquered Italy and sacked Rome in 410. Driven to the north banks of the Danube by the Huns, the Goths begged Valens, the caesar of the East, for admittance into the empire in 376. Gibbon estimates a population of nearly a million men, women, and children from the 200,000 Gothic warriors reported by the contemporary historian. When agreement was reached that they would settle in Thrace and defend the empire, the Romans began to ferry this multitude across the badly swollen river in canoes and boats of all sizes for many days and nights, losing many in the rapid current. Valens and his

counselors, whom Gibbon calls slaves decorated with the titles of prefects and generals, looked on the settlement as a rich bargain, since they could now keep and spend the gold the provinces sent in as taxes to hire mercenaries.

But this was only the beginning of Roman greed and moral decay in the Gothic story. Valens had decreed that the warriors must surrender their arms before crossing the river and that they must give up their children to be sent to distant cities where they would be civilized and would serve as hostages to keep the Goths in line. But the Goths, whose weapons were their hereditary honour, bribed the Roman officials with their wives, daughters, sons, carpets, and linen, and entered the boats with weapons in hand.

> Topic
> Sentence:
> Inner and
> Outer
> Combine

Then Roman greed went farther. Instead of feeding the Goths as Valens had ordered, the officials sold them bread, dog meat, and meat from cattle killed by disease at outrageous prices—a slave for a loaf of bread, ten pounds of gold for a little bad meat. The Goths finally rebelled, devastated the country, fought Valens to a standstill, and settled independently in Thrace, where, though they became Christians, their hatred for the Romans smoldered until Alaric led them westward to conquer Italy and sack the ancient capital in A.D. 410. Aside from other forays into Italy, Alaric's victory illustrates clearly how moral decay combines with outer attack to contribute a major plunge in the long continuing fall of the Roman Empire.

> Topic
> Sentence

> Clincher

A LITERARY QUESTION

2. Discuss the role of the senses in Wordsworth's philosophy, identifying and analysing the following passage:

> Therefore I am still
> A lover of the meadows and the woods,
> And mountains; and of all that we behold
> From this green earth; of all the mighty world
> Of eye, and ear,—both what they half create,
> And what perceive; well pleased to recognize
> In nature and the language of the sense
> The anchor of my purest thoughts, the nurse,
> The guide, the guardian of my heart, and soul
> Of all my moral being.

One-Sentence Answer

In this important passage from "Tintern Abbey," Wordsworth makes his clearest statement about the role of the senses in perceiving the natural world and establishing —or "nursing"—the inner being.

Jotted Outline—on another sheet, or in margin

1. Outer nature—wild, cultivated (cottages)
2. Inner nature—world of eye and ear
3. Reality
4. Senses as creators
5. Senses as perceivers
6. Nature plus senses—soul and being
7. Perceived and created reality
8. Poetry—iambic pent—sincerity

Answer

Thesis

In this important passage from "Tintern Abbey," Wordsworth makes his clearest statement about the role of the senses in perceiving the natural world and establishing

Background Knowledge

—or "nursing"—the inner being. He has previously in this poem acknowledged the point with which he opens his "Immortality" ode that the unconscious and joyful impressions of boyhood, when he ran and jumped through these hills, have faded to the calmer impressions of maturity, which

Thesis Clinched

have mixed a sense of humanity (a "sad music") with the youthful joys in wild non-human nature.

Topic Sentence

He has visited this same scene five years before, as he says at the beginning, and the impressions from that visit have nourished him as they recurred to his mind—actual pictures popping into his thoughts—in the frenzy of the city and times of depression (his own depressed feelings). These recollections have brought to him the same tranquil mood that now fills his soul and gives the impression of harmony with nature and a feeling that he "sees into the life of things." He says that his present recapturing of the scene and mood is made even better because he knows that this present visit, a kind of recharging of batteries, will similarly sustain him in the future.

Topic Sentence

In this quoted passage, he tries to analyze the psychological process and the nature of reality—a very important statement. Here the uninhabited wilds of youthful joy have become "meadows and the woods and mountains." This is the more inhabited part of the view already mentioned in the cottages here and there among the woods, with smoke rising, still suggesting calm solitude, and the pastures divided by wild rows of heath. He refers to "this green earth," which again suggests cultivated fields and pastures rather than the surrounding wild woods.

All of this "mighty world," which is all of external reality, is perceived by eye and ear—the senses. But in fact, he says, these same senses "half-create" reality too. From this psychological exchange between external physical nature and the "language of the sense," which seems to half-perceive and half-create in a kind of dialogue, he nourishes his soul and moral being. He even seems to say, at the end, that this sensory experience *is* the soul of his moral being.

Topic Sentence

But he also speaks of this interchange with nature, through the senses, as an anchor, a nurse, a guide, and a guardian, implying that his soul and being are something separate that the sensory experience works on. He seems uncertain what this entity "nature and the language of the sense" really is—an anchor, a nurse, a guide (a leader), or a guardian (a protector). These lines, I think, show Wordsworth working very hard to explain something he feels deeply, but which is hard to explain. These lines, which seem almost like prose statements, yet scan as iambic pentameter, convey the deep sincerity typical of Wordsworth's poetry and his ideas.

Thesis Amplified

Clincher

A QUESTION IN THE SOCIAL SCIENCES

3. Brewer and Brewer contrast Freudian and Jungian ideas as the essential poles of psychological theory. Describe the basic similarities and contrasts.

One-Sentence Answer

Both Freud and Jung agree in the primacy of subconscious ideas, but Freud finds this realm of dreams and lost remembrances sexual and socially destructive, a negative pole, whereas Jung finds it archetypical and positive.

Jotted Outline

1. Freud-hypnosis-dualistic psychology
2. Jung's buried treasure
3. Archetypes
4. Schubert
5. Dementia praecox (schizophrenia)
6. Superego-Ego-Id
7. Freud negative—Jung positive

Answer

Thesis

    Both Freud and Jung agree in the validity of unconscious or subconscious ideas, but Freud sets dreams and lost remembrances as a negative pole to social life, whereas Jung finds them archetypal and positive. Freud, starting with hypnosis to get at the suppressed traumas of hysteria, became convinced that evidence from dreams was crucially informative. Jung, Adler, and others joined him. But Jung, analysing his own dreams, as Freud had done, found joy, as if discovering buried secrets, rather than the fear and aversion in Freud's interpretations. Consequently, their polar split was between Freud's negative and Jung's positive views.

Thesis
Amplified

Topic
Sentence:
First Half

    Freud had actually built on the predominating psychology of G. H. Schubert, which saw, as in Stevenson's *Dr. Jekyll and Mr. Hyde,* a good daytime personality suppressing a nocturnal and savage one. Freud adopted this as he described infantile sexuality as the seat of evil, or antisocial impulses, to be repressed in maturity—sexual love of one's mother, murderous hatred of one's father, the famous Oedipus complex. Freud converted the, to him, traditional two-level psychology into three. Instead of a good surface and a destructive subsurface, he described a *superego,* the socially acceptable good set of values, and the *id,* the hidden sexual and violent side of personality, with the *ego,* or personal identity, negotiating and defining itself between the two.

Topic
Sentence:
Second Half

    Jung, beginning with work on dementia praecox, or schizophrenia, evidently a deeper psychic trouble than hysteria, was attracted to Freud's work, joined him in editing a new journal, and in a new international psychoanalytic society. But Jung broke with Freud on the interpretation of dreams. Where Freud saw suppressed and unacceptable sexual drives, Jung saw archetypal patterns, built into the brain's caverns by evolution, up from savagery.

Jung sees two psychic levels in the unconscious where Freud sees only the libido (the *id*) containing rebellious infantile sexuality. Jung, like Freud, sees the unconscious retaining repressed drives, as expressed in dreams. But he sees these repressions as more broadly personal than explicitly sexual. This is the first level of Jung's unconscious, the somewhat negative and Freudian one. Beneath this is the collective unconscious, the positive reservoir of human experience built into the brain by evolution, which all people share, beyond or beneath the personal.

In short, Freud sees the unconscious as a threat, shared by all but built from personal traumas. Jung sees it more positively, containing personal and threatening suppressions, but supported by a positive and archetypical human consciousness built into human awareness by evolution, not so much suppressed as forgotten, a positive, universal, and archetypal source of energy that can be tapped through dreams and psychoanalysis.

Topic Sentence

Thesis Restated as Clincher

14
A Glossary of Usage

Speech keeps a daily pressure on writing, and writing returns the compliment, exacting sense from new twists in the spoken language and keeping old senses straight. Usage, generally, is "the way they say it." Usage is the current in the living stream of language; it keeps us afloat, it keeps us fresh—as it sweeps us along. But to distinguish yourself as a writer, you must always swim upstream. You may say, *hoojaeatwith?;* but you will write: *With whom did they compare themselves? With the best, with whoever seemed admirable.* Usage is, primarily, talk; and talk year by year gives words differing social approval, and differing meanings. Words move from the gutter to the penthouse, and back down the elevator shaft. *Bull,* a four-letter Anglo-Saxon word, was unmentionable in Victorian circles. One had to say *he-cow,* if at all. Phrases and syntactical patterns also have their fashions, mostly bad. *Like unto me* changes to *like me* to *like I do; this type of thing* becomes *this type thing; -wise,* after centuries of dormancy in only a few words *(likewise, clockwise, otherwise),* suddenly sprouts out the end of everything: *budgetwise, personalitywise, beautywise, prestigewise. Persuade them to vote* becomes *convince them to vote.* Suddenly, everyone is saying *hopefully.* As usual, the marketplace changes more than your money.

But the written language has always refined the language of the marketplace. The Attic Greek of Plato and Aristotle (as Aristotle's remarks about local usages show) was distilled from commercial exchange. Cicero and Catullus and Horace polished their currency against the archaic and the Greek. Mallarmé claimed that Poe had given *un sens plus pur aux mots de la tribu*—which Eliot rephrases for himself: "to purify the dialect of the tribe." It is the

very nature of writing so to do; it is the writer's illusion that he
has done so:

> I have laboured to refine our language to grammatical pu-
> rity, and to clear it from colloquial barbarisms, licentious
> idioms, and irregular combinations. Something, perhaps, I
> have added to the elegance of its construction, and some-
> thing to the harmony of its cadence.

—wrote Samuel Johnson in 1752 as he closed his *Rambler* papers.
And he had almost done what he hoped. He was to shape English
writing and speech for the next hundred and fifty years, until it
was ready for another dip in the stream and another purification.
His work, moreover, lasts. We would not imitate it now; but we
can read it with pleasure, and imitate its enduring drive for excellence and meaning—making words mean what they say.

Johnson goes on to say that he has "rarely admitted any word
not authorized by former writers." Writers provide the second
level of usage, the paper money. But even this usage requires
principle. If we accept "what the best writers use," we still cannot
tell whether it is valid: we may be aping their bad habits. Usage
is only a court of first appeal, where we can say little more than
"He said it." Beyond that helpless litigation, we can test our
writing by asking what the words mean, and by simple principles:
clarity is good, economy is good, ease is good, gracefulness is
good, fullness is good, forcefulness is good. As with all predica-
ments on earth, we judge by appeal to meanings and principles,
and we often find both in conflict. Do *near* and *nearly* mean the
same thing? Do *convince* and *persuade*? *Lie* and *lay*? Is our writing
economical but unclear? Is it full but cumbersome? Is it clear but
too colloquial for grace? Careful judgment will give the ruling.

THE GLOSSARY

A, an. *A* goes before consonants and *an* before vowels. But use
a before *h* sounded in a first syllable: *a hospital, a hamburger.* Use *an* before a silent *h*: *an honour, an heir, an
hour.* With *h*-words accented on the second syllable, most
ears prefer *an*: *an hypothesis, an historical feat.* But *a hypothe-*

sis is fully acceptable. Use *a* before vowels pronounced as consonants: *a use, a euphemism.*

Abbreviations. Use only those conventional abbreviations your reader can easily recognize: *Dr., Mr., Mrs., Ms., Messrs.* (for two or more men, pronounced "messers," as in *Messrs. Adams, Pruitt, and Williams*), *Jr., St., Esq.* (Esquire, following a British gentleman's name, or, occasionally, a U.S. attorney's, between commas and with *Mr.* omitted), *S.J.* (Society of Jesus, also following a name). All take periods. University degrees are usually recognizable: *B.A., M.A., Ph.D., D.Litt., M.D., LL.D.* Similarly, dates and times: B.C., A.D., A.M., P.M. Though these are conventionally printed as small capitals, regular capitals in your classroom papers are perfectly acceptable as are "lowercase" letters for a.m. and p.m. *A.D.* precedes its year *(A.D. 1066); B.C.* follows its year. Write them without commas: *2000 B.C. was Smith's estimate.* A number of familiar abbreviations go without periods: *TV, NDP, USSR, USA, YMCA,* though periods are perfectly OK or O.K. Certain scientific phrases also go without periods, especially when combined with figures: *55 mph, 300 rpm, 4000 kwh.* But *U.N.* and *U.S. delegation* are customary. Note that in formal usage *U.S.* serves only as an adjective; write out *the United States* serving as a noun.

Abbreviations conventional in running prose, unitalicized, are "e.g." (*exempli gratia,* "for example"), "i.e." (*id est,* "that is"), "etc." (*et cetera,* better written out "and so forth"), and "viz." (*videlicet,* pronounced "vi-DEL-uh-sit," meaning "that is," "namely"). These are followed by either commas or colons after the period:

The commission discovered three frequent errors in management, i.e., failure to take appropriate inventories, erroneous accounting, and inattention to costs.

The term included some outstanding extracurricular programs, e.g.: a series of lectures on civil rights, three concerts, and a superb performance of *Oedipus Rex.*

The abbreviation *vs.,* usually italicized, is best spelled out, unitalicized, in your text: "The antagonism of Capulet versus Montague runs throughout the play." The abbreviation c. or ca., standing for *circa* ("around") and used with approximate dates in parentheses, is not italicized: "Higden wrote *Polychronicon* (c. 1350)." See also 166–68.

Above. For naturalness and effectiveness, avoid such references as "The above statistics are . . . ," and "The above speaks for itself." Simply use "These" or "This."

Action. A horribly overused catchall. Be specific: *invasion, rape, murder, intransigence, boycott.*

Adapt, adopt. To *adapt* is to modify something to fit a new purpose. To *adopt* is to take it over as it is.

Advice, advise. Frequently confused. *Advice* is what you get when advisers *advise* you.

Affect, effect. *Affect* means "to produce an *effect.*" Avoid *affect* as a noun; just say *feeling* or *emotion. Affective* is a technical term for *emotional* or *emotive,* which are clearer.

Aggravate. Means to add gravity to something already bad enough. Avoid using it to mean "irritate."

WRONG	RIGHT
He aggravated his mother.	The rum aggravated his mother's fever.

All, all of. Use *all* without the *of* wherever you can to economize: *all this, all that, all those, all the people, all her lunch.* But some constructions need *of: all of them, all of Laurence.*

All ready, already. Two different meanings. *All ready* means that everything is ready; *already* means "by this time."

All right, alright. *Alright* is not *all right;* you are confusing it with the spelling of *already.*

Allusion, illusion, disillusion. The first two are frequently confused, and *disillusion* is frequently misspelled *disallusion.* An *allusion* is a reference to something; an *illusion* is a mistaken conception. You disillusion someone by bringing him back to hard reality from his illusions.

Alot. You mean *a lot,* not *allot.*

Among. See *Between.*

Amount of, number of. Use *amount* with general heaps of things; use *number* with amounts that might be counted: *a small amount of interest, a large number of votes.* Use *number* with living creatures: *a number of applicants,* a *number of squirrels.*

And/or. An ungainly thought stopper. See *Virgule,* 229.

Anxious. Use to indicate *Angst,* agony, and anxiety. Does not mean cheerful expectation: "He was *anxious* to get started." Use *eager* instead.

Any. Do not overuse as a modifier.

POOR	GOOD
She was the best of any girl in the class.	She was the best girl in the class.
If any people know the answer, they aren't talking.	If anyone knows the answer, he's not talking.

Add *other* when comparing likes: "She was better than *any other* girl in the class." But "This girl was better than any boy."

Any more. Written as two words, except when an adverb in negatives and questions:

She never wins *anymore.*
Does she play *anymore?*

Anyplace, someplace. Use *anywhere* and *somewhere* (adverbs), unless you mean "any *place*" and "some *place*."

Appear. Badly overworked for *seem.*

Appreciate. Means "recognize the worth of." Do not use to mean simply "understand."

LOOSE	CAREFUL
I *appreciate* your position.	I *understand* your position.
I *appreciate* that your position is grotesque.	I *realize* your position is grotesque.

Area. Drop it. *In the area of finance* means *in finance,* and *conclusive in all areas* means simply *conclusive,* or *conclusive in all departments (subjects, topics).* Be specific.

Around. Do not use for *about:* it will seem to mean "surrounding."

POOR	GOOD
Around thirty people came.	*About* thirty people came.
He sang at *around* ten o'clock.	He sang at *about* ten o'clock.

As. Use where the cigarette people have *like:* "It tastes good, *as* a goody should," or "it tastes good the way a goody should." (See also *Like.*)

Do not use for *such as:* "Many things, *as* nails, hats, toothpicks. . . ." Write "Many things, *such as* nails. . . ." Do not use *as* for *because* or *since;* it is ambiguous:

AMBIGUOUS	PRECISE
As I was walking, I had time to think.	Because I was walking, I had time to think.

As if. Takes the subjunctive: ". . . as if he *were* cold."
As of, as of now. Avoid, except for humour. Use *at,* or *now,* or delete entirely.

POOR	IMPROVED
He left, as of ten'o'clock.	He left at ten o'clock.
As of now, I've sworn off.	I've just sworn off.

As to. Use only at the beginning of a sentence: "As to his first allegation, I can only say. . . ." Change it to *about,* or omit it, within a sentence: "He knows nothing *about* the details"; "He is not sure [whether] they are right."
As well as. You may mean only *and.* Check it out. Avoid such ambiguities as *The Commons voted as well as the Lords.*
Aspect. Overused. Try *side, part, portion.* See *Jargon.*
At. Do not use after *where.* "Where is it at?" means "Where is it?"
Awhile, a while. You usually want the adverb: *linger awhile, the custom endured awhile longer.* If you want the noun, emphasizing a period of time, make it clear: *the custom lasted for a while.*
Bad, badly. *Bad* is an adjective: *a bad trip. Badly* is an adverb: *he wrote badly.* Linking verbs take *bad: he smells bad; I feel bad; it looks bad.*
Balance, bulk. Make them mean business, as in "He deposited the balance of his allowance" and "The bulk of the crop was ruined." Do not use them for people:

POOR	IMPROVED
The *balance* of the class went home.	The *rest* of the class went home.
The *bulk* of the crowd was indifferent.	*Most* of the crowd was indifferent.

Basis. Drop it: *on a daily basis* means *daily.*
Be sure and. Write *be sure to.*

Because of, due to. See *Due to.*

Besides. Means "in addition to," not "other than."

POOR	IMPROVED
Something *besides* smog was the cause [unless smog was also a cause].	Something *other than* smog was the cause.

Better than. Unless you really mean *better than*, use *more than.*

POOR	IMPROVED
The lake was *better than* two miles across.	The lake was *more than* two miles across.

Between, among. *Between* ("by twain") has *two* in mind; *among* has more than two. *Between*, a preposition, takes an object; *between us, between you and me.* ("Between you and I" is sheer embarrassment; see *Me*, below.) *Between* also indicates geographical placing: "It is midway between Toronto, Ottawa, and Montreal." "The grenade fell between Jones and me and the gatepost"; but "The grenade fell among the fruit stands." "Between every building was a plot of petunias" (or "In between each building. . . .") conveys the idea, however nonsensical "between a building" is. "Between all the buildings were plots of petunias" would be better, though still a compromise.

Bimonthly, biweekly. Careless usage has damaged these almost beyond recognition, confusing them with *semimonthly* and *semiweekly.* For clarity, better say "every two months" and "every two weeks."

But, cannot but. "He can but fail" is old but usable. After a negative, however, the natural turn in *but* causes confusion:

POOR	IMPROVED
He cannot but fail.	He can only fail.
He could not doubt but that it. . . .	He could not doubt that it. . . .
He could not help but take. . . .	He could not help taking. . . .

When *but* means "except," it is a preposition. "Everybody laughed but me."

But that, but what. Colloquial redundancies.

POOR	IMPROVED
There is no doubt but that John's is the best steer.	There is no doubt that John's is the best steer.
	John's is clearly the best steer.
There is no one but what would enjoy it.	Anyone would enjoy it.

Can, may (could, might). *Can* means ability; *may* asks permission, and expresses possibility. *Can I go?* means, strictly, "Have I the physical capability to go?" In speech, *can* usually serves for both ability and permission, though the clerk will probably say, properly, "May I help you?" In assertions, the distinction is clear: "He can do it." "He may do it." "If he can, he may." Keep these distinctions clear in your writing.

Could and *might* are the past tenses, but when used in the present time they are subjunctive, with shades of possibility, and hence politeness: *"Could* you come next Tuesday?" *Might* I inquire about your plans?" *Could* may mean ability almost as strongly as *can:* "I'm sure he could do it." But *could* and *might* are usually subjunctives, expressing doubt:

Perhaps he could make it, if he tries.
I might be able to go, but I doubt it.

Cannot, can not. Use either, depending on the rhythm and emphasis you want. *Can not* emphasizes the *not* slightly.
Can't hardly, couldn't hardly. Use *can hardly, could hardly,* since *hardly* carries the negative sense.
Can't help but. A marginal mixture in speech of two clearer and more formal ideas, *I can but regret* and *I can't help regretting.* Avoid it in writing.
Capital, capitol. Frequently confused. You mean *capital,* the head thing, unless describing the Capitol Building and Hill in Washington, D.C., the *capital* of the United States, or the *Capitol* in Rome.
Case. Chop out this deadwood:

POOR	IMPROVED
In many cases, ants survive. . . .	Ants often. . . .
In such a case, surgery is recommended.	Then surgery is recommended.
In case he goes. . . .	If he goes. . . .
Everyone enjoyed himself, except in a few scattered cases.	Almost everyone enjoyed himself.

Cause, result. Since *all* events are both causes and results, suspect yourself of wordiness if you write either word.

WORDY	ECONOMICAL
The invasions caused depopulation of the country.	The invasions depopulated the country.
He lost as a result of poor campaigning.	He lost because his campaign was poor.

Cause-and-effect relationship. Verbal adhesive tape. Recast the sentence, with some verb other than the wordy *cause:*

POOR	IMPROVED
Othello's jealousy rises in a cause-and-effect relationship when he sees the handkerchief.	Seeing the handkerchief arouses Othello's jealousy.

Censor, censure. Frequently confused. A *censor* cuts out objectionable passages. *To censor* is to cut or prohibit. *To censure* is to condemn: "The *censor censored* some parts of the play, and *censured* the author as an irresponsible drunkard."

Centre around. A physical impossibility. Make it *centres on,* or *revolves around,* or *concerns,* or *is about.*

Clichés. Don't use unwittingly. But they can be effective. There are two kinds: (1) the rhetorical—*tried and true, the not too distant future, sadder but wiser, in the style to which she had become accustomed;* (2) the proverbial—*apple of his eye, skin of your teeth, sharp as a tack, quick as a flash, twinkling of an eye.* The rhetorical ones are clinched by sound alone; the proverbial are metaphors caught in the popular fancy. Proverbial clichés can lighten a dull passage. You may even revitalize them, since they are frequently dead metaphors (see 138–39). Avoid the rhetorical clichés unless you turn them to your advantage; *tried and untrue, gladder and wiser, a future not too distant.*

Compare to, compare with. To compare *to* is to show similarities (and differences) between different kinds; to compare *with* is to show differences (and similarities) between like kinds.

> **Composition has been compared *to* architecture.**
> **He compares favorably *with* W. O. Mitchell.**
> **Compare Shakespeare *with* Ben Johnson.**

Complement, compliment. Frequently confused. *Complement* is a completion; *compliment* is a flattery: "When the regiment reached its full *complement* of recruits, the general gave it a flowery *compliment.*"

Concept. Often jargonish and wordy.

POOR	IMPROVED
The concept of multiprogramming allows. . . .	Multiprogramming allows. . . .

Connotation, denotation. Words denote things, acts, moods, whatever: *tree, house, running, anger.* They usually also *connote* an attitude toward these things. *Tree* is a purely neutral denotation, but *oak* connotes sturdiness and *willow* sadness in addition to denoting different trees. *A House Is Not a Home,* wrote a certain lady, playing on connotations and a specific denotation: a house of prostitution. *Woman* and *lady* both denote the human female, but carry connotations awakened in differing contexts:

> A *woman* usually outlives a man. (Denotation)
> She is a very able *woman.* (Connotation positive)
> She is his *woman.* (Connotation negative)
> She acts more like a *lady* than a *lady* of pleasure. (Connotations plus and minus)

Usage changes denotations: *a gay party* changes from a festive to a homosexual gathering. Usage also changes connotations. *Negro,* once polite, is now taboo for the once impolite *black. Chairman,* once a neutral denoter, now has acquired enough negative connotations to change a number of letterheads and signatures.

Beware of unwanted, or exaggerated, or offensive connotations: your reader may find you prejudiced.

Contact. Don't *contact* anyone: call, write, find, tell him.

Continual, continuous. You can improve your writing by *continual* practice, but the effort cannot be *continuous.* The first means "frequently repeated"; the second, "without interruption."

> **It requires *continual* practice.**
> **There was a *continuous* line of clouds.**

Contractions. We use them constantly in conversation: *don't, won't, can't, shouldn't, isn't.* Avoid them in writing, or your prose will seem too chummy. But use one now and then when you want some colloquial emphasis: *You can't go home again.*

Convince, persuade. *Convince* THAT and *persuade* TO are the standard idioms. *Convince* OF is also standard. *Convince* is wrongly creeping in before infinitives with *to.*

WRONG	**RIGHT**
They *convinced* him to run.	They *persuaded* him *to* run.
	They *convinced* him *that* he should run.
	They *convinced* him *of* their support.

Could, might. See *Can, may.*

Could care less. You mean *couldn't care less.* Speech has worn off the *n't,* making the words say the opposite of what you mean. A person who cares a great deal could care a great deal less; one who does not care *"couldn't* care less": he's already at rock bottom.

Could of, would of. Phonetic misspellings of *could've* ("could have"), and *would've* ("would have"). In writing, spell them all the way out: *could have* and *would have.*

Couldn't hardly. Use *could hardly.*

Council, counsel, consul. *Council* is probably the noun you mean: a group of deliberators. *Counsel* is usually the verb "to advise." But *counsel* is also a noun: an adviser, an attorney, and their advice. Check your dictionary to see that you are writing what you mean. A *counsellor* gives you his *counsel* about your courses, which may be submitted to an academic *council.* A *consul* is an official representing your government in a foreign country.

Curriculum. The plural is *curricula,* though *curriculums* will get by in informal prose. The adjective is *curricular.*

Definitely. A high-school favourite, badly overused.

Denotation, Connotation. See *Connotation.*

Different from, different than. Avoid *different than,* which confuses the idea of differing. Things differ *from* each other. Only in comparing several differences does *than* make clear sense: "All three of his copies differ from the original, but his last one is *more* different *than* the others." But here *than* is controlled by *more,* not by *different.*

WRONG	RIGHT
It is different *than* I expected.	It is different *from* what I expected.
	It is not what I expected.
He is different *than* the others.	He is different *from* the others.

Discreet, discrete. Frequently confused. *Discreet* means someone tactful and judicious; *discrete* means something separate and distinct: "He was *discreet* in examining each *discrete* part of the evidence."

Disinterested. Does not mean "uninterested" nor "indifferent." *Disinterested* means impartial, without private interests in the issue.

WRONG	RIGHT
You seem disinterested in the case.	You seem uninterested in the case.
	The judge was disinterested and perfectly fair.
He was disinterested in it.	He was indifferent to it.

Double negative. A negation that cancels another negation, making it accidentally positive: "He couldn't hardly" indicates that "He could easily," the opposite of its intended meaning. "They can't win nothing" really says that they *must* win something.

But some doubled negations carry an indirect emphasis —a mild irony, really—in such tentative assertions as "One cannot be certain that she will not prove to be the century's greatest poet," or "a not unattractive offer."

Due to. Never begin a sentence with *"Due* to circumstances beyond his control, he. . . ." *Due* is an adjective and must always relate to a noun or pronoun: "The catastrophe *due* to circumstances beyond his control was unavoidable," or "The catastrophe was *due* to circumstances beyond his control" (predicate adjective). But you are still better off with *because of, through, by,* or *owing to. Due to* is usually a symptom of wordiness, especially when it leads to *due to the fact that,* a venerable piece of plumbing meaning *because.*

WRONG	RIGHT
He resigned *due to* sickness.	He resigned *because of* sickness.
He succeeded *due to* hard work.	He succeeded *through* hard work.
He lost his shirt *due to* leaving it in the locker room.	He lost his shirt *by* leaving it in the locker room.
The Far East will continue to worry the West, *due to* a general social upheaval.	The Far East will continue to worry the West, *owing to* a general social upheaval.
The program failed *due to the fact that* a recession had set in.	The program failed *because* a recession had set in.

Effect. See *Affect.*

Either, neither. One of two, taking a singular verb: *Either is a good candidate, but neither speaks well. Either . . . or (neither . . . nor)* are paralleling conjunctions. See 110.

Eminent, imminent, immanent. Often confused. *Eminent* is something that stands out; *imminent* is something about to happen. *Immanent,* much less common, is a philosophical

term for something spiritual "remaining within, indwelling."
You usually mean *eminent.*

Enormity. Means "atrociousness"; does not mean "enormous-
ness."

> the *enormity* of the crime
> the *enormousness* of the mountain

Enthuse. Don't use it; it coos and gushes.

WRONG	RIGHT
She *enthused* over her new dress.	She gushed on and on about her new dress.
He was *enthused.*	He was *enthusiastic.*

Environment. Frequently misspelled *enviorment* or *envirnment.* It
is business jargon, unless you mean the world around us.

WORDY	IMPROVED
in an MVT environment	in MVT; with MVT; under MVT
He works in an environment of cost analysis.	He analyses cost.

Equally as good. A redundant mixture of two choices, *as good
as* and *equally good.* Use only one of these at a time.

Etc. Substitute something specific for it, or drop it, or write "and
so forth."

Euphemism. Substituting positive for negative connotations:
passed away for *died; put to sleep* for *killed; imbibed occasionally* for
drank constantly.

Everyday, every day. You wear your *everyday* clothes *every day.*

Everyone, everybody. Avoid the common mismatching *their:*

> "Everyone does *his* [or *her* but not *their*] own thing."

Exists. Another symptom of wordiness.

POOR	IMPROVED
a system like that which exists at university	a system like that at university

The fact that. Deadly with *due to,* and usually wordy by itself.

POOR	IMPROVED
The fact that **Rome fell** *due to* **moral decay is clear.**	*That* **Rome fell** *through* **moral decay is clear.**
This disparity is in part *a result of the fact that* **some of the best indicators make their best showings in an expanding market.**	**This disparity arises in part** *because* **some of the best indicators. . . .**
In view of the fact that **more core is used. . . .**	**Because more core. . . .**

Factor. Avoid it. We've used it to death. Try *element* when you mean "element." Look for an accurate verb when you mean "cause."

POOR	IMPROVED
The increase in female employment is a factor in juvenile delinquency.	**The increase in female employment has contributed to juvenile delinquency.**
Puritan self-sufficiency was an important factor in the rise of capitalism.	**Puritan self-sufficiency favoured the rise of capitalism.**

Farther, further. The first means distance, actual or figurative; the second means more in time or degree. You look *farther* and consider *further,* before you go *farther* into debt.
Feasible. See *Viable.*
Fewer, less. See *Less, few.*
The field of. Try to omit it—you usually can—or bring the metaphor to life. It is trite and wordy.

POOR	IMPROVED
He is studying in the field of geology.	**He is studying geology.**

Firstly. Archaic. Trim all such terms to *first, second,* and so on.
Flaunt, flout. *Flaunt* means to parade, to wave impudently; *flout* means to scoff at. The first is metaphorical; the second, not: "She *flaunted* her wickedness and *flouted* the police."

Flounder, founder. Frequently confused. *Flounder* means to wobble clumsily, to flop around; *founder,* to sink (*The ship foundered*), or, figuratively, to collapse, or go lame (said of horses).

For. See 219.

Former, latter. Passable, but they often make the reader look back. Repeating the antecedents is clearer:

POOR	IMPROVED
The Athenians and Spartans were always in conflict. *The former* had a better civilization; *the latter* had a better army.	The Athenians and Spartans were always in conflict. Athens had the better culture; Sparta, the better army.

Fun. A noun. Avoid it as an adjective: *a fun party* ("The party was fun").

Further. See *Farther.*

Good, well. *Good* is the adjective: *good time. Well* is the adverb: *well done.* In verbs of feeling, we are caught in the ambiguities of health. *I feel good* is more accurate than *I feel well,* because *well* may mean that your feelers are in working order. But *I feel well* is also an honest statement: "I feel that I am well." Ask yourself what your readers might misunderstand from your statements, and you will use these two confused terms clearly.

Got, gotten. Both acceptable. Your rhythm and emphasis will decide. America prefers the older *gotten* in many phrases; Britain goes mainly for *got.*

Hanged, hung. *Hanged* is the past of *hang* only for the death penalty.

They hung the rope and hanged the man.

Hardly. Watch the negative here. "I can't *hardly*" means "I *can* easily." Write: "One can hardly conceive the vastness."

Healthy, healthful. Swimming is *healthful;* swimmers are *healthy.*

His/her, his (her). Shift to the neutral plural ("Students should sign their papers on the first page."), employ an *occasional* "his or her," or otherwise rephrase: *s/he* is cumbersome. *His* is still respectable when standing for both sexes so long as your reader can reasonably infer both. Something like "Men and women in science" near your beginning will help. You should, however, avoid these traps: "Any *man* who has endured privation in service . . . ," or "The secretary trying to please *her* boss . . . ," unless you are clearly writing *only* about men or women.

Historically. A favourite windy throat-clearer. Badly overused.

History. The *narrative,* written or oral, of events, not the events themselves. Therefore, avoid the redundancy *"recorded* history," likewise *"annals* of history," *"chronicles* of history." *History* alone can suffice or even itself disappear. "Archaeologists have uncovered evidence of events previously unknown to history" would be better without the misleading *to history.*

Hopefully. An inaccurate dangler, a cliché. "Hopefully, they are at work" does not mean that they are working hopefully. Simply use "I hope" or "one hopes" (but *not* "it is hoped"); not "They are a symbol of idealism, and, hopefully, are representative," but "They are a symbol of idealism and are, one hopes, representative."

However. Initial *however* should be an adverb: "However long the task takes, it will be done." For the "floating" *however,* and *however* versus *but,* see 222.

Hung. See *Hanged.*

The idea that. Like *the fact that*—and the cure is the same. Cut it.

If, whether. *If* is for uncertainties; *whether,* for alternatives. Usually the distinction is unimportant: *I don't know if it will rain; I don't know whether it will rain [or not].*

Imminent, immanent. See *Eminent.*

Imply, infer. The author *implies;* you *infer* ("carry in") what you think he means.

He *implied* **that all women are hypocrites.**
From the ending, we *infer* **that tragedy ennobles as it kills.**

Importantly. Often an inaccurate (and popular) adverb, like *hopefully.*

INACCURATE	IMPROVED
More importantly, he walked home.	*More important,* he walked home.

In connection with. Always wordy. Say *about.*

POOR	IMPROVED
They liked everything *in connection with* university.	They liked everything *about* university.

Includes. Jargonish, as a general verb for specific actions.

POOR	IMPROVED
The report includes rural and urban marketing.	The report analyses rural and urban marketing.

Individual. Write *person* unless you really mean someone separate and unique.

Infer. See *Imply, infer.*

Ingenious, ingenuous. Sometimes confused. *Ingenious* means clever; *ingenuous,* naïve. *Ingenius* is a common misspelling for both.

Instances. Redundant. *In many instances* means *often, frequently.*

Interesting. Make what you say interesting, but never tell the reader *it is interesting:* he may not believe you. *It is interesting* is merely a lazy preamble.

POOR	IMPROVED
It is interesting to note that nicotine is named for Jean Nicot, who introduced tobacco into France in 1560.	Nicotine is named for Jean Nicot, who introduced tobacco into France in 1560.

Irregardless. A faulty word. The *ir-* (meaning *not*) is doing what the *-less* already does. You are thinking of *irrespective,* and trying to say *regardless.*

Irregular verbs. Here are some to watch; learn to control their past and past-participial forms. (See, also, *Hanged, hung; Lay; Rise, raise; Set, sit.*) Alternate forms are in parentheses.

arise, arose, arisen
awake, awoke, awaked
   (*but* was awakened)
bear, bore, borne

beat, beat, beaten
begin, began, begun
bid ("order"), bade,
   bidden

bid ("offer"), bid, bid
burst, burst, burst
drag, dragged (not drug),
  dragged
fit, fitted (fit, *especially*
  intransitively), fitted
  (*but* a fit person)
fling, flung, flung
get, got, got (gotten)
lay, laid, laid
lie, lay, lain
light, lit (lighted), lit
  (lighted)
prove, proved, proven
  (proved)
ride, rode, ridden

sew, sewed, sewn (sewed)
shine ("glow"), shone,
  shone
shine ("polish"), shined,
  shined
show, showed, shown
  (showed)
shrink, shrank (shrunk),
  shrunk (shrunken)
sow, sowed, sown (sowed)
spring, sprang, sprung
swim, swam, swum
swing, swung, swung
wake, woke (waked)
  waked
waken, wakened, wakened

Is when, is where. Avoid these loose attempts:

LOOSE	SPECIFIC
Combustion is when [where] oxidation bursts into flame.	**Combustion is oxidation bursting into flame.**

It. Give it a specific reference, as a pronoun. See 122–23, 208–09.

Its, it's. Don't confuse *its,* the possessive pronoun, with *it's,* the contraction of *it is.*

-ize. A handy way to make verbs from nouns and adjectives *(patron-ize, civil-ize).* But handle with care. Manufacture new *-izes* only with a sense of humour and daring ("they Harvardized the party"). Business overdoes the trick: *finalize,* a relative newcomer, has provoked strong disapproval from writers who are not commercially familiarized.

Jargon. A technical, wordy phraseology that becomes characteristic of any particular trade, or branch of learning, frequently with nouns modifying nouns, and in the passive voice. Break out of it by making words mean what they say.

JARGON	CLEAR MEANING
The *plot structure* of the play provides no *objective correlative.*	The play fails to act out and exhibit the hero's inner conflicts.

	The plot is incoherent.
	The structure is lopsided.
The *character development* of the heroine is excellent.	The author sketches and deepens the heroine's personality skillfully. The heroine matures convincingly.
Three *motivation profile studies* were developed *in the area of production management.*	The company studied its production managers, and discovered three kinds of motivation.
He *structured* the meeting.	He organized (planned, arranged) the meeting.

Kind of, sort of. Colloquialisms for *somewhat, rather, something,* and the like. Usable, but don't overuse.

Lay. Don't use *lay* to mean *lie. To lay* means "to put" and needs an object; *to lie* means "to recline." Memorize both their present and past tenses, frequently confused:

> I *lie* down when I can; I *lay* down yesterday; I have *lain* down often. [Intransitive, no object.]
> The hen *lays* an egg; she *laid* one yesterday; she has *laid* four this week. [Transitive, *lays* an object.]
> Now I *lay* the book on the table; I *laid* it there yesterday; I have *laid* it there many times.

Lead, led. Because *lead* (being in front) is spelled like the *lead* in *lead pencil,* people frequently misspell the past tense, which is *led.*

Lend, loan. Don't use *loan* for *lend. Lend* is the verb; *loan,* the noun: "Please *lend* me a five; I need a *loan* badly." Remember the line: "I'll *send* you to a *friend* who'll be willing to *lend.*"

Less, few. Don't use one for the other. *Less* answers "How much?" *Few* answers "How many?"

| **WRONG** | **RIGHT** |
| We had *less* people than last time. | We had *fewer* people this time than last. |

Level. Usually redundant jargon. *High level management* is *top management* and *university level courses* are *university courses.* What is a *level management,* or a *level course* anyway?

Lie, lay. See *Lay.*

Lighted, lit. Equally good past tenses for *light* (both "to ignite" and "to descend upon"), with *lit* perhaps more frequent. Rhythm usually determines the choice. *Lighted* seems preferred for adverbs and combinations: *a clean well-lighted place; it could have been lighted better.*

Like, as, as if. Usage blurs them, but the writer should distinguish them before he decides to go colloquial. Otherwise, he may throw his readers off.

> **He looks *like* me.**
> **He dresses *as* [the way] I do.**
> **He acts *as if* he were high.**

Note that *like* takes the objective case, and that *as,* being a conjunction, is followed by the nominative:

> **She looks like *her.***
> **He is as tall as *I* [am].**
> **He is tall, like *me.***

Like sometimes replaces *as* where no verb follows in phrases other than comparisons *(as . . . as):*

> **It works *like* a charm. (. . . *as* a charm *works.*)**
> **It went over *like* a lead balloon. (. . . *as* a lead balloon *does.*)**
> **They worked *like* beavers. (. . . *as* beavers *do.*)**

Literally. Often misused, and overused, as a general emphasizer: "We *literally* wiped them off the field."

Loan. See *Lend.*

Loose, lose. You will *lose* the game if your defense is *loose.*

Lots, lots of, a lot of. Conversational for *many, much, great, considerable.* Try something else. See *Alot.*

Majority. Misused for *most:* "The *majority* of the play is comic" [wrong].

Maximum (minimum) amount. Drop *amount.* The minimum and the maximum *are* amounts. Don't write *a minimum of* and *as a minimum:* write *at least.*

May. See *Can, may.*

Maybe. Conversational for *perhaps*. Sometimes misused for *may be*. Unless you want an unmistakable colloquial touch, avoid it altogether.

Manner. A sign of amateur standing. Use *way*, or *like this*, not *in this manner*.

Me. Use *me* boldly. It is the proper object of verbs and prepositions. Nothing is sadder than faulty propriety: "between you and *I*," or "They gave it to John and *I*," or "They invited my wife and *I*." Test yourself by dropping the first member "between I" *(no)*, "gave it to I" *(no)*, "invited I" *(no)*. And do NOT substitute *myself*.

Medium, media. The singular and the plural. Avoid *medias*, and you will distinguish yourself from the masses.

Might. See *Can, may*.

Most. Does not mean *almost*.

WRONG	RIGHT
Most everyone knows.	*Almost* everyone knows.

Must, a must. A *must* is popular jargon. Try something else:

JARGON	IMPROVED
Beatup is really a *must* for every viewer.	Everyone interested in film should see *Beatup*.
This is a *must* course.	Everyone should take this course.

Myself. Use it only reflexively ("I hurt *myself*"), or intensively ("I *myself* often have trouble"). Fear of *me* leads to the incorrect "They gave it to John and *myself*." Do not use *myself, himself, herself, themselves* for *me, him, her, them*.

Nature. Avoid this padding. Do not write *moderate in nature, moderate by nature, of a moderate nature;* simply write *moderate*.

Near. Avoid using it for degree.

POOR	IMPROVED
a *near* perfect orbit	a *nearly* perfect orbit
	an *almost* perfect orbit
It was a *near* disaster.	It was *nearly* a disaster [or **nearly disastrous**].

Neither. See *Either.*

No one. Two words in Canada, not *noone,* or *no-one* (British).

None. This pronoun means "no one" and takes a singular verb, as do *each, every, everyone, nobody,* and other distributives. See 201.

Nowhere near. Use *not nearly,* or *far from,* unless you really mean *near:* "He was nowhere, near the end." See *Near.*

Number of. Usually correct. See *Amount of.*

Numbers. Spell out those that take no more than two words *(twelve, twelfth, twenty-four, two hundred);* use numerals for the rest *(101, 203, 4510).* Spell out *all* numbers beginning a sentence. But use numerals to make contrasts and statistics clearer: *20 as compared to 49; only 1 out of 40; 200 or 300 times as great.* Change a two-word number to numerals when it matches a numeral: *with 400* [not *four hundred*] *students and 527 parents.* Numbers are customary with streets: *42nd Street, 5th Avenue,* which may also be spelled out for aesthetic reasons: *Fifth Avenue.* Use numbers also with dates, times, measurements, and money: *1 April 1986; 6:30* A.M. (but *half-past six); 3 × 5 cards; 240 by 100 feet; 6'3"* (but *six feet tall); $4.99; $2 a ticket* (but *16 cents a bunch*).

You may use Roman numerals (see your dictionary) with Arabic to designate parts of plays and books: "Romeo's mistake (II. iii. 69)"; "in *Tom Jones* (XII. iv. 483)." But the new style is all Arabic: (2.3.69), (12.4.483). See 168. Also see *Per cent, percent, percentage.*

Off of. Write *from:* "He jumped *from* his horse."

On the part of. Wordy.

POOR	IMPROVED
There was a great deal of discontent *on the part of* those students who could not enroll.	The students who could not enroll were deeply discontented.

One. As a pronoun—*"One* usually flunks the first time"—see 8–9. Avoid the redundant numeral:

POOR	IMPROVED
One of the most effective ways of writing is rewriting.	The best writing is rewriting.

The Stone Angel **is one of the most interesting of Laurence's books.**	*The Stone Angel* **is Laurence at her best.**
The meeting was obviously a poor one.	**The meeting was obviously poor.**

In constructions such as "one of the best that . . ." and "one of the worst who . . . ," the relative pronouns often are mistakenly considered singular. The plural noun of the prepositional phrase *(the best, worst)*, not the *one*, is the antecedent, and the verb must be plural too:

WRONG	**RIGHT**
one of the best [*players***] who *has* ever swung a bat**	**one of the best [***players***] who *have* ever swung a bat**

Only. Don't put it in too soon; you will say what you do not mean.

WRONG	**RIGHT**
He *only liked* mystery stories.	**He liked *only* mystery stories.**

Overall. Jargonish. Use *general,* or rephrase.

DULL	**IMPROVED**
The overall quality was good.	**The lectures were generally good.**

Oversight. An unintentional omission: "Leaving you off the list was an *oversight.*" Unfortunately, officialdom has started to use it for *overview* or *supervisory.* Congress now has an Oversight Committee (perhaps several)—which sounds like a committee set up to catch omissions. Avoid this ambiguity. Keep your *oversights* meaning *oversights.*

Parent. One of those nouns aping a verb: *to rear, bring up, supervise, raise, love.*

Per. Use *a:* "He worked ten hours *a* day." *Per* is jargonish, except in conventional Latin phrases: *per diem, per capita* (not italicized in your running prose).

POOR	IMPROVED
This will cost us a manhour *per* machine *per* month a year from now.	A year from now, this will cost us a manhour a machine a month.
As *per* your instructions.	According to your instructions.

Per cent, percent, percentage. *Percent* (one word) seems preferred, though *percentage,* without numbers, still carries polish: "A large *percentage of* nonvoters attended." Use both the % sign and numerals only when comparing percentages as in technical reports; elsewhere, use numerals with *percent* when your figures cannot be spelled out in one or two words (2½ percent, 150 percent, 48.5 percent). Otherwise, spell out the numbers as well: *twenty-three percent, ten percent, a hundred percent.* See *Numbers.*

Perfect. Not "more perfect," but "more nearly perfect."

Personally. Almost always superfluous.

POOR	IMPROVED
I want to welcome them *personally.*	I want to welcome them [myself].
Personally, I like it.	I like it.

Phase. Do not use when *part* is wanted; *"a phase* of the organization" is better put as "a *part* of the organization." A phase is a stage in a cycle, as of the moon, of business, of the financial markets.

Phenomena. Frequently misused for the singular *phenomenon:* "This is a striking *phenomenon"* (not *phenomena*).

Phenomenal. Misused for a general intensive: "His popularity was *phenomenal."* A phenomenon is a fact of nature, in the ordinary nature of things. Find another word for the extraordinary: "His success was *extraordinary" (unusual, astounding, stupendous).*

Plan on. Use *plan to.* "He planned on going" should be "He planned to go."

Prejudice. When you write "He was *prejudice,"* your readers may be *puzzle.* Give it a *d:* "He was *prejudiced";* then they won't be *puzzled.*

Presently. Drop it. Or use *now.* Many readers will take it to mean *soon:* "He will go *presently.* " It is characteristic of official jargon:

POOR	IMPROVED
The committee is meeting *presently.*	The committee is meeting. The committee is meeting *soon.*
He is *presently* studying Greek.	He is studying Greek.

Principle, principal. Often confused. *Principle* is a noun only, meaning an essential truth, or rule: "It works on the *principle* that hot air rises." Princi*pal* is the *a*djective: The high-school *principal* acts as a noun because usage has dropped the *person* the adjective once modified. Likewise, *principal* is the principal amount of your money, which draws interest.

Process. Often verbal fat. For example, the following can reduce more often than not: *production process,* to *production; legislative* (or *legislation*) *process,* to *legislation; educational* (or *education*) *process,* to *education; societal process* to *social forces.*

Proof, evidence. *Proof* results from enough *evidence* to establish a point beyond doubt. Be modest about claiming proof:

POOR	IMPROVED
This *proves* that Fielding was in Bath at the time.	Evidently, Fielding was in Bath at the time.

Provide. If you *absolutely cannot* use the meaningful verb directly, you may say *provide,* provided you absolutely cannot *give, furnish, allow, supply, enable, authorize, permit, facilitate, force, do, make, effect, help, be, direct, encourage. . . .*

Providing that. Use *provided,* and drop the *that. Providing,* with or without *that,* tends to make a misleading modification.

POOR	IMPROVED
I will drop, *providing that* I get an incomplete.	I will drop, *provided* I get an incomplete.

In "I will drop, *providing that* I get an incomplete," *you* seem to be providing, contrary to what you mean.

Put across. Try something else: *convinced, persuaded, explained, made clear. Put across* is badly overused.

Quality. Keep it as a noun. Too many *professional quality writers* are already producing *poor quality prose,* and *poor in quality* means *poor.*

Quite. An acceptable but overused emphatic: *quite good, quite expressive, quite a while, quite a person.* Try rephrasing it now and then: *good, very good, for some time, an able person.*

Quote, quotation. Quote your quotations, and put them in quotation marks. Distinguish the verb from the noun. The best solution is to use *quote* only as a verb and to find synonyms for the noun: *passage, remark, assertion.*

WRONG	RIGHT
As the following *quote* from Milton shows: . . .	As the following *passage* [*or* quotation] from Milton shows: . . .

Raise. See *Rise, raise.*

Rarely ever. Drop the *ever:* "Shakespeare *rarely* misses a chance for comedy."

Real. Do not use for *very. Real* is an adjective meaning "actual":

WRONG	RIGHT
It was *real* good.	It was *very* good.
	It was *really* good.

Reason . . . is because. Knock out *the reason . . . is,* and *the reason why . . . is,* and you will have a good sentence.

[The reason] they have difficulty with languages [is] because they have no interest in them.

Regarding, in regard to. Redundant or inaccurate.

POOR	IMPROVED
Regarding the banknote, Jones was perplexed. [Was he *looking* at it?]	Jones was perplexed by the banknote.
He knew nothing *regarding* money.	He knew nothing about money.
She was careful *in regard to* the facts.	She respected the facts.

Regardless. This is correct. See *Irregardless* for the confusion.
Respective, respectively. Usually redundant.

POOR	IMPROVED
The armies retreated to their *respective* trenches.	The armies retreated to their trenches.
Smith and Jones won the first and second prize *respectively*.	Smith won the first prize; Jones, the second.

Reverend, Honourable. Titles of clergymen and members of the Privy Council (among others). The fully proper forms, as in the heading of a letter (*the* would not be capitalized in your running prose), are *The Reverend Mr. Claude C. Smith; The Honourable Adam A. Jones.* In running prose, *Rev. Claude Smith* and *Hon. Adam Jones* will get by, but the best procedure is to give the title and name its full form for first mention, then continue with *Mr. Smith* and *Mr. Jones.* Do not use "Reverend" or "Honourable" with the last name alone.

Rise, raise. Frequently confused. *Rise, rose, risen* means to get up. *Raise, raised, raised* means to lift up. "He *rose* early and *raised* a commotion."

Sanction. Beatifically ambiguous, now meaning both "to approve" and "to penalize." Stick to the root; use it only "to bless," "to sanctify," "to approve," "to permit." Use *penalize* or *prohibit* when you mean just that. Instead of "They exacted *sanctions,*" say "They exacted *penalties*" or "enacted *restrictions.*"

Sarcasm. A cutting remark. Wrongly used for any irony.

Seldom ever. Redundant. Cut the *ever.* (But *seldom if ever* has its uses.)

Set, sit. Frequently confused. You *set* something down; you yourself *sit* down. Confine *sitting* mostly to people *(sit, sat, sat),* and keep it intransitive, taking no object. *Set* is the same in all tenses *(set, set, set).*

CONFUSED	CLARIFIED
The house *sets* too near the street.	The house *stands* [*sits*] too near the street.
The package *set* where he left it.	The package *lay* [*sat*] where he left it.
He *has set* there all day.	He *has sat* there all day.

Shall, will; should, would. The older distinctions—*shall* and
should reserved for *I* and *we*—have faded; *will* and *would* are
usual: "I will go"; "I would if I could"; "he will try"; "they
all would." But *shall* remains in first-person questions: *Shall
I call you tomorrow? Shall* in the third person expresses deter-
mination: "They shall not pass." *Should,* in formal usage, is
actually ambiguous: *We should be happy to comply,* intended to
mean "would be happy," seems to say "ought to be happy."

Should of. See *Could of, would of.*

Similar to. Use *like:*

POOR	IMPROVED
This is *similar* to that.	This is *like* that.

Sit. See *Set, sit.*

Situate. Usually wordy and inaccurate. Avoid it unless you mean,
literally or figuratively, the act of determining a site, or placing a building: "Do not *situate* heavy buildings on loose soil."

FAULTY	IMPROVED
He is well *situated.*	He is rich.
Stratford is a town *situated* on the Avon River.	Stratford is a town on the Avon River.
The control panel is *situated* on the right.	The control panel is on the right.
The company is well *situated* to meet the competition.	The company is well prepared to meet the competition.

Situation. Usually jargon. Avoid it. Say what you mean: *state,
market, mess, quandary, conflict, predicament.*

Size. Often redundant. A *small-sized country* is *a small country. Large
in size* is *large.*

Slow. Go slow is what the street signs and the people on the
street all say, but write "Go slowly."

So. Should be followed by *that* in describing extent: "It was
so foggy *that* traffic almost stopped." Avoid its incomplete
form, the gushy intensive—*so nice, so wonderful, so pretty*—
though occasionally this is effective.

Someplace, somewhere. See *Anyplace.*

Sort of. See *Kind of, sort of.*

Split infinitives. Improve them. They are cliché traps: *to really know, to really like, to better understand.* They are one of the signs of a wordy writer, and usually produce redundancies: *to really understand* is *to understand.* The quickest cure for split infinitives is to drop the adverb. See 88–89, 212.

    For a gain in grace, and often for a saving of words, you can sometimes change the adverb to an adjective.

POOR	IMPROVED
to adequately *think* out solutions	*to think* out adequate solutions
to enable us *to* effectively *plan* our advertising	*to* enable us *to plan* effective advertising

Structure. See *Jargon.*
Sure. Too colloquial for writing: "It is *sure* a good plan." Use *surely* or *certainly,* or rephrase.
Tautology. Several words serving where fewer—usually one— are needed, or wanted: useless repetition. Some examples:

attach [together]	mix [together]
[basic] essentials	[pair of] twins
consecutive days [in a row]	(but, two *sets* of twins)
[early] beginnings	[past] history
[final] completion	refer [back]
[final] upshot	repeat [again]
[first] beginnings	sufficient [enough]
[just] merely	whether [or not]

That, which, who. *That* defines and restricts; *which* is explanatory and nonrestrictive; *who* stands for people, and may be restrictive or nonrestrictive. See *Who,* and 105, 124, 220–221.
There is, there are, it is. However natural and convenient—it is WORDY. Notice that *it* here refers to something specific, differing distinctly from the *it* in "It is easy to write badly." (Better: "Writing badly is easy.") This indefinite subject, like *there is* and *there are,* gives the trouble. Of course, you will occasionally need an *it* or a *there* to assert existences:

There are ants in the cupboard.	There are craters on the moon.
There is only one Kenneth.	It is too bad.

They. Often a loose indefinite pronoun; tighten it. See 208, 209.

Till, until. Both are respectable. Note the spelling. Do not use *'til.*

Too. Awful as a conjunctive adverb: "Too, it was unjust." Also poor as an intensive: "They did not do too well" (note the difference in Shakespeare's "not wisely but too well"—he really means it). Use *very,* or (better) nothing: "They did not do well" (notice the nice understated irony).

Tool. Overused for "means." Try *instrument, means.*

Toward, towards. *Toward* is the better (towards in Britain), though both are acceptable.

Trite. From Latin *tritus:* "worn out." Many words get temporarily worn out and unusable: *emasculated, viable, situation,* to name a few. And many phrases are permanently frayed; see *Clichés.*

Type. Banish it, abolish it. If you must use it, insert *of:* not *that type person* but *that type OF person,* though even this is really jargon for *that kind of person, a person like that.* See 127.

Unique. Something *unique* has nothing in the world like it.

WRONG	RIGHT
The *more unique* the organization. . . .	The *more nearly unique.* . . .
the *most unique* man I know	the *most unusual* man I know
a *very unique* personality	a *unique* personality

Use, use of. A dangerously wordy word. See 124–25.

Use to. A mistake for *used to.*

Utilize, utilization. Like *use,* wordy. See 125.

POOR	IMPROVED
He *utilizes* frequent dialogue to enliven his stories.	Frequent dialogue enlivens his stories.
The *utilization* of a scapegoat eases their guilt.	A scapegoat eases their guilt.

Very. Spare the *very* and the *quite, rather, pretty,* and *little.* I would hate to admit (and don't care to know) how many of these

qualifiers I have cut from this text. You can do without them
entirely, but they do ease a phrase now and then.

Viable. With *feasible,* overworked. Try *practicable, workable, possible.*

Ways. Avoid it for distance. Means *way:* "He went a short
way into the woods."

Well. See *Good.*

Whether. See *If.*

Which. See *Who, which, that.*

While. Reserve for time only, as in *"While* I was talking, she
smoked constantly." Do not use for *although.*

WRONG	RIGHT
While I like her, I don't admire her.	*Although* I like her, I don't admire her.

Who, which, that. *Who* may be either restrictive or nonrestrictive: "The ones *who win* are lucky"; "The players, *who are all outstanding,* win often." *Who* refers only to persons. Use *that* for all other restrictives; *which* for all other nonrestrictives. Cut every *who, that,* and *which* not needed. See 119, 123, "the *of-and-which* disease" (123–124), and, on restrictives, and nonrestrictives, 124.

Avoid *which* in loose references to the whole idea preceding, rather than to a specific word, since you may be unclear:

FAULTY	IMPROVED
He never wore the hat, which his wife hated.	His wife hated his going bareheaded.
	He never wore the hat his wife hated.

Whom, whomever. The objective forms, after verbs and prepositions; but each is often wrongly put as the subject of a clause (206).

WRONG	RIGHT
Give the ticket to *whomever* wants it.	Give the ticket to *whoever* wants it. [The whole clause is the object of

The president, *whom* he said would be late. . . .	*to*; whoever is the subject of *wants.*] The president, *who* he said *would be late.* . . . [Commas around *he said* would clear the confusion.]
Whom shall I say called?	*Who* shall I say called?

BUT:
They did not know *whom* to elect. [The infinitive takes the objective case.]

Who's, whose. Sometimes confused in writing. *Who's* means "who is?" in conversational questions: *"Who's* going?" Never use it in writing (except in dialogue), and you can't miss. *Whose* is the regular possessive of *who:* "The committee, *whose* work was finished, adjourned."

Will. See *Shall.*

-wise. Avoid all confections like *marketwise, customerwise, pricewise, gradewise, confectionwise*—except for humour.

Would. For habitual acts, the simple past is more economical:

POOR	IMPROVED
The parliament *would meet* only when called by the king.	The parliament *met* only when called by the king.
Every hour, the watchman *would make* his round.	Every hour, the watchman *made* his round.

Would sometimes seeps into the premise of a supposition. Rule: Don't use *would* in an *if* clause.

WRONG	RIGHT
If he *would have* gone, he would have succeeded.	If he *had* gone, he would have succeeded.
	Had he gone, he would have succeeded [more economical].

Would of. See *Could of, would of.*

You (I, we, one). See 8–9.

Canadian Reference Sources

Included in the following list is a brief selection of basic Canadian reference sources, based largely on Dorothy Ryder's *Canadian Reference Sources,* including the supplement. Students interested in Canadian sources in particular are advised to consult this work for more extensive bibliographical guidance; for materials developed since 1973, students should consult the reference librarian.

Avis, Walter S. *A Bibliography of Writings on Canadian English* (1857–1965). Toronto: W. J. Gage, 1965.

Books in Canada. Toronto: Canadian Review of Books. Periodical discusses books in the social sciences and humanities.

Canadiana. Ottawa: National Library of Canada. Canada's official national bibliography lists publications of Canadian interest received by the National Library.

Canadian Books in Print. Toronto: Canadian Books in Print Committee.

Canadian Historical Review. Toronto: University of Toronto Press. Lists recent publications relating to Canadian history, economics, geography, statistics, education, religion, ethnology, and folklore.

Canadian News Index (formerly *Canadian Newspaper Index*). Toronto: Micromedia Ltd.

Canadian Periodical Index. Ottawa: Canadian Library Association.

Catalogue de l'edition au Canada français. Montreal: Le Conseil superieur du livre. Includes the in-print publications of French Canada in subject order.

Dictionary of Canadian Biography. Toronto: University of Toronto Press. In progress. French edition, *Dictionnaire biographique du Canada.* Quebec: Les Presses de l'Universite Laval.

Dictionary of Canadian English. Toronto: W. J. Gage. Continuous revision.

Encyclopedia Canadiana. Toronto: Grolier of Canada. Continuous revision. Comprehensive reference work on Canada with short bibliographies given with articles.

L'Encyclopedia du Canada français. Montreal: Cercle du livre. A series of volumes, each dealing with some aspect of French Canada.

Klinck, C. F. *Literary History of Canada.* Toronto: University of Toronto Press, 1977.

Story, N. *The Oxford Companion to Canadian History and Literature.* Toronto: Oxford University Press, 1967.

Tanghe, R. *Bibliography of Canadian Bibliographies.* Toronto: University of Toronto Press, 1960. Revised in 1972 by Douglas Lochkead.

Thibault, Claude. *Bibliographia Canadiana.* Don Mills: Longman's of Canada, 1973.

University of Toronto Quarterly. Toronto: University of Toronto Press. *Letters in Canada* published annually since 1935–1936; a critico-historical survey of publications in the social sciences and humanities.

Watters, R. E., and I. F. Bell. *On Canadian Literature.* Toronto: University of Toronto Press, 1966. Checklist of articles, books, and theses on English Canadian language and literature, 1806–1960.

Index

291